Ecology of Vocation

Ecology of Vocation

Recasting Calling in a New Planetary Era

Kiara A. Jorgenson

LEXINGTON BOOKS/FORTRESS ACADEMIC
Lanham • Boulder • New York • London

Published by Lexington Books/Fortress Academic
Lexington Books is an imprint of The Rowman & Littlefield Publishing Group, Inc.
4501 Forbes Boulevard, Suite 200, Lanham, Maryland 20706
www.rowman.com

6 Tinworth Street, London SE11 5AL, United Kingdom

Copyright © 2020 by The Rowman & Littlefield Publishing Group, Inc.

All rights reserved. No part of this book may be reproduced in any form or by any electronic or mechanical means, including information storage and retrieval systems, without written permission from the publisher, except by a reviewer who may quote passages in a review.

British Library Cataloguing in Publication Information Available

Library of Congress Cataloging-in-Publication Data Available

ISBN 9781978700215 (cloth)
ISBN 9781978700239 (pbk)
ISBN 9781978700222 (electronic

Contents

List of Abbreviations		vii
Acknowledgments		ix
Introduction		1
1	Surveying the Land: The Shape of Discourse in Christian Ecological Ethics	11
2	Vocation as Kinship with Clod and Ape: The Planetary Promise of H. Richard Niebuhr's Responsibility Ethic	43
3	New Decalogues: Luther, Calvin, and the Democratization of Vocation	57
4	Embodied Work: Ecology and the Protestant Doctrine of Vocation Since the Reformers	75
5	Voices From the Wilderness: Critical Principles for Contemporary Christian Vocation From the Perspective of a Pastor, Scholar, and Poet	103
6	Ecology of Vocation: The Reclamation and Reformation of a Vital Protestant Doctrine	127
Epilogue		157
Bibliography		161
Index		171
About the Author		177

List of Abbreviations

C2ES	Pew Center for Climate and Energy Solutions
CD	Church Dogmatics
EIA	U.S. Energy Information Administration
ELCA	Evangelical Lutheran Church in America
EPA	Environmental Protection Agency
IPCC	International Panel on Climate Change
LW	Luther's Works

Acknowledgments

In this kind of project, those who have most decidedly influenced the work are rarely, if at all, mentioned in the footnotes. First, thanks go to those who fostered my sense of Christian vocation from an early age. Sherry Larson, John Folkerds, and the late Ed Blair were the first to formally introduce me to the concept of calling and (against all odds) demonstrated a knack for making middle-school catechesis fun. Later mentors DeAne Lagerquist, the late Jennifer Koenig, Dave Jarvis, and Kelly Chatman all played key roles in nurturing my Protestant identity and emergent call to activism. Evangelical colleagues from Denver Seminary days renewed my love of the Scriptures in a spiritually weary season of life and taught me about the importance of tethering theology to biblical studies. Key among them were Elodie Emig, Steve Garcia, Danny Carroll Rodas, and Jim Howard.

I am grateful to those who accompanied me in graduate school and offered invaluable feedback on the development of the ideas within this book. Time and again Lois Malcolm pushed me to clarify the nature of my inquiry. Alan Padgett faithfully and pastorally advised the dissertation that is the foundation of this book. When I needed encouragement to find my own voice as a scholar-activist, Cynthia Moe-Lobeda listened well and asked just the right questions. I thank Peter Susag for editing the earliest versions of this work and my Luther Seminary peers and friends (especially the self-proclaimed Theologians of the Round) for assuaging my fear that an academic life would prove a lonely one. To my colleagues at Au Sable, Lutherans Restoring Creation, the EcoFaith Network of the Minneapolis Synod of the ELCA, and Augsburg and St. Olaf Colleges, thank you for sharing my passion for God's beautiful and verdant creation and broadening my academic repertoire, without which significant portions of this project would have remained underdeveloped.

The present text would be far poorer without the important advice of readers from Fortress Academic/Lexington Press, especially Michael Gibson, Neil Elliott, and my St. Olaf colleague, the late Douglas Schuurman. Thanks to a generous publication grant from the American Association of University Women I was able to partner with Carla Foote of Fine Point Editorial, whose theological acumen coupled with a keen eye for straight talk helped make this work more accessible, and Katie Clymer, whose creative genius on the cover beautifully captures the connectivity of life I've sought to lift up within this work.

Contented and flourishing children are essential to the completion of any mother's work. I give thanks to my mama-Ph.D. friends Kim Radersma, Erin Heim, and Dana Scopatz who have offered tips on navigating mammademia, shared many a conference hotel room, and extended empathy when I had to leave my babies to return to work. To Betsy Mevissen, who provided a safe haven for my oldest while in graduate school residency, and Gloria Allie, whose no-nonsense love of my girls has provided added stability, thank you. A big thanks to my mother-in-law, Linda, who with selfless joy took on days of childcare and in ways seen and unseen made our home a more comfortable one during this season.

With the origins of my interest in theology and nature I credit my three parents. My father, Roger Esterbooks, has modeled critical thinking about matters of importance and demonstrated a humbling and steady confidence in my abilities. At an early age my mother, Connie Wahlstrom, granted me freedom to spend hours in the wooded wetland behind our house and fostered within me a curiosity about the natural world. And to the late and beloved Vern Wahlstrom, who without exhaustion entertained my love of trees, I thank for the example of stewardship; his multifaceted vocation was truly something extraordinary.

My final acknowledgments, to my husband and daughters, must be of a different sort. In ways that I am probably last to recognize, each of them has contributed critical ingredients to my work. Andrew has literally crafted his own vocation to support and undergird mine, frequently and generously sharing his astute theological mind. When overcome by the uncertainties of academia, his attention and affection have grounded me. The very presence of my daughters, Olia and Ingrid, reminds of life's fragility and like nothing else inspires me to care for it in ways big and small. I am beyond grateful for these dear ones, not least of all for the ways they embody the joy set before us all. But in reality, my family has done something more. They have let my work go on and have even encouraged my devotion to it. For this, I'm not sure how to give adequate thanks, except to say that God has called me to no greater work than learning to love these three well. It is to them that I lovingly dedicate this book.

Introduction

Concern for the ecological problems facing the world is a subject of popular dialogue in the United States, but despite growing concerns actual lifestyle changes are limited. The prefix "eco" is now joined with a variety of business endeavors, education ventures, and political conversations related to energy independence. At a cursory glance, the aggregate of such paradigmatic shifts suggests U.S. citizens have made an ecological about-face and are beginning to address the grave challenges of the Anthropocene, a proposed and contested new ecological epoch named for human impact on earth's systems. Yet, closer examination of the average North American lifestyle quickly unravels such optimism, as does a sober look at our ecological realities. In 2017, U.S. citizens, who constitute less than 5 percent of the world's total population, used 90 percent more energy than the average Chinese citizen and 50 percent more than the average European, resulting in a whopping 24 percent use of the world's coal, natural gas, and petroleum products.[1] Contemporary ecologists and climate scientists estimate that in order to level off the downward trend of global warming, Americans alone would need to reduce their use of fossil fuels by 70 percent.[2] As climate activist and scholar Bill McKibben suggests, such a shift not only requires more attention to ecological matters, but more so, a "change in the ways we move ourselves around, the spaces we live in, the jobs we perform, the food we eat."[3] In short, the realities of climate change call for nothing less than the radical reformation of both private and public life.

    The Christian church can and must play an integral role in the emergence of such progressive change. This isn't because the methods of environmental science prove metaphysically and existentially void, needful of some infusion of spiritual purpose, as some have suggested. Nor is it because Christianity provides a moral structure unlike any other philosophical or religious tradition. Rather, as a powerful vehicle of social agency with its own sorted natural history, the church offers resources for rethinking and refeeling our destiny.[4] Contributing to the larger cause of rethinking and refeeling the ecological viability of religious foundations, this book focuses on the North American church's fractured and failed attempts to practically address contemporary environmental challenges. Though the church has begun to attend to ecological matters more seriously and has made headway in its eco-ethical engagement, the majority of the church's conversations have sought to locate one common methodological approach. Efforts to locate one common methodological approach has inhibited actual movement within the Christian community and left our ethical conversations unresolved and hollow. Often speaking past one another, Christian eco-theologians and ethicists have underestimated the power of a plurality of approaches to Christian ecological ethics and have therefore failed to leverage the diversity of theological resources at the church's disposal.

With an aim to strategically position the church as an embodied prophetic presence in our nation and world, this book explores how and why a dialogical approach to ecological ethics *vis-à-vis* the Protestant doctrine of vocation provides practical help for the North American church seeking to better fulfill its shared ecological calling. Another issue is the way the Protestant doctrine of vocation has been too readily identified with industrialized concepts of work, which have evacuated the ecological promise of the doctrine in modern ecologically perilous times. Suggesting that our understanding of the neighbor extend beyond humanity as we now know it, I argue that a critical retrieval and reformation of the rich and dynamic Protestant doctrine can give form and language to a practical ethic mediated by our very creatureliness. It offers theological form for the ways it connects creation and redemption and holds critical tenets of both in tension. And vocation provides ethical language with its emphasis on right relationship over and above right behavior or right intentions. When related to but distinguished from the particular aim of work and rebranded by the moral complexities emerging as a result of our rapidly changing planet, the doctrine offers the church a conceptual framework to consider the interrelatedness of the myriad roles one inhabits and enact personal and corporate environmental responsibility in this anthropocenic era.

WORKING ASSUMPTIONS

Inherent to this project are two working assumptions. First, a faith-seeking-understanding approach to the larger conversation between religion and science is espoused. Because global environments are rapidly changing due in large measure to human belief and behavior, any and all social scientific resources must be tapped into, including those within the religious realm. Building upon the legacy of Ian Barbour's proposed integrative method in *Religion in an Age of Science* and subsequent titles by way of Alan Padgett's modification as articulated in *Science and the Study of God: A Mutuality Model for Theology and Science*, Christian ethics in particular has a place in the larger environmental conversation.[5] I argue for this not only because of the merits of Christian ethics, wherein virtues like temperance, mutuality, and justice can be useful and easily applied to the field of ecology, but also because Christian ethics as a form of discourse has historically examined the correlative relationship between sacred text, thought, and practice on individual and corporate levels and as such can shed great light on the formation of value in various traditions of knowledge, *scientia* (science) and *sapientia* (wisdom) alike.

A second working assumption relates to the scientific literature utilized throughout. Because this work is not scientific in scope and methodology, a heavy reliance is placed upon majority-view, peer-reviewed scientific findings. For example, the realities of global climate change are assumed, the nature of which are examined primarily through the Intergovernmental Panel on Climate Change's (IPCC) 2014 report, as well as findings from the reputable Pew Center for Climate and Energy Solutions (C2ES). When discussing the interrelated nature of the environmental challenges we presently face, I call upon reports produced by several government agencies, such as the U.S. Energy Information Administration (EIA), the U.S. Environmental Protection Agency (EPA), and Stanford University's Woods Institute for the Environment. Seeking to contextualize such information theologically, I explore the ways that vocation might translate to the field of ecological ethics at large.

DEFINITION OF TERMS

The astute reader will note my deliberate use of the term ecological ethics, as opposed to environmental ethics, eco-ethics, ethics of nature, etc. By using this term, I bypass delineations frequently made within environmental ethics (animal ethics, ethics of sentience, holistic entities, etc.), all of which understand the object of moral obligation as external to the self. Like many secular ethicists hailing from more radical perspectives, I question whether the extension of moral standing to the other-than-human world is enough. I do not find recast deontologies, or rule-based ethical systems, to be normatively sufficient. Beyond extensionism, which merely extends normative ethical traditions to the realm of animals, plants, and ecosystems, a broader philosophical perspective is required wherein fundamental changes can take place within the realm of attitude and our understandings of reality. American

Christians in particular must reexamine identity in light of global challenges and in so doing charter territory beyond the arena of personal ethics to the political stage. The perspective of *oikos*—the household—necessarily impacts the *demos*—the state. A familiar theological example of such radical approaches is deep ecology, which I engage in chapter 1. Deep ecologists of the Christian ilk focus more on the Church's emergent ecological consciousness than any said moral obligations to the environment. While their principles frequently lack practical application and can prove elementary in their engagement of complex environmental quandaries, deep ecologists' clear attention to interrelationality is particularly valuable to the Christian ethicist. The question for any ethicist is "What is the appropriate, fitting, or right action or posture?" The question for the *Christian* ethicist goes a step further to, "What is the appropriate, fitting, or right relationship to God and other?" First and foremost, the Christian must engage environmental questions from the vantage of relationship, and the term ecological ethics highlights that priority more clearly than environmental ethics or any of the other aforementioned terms.

In chapter 1, I repeatedly use a novel term, terreology, to refer to the respective theologies Christians use to understand life on earth. Discourse on Christian ecological ethics frequently uses the term "theoretical" or "cosmological" to describe such approaches and contrasts them with more practical ones. To avoid confusion, particularly surrounding the term "cosmology" which traditionally refers to the origin and development of the universe, I introduce terreology. By this term I am referring to theoretical, abstract perspectives on our lived earth-bound (*terre*) experience within Christian ecological ethics.

The definition of vocation is also essential in this discussion. As will become clear throughout, within the Christian community this term has come to mean anything from an internal inclination to a legalized responsibility, a God-given gift to a necessary job. Because this project specifically focuses on the Protestant doctrine, the term vocation will follow the early Reformers' definition, which extended calling (*qārā, kaleō*, and later *vocare*) beyond the clerical to all and emphasized God's agency.[6] I adopt Luther and Calvin's two-fold understanding of the doctrine (internal and external), addressed in detail in chapter 3. Their understanding of an internal or spiritual vocation referred to God's calling of a person unto God's self; thus having more soteriological implications.[7] External vocation, on the other hand, refers to the specific tasks, offices, relationships, and responsibilities one is led to by God, perhaps most clearly explicated by Pauline bodily metaphors.[8] While the connection between the two aspects of calling is made clear in chapter 3, where I adopt Gustaf Wingmen's reading of Luther and describe vocation as a doctrinal bridge between creation and redemption, generally I don't speak of vocation as a measure of God's prevenient grace. Unless overtly referring to vocation in soteriological terms, I use calling to connote the latter aspect, understanding that external vocation is always the amalgamation and interconnectedness of one's myriad roles, including but not limited to work.

POTENTIAL LIMITATIONS OF THIS STUDY

Drawing upon the biblical narrative and sixteenth-century thinkers to develop a contemporary definition of vocation brings about potential limitations. In the application of key theological themes, the hazard of anachronism looms large. Using historical-critical methods of reading biblical texts, I seek to uncover principles of eco-redemptive hermeneutics and then attempt to apply them to the contemporary context. The approach is largely dialogical rather than prescriptive. As developed in the first chapter, particular attention is given to the ways in which humans participate within creation and the ways in which God of the Scriptures is immanently revealed within creation. Helpful guides here include the work of Richard Bauckham, David Horrell, and Ellen Davis, among others.[9]

To avoid "ecologizing" or greening the work of the Reformers and the other thinkers writing on the doctrine of vocation, the historical chapters focus on working understandings of nature as they relate to thinkers' theologies of creation and redemption respectively. Situating vocation within a larger discussion on nature, particular attention is paid to helpful theological trajectories such as the democratization of vocation. From there promising insights and perspectives are highlighted, many of which are practically taken up in the final constructive chapter of the book.

THE NEED FOR THIS STUDY

The 1990s ushered in many North American religious studies on work as vocation. Eco-theological scholarship has burgeoned in the twenty-first century and is becoming a topic of growing concern in Christian contexts in particular. However, very little work has explicitly examined the connection between Christian concepts of calling and environmental concern, despite the growing number of works referencing ecological vocation or calling to environmental responsibility.[10] These works, while helpful in their descriptions of institutional politics, are not explicitly ethical in scope. They neither mediate between ethical perspectives nor provide practical measures for the Christian in society. Ethical works that evoke the topic of calling are also surprisingly ambiguous as to their understanding of ecological vocation.[11] To date, the work that most closely resembles the project at hand is Cynthia Moe-Lobeda's book, *Resisting Structural Evil: Love as Ecological-Economic Vocation*. However, because Moe-Lobeda understands vocation through the

Protestant lens of love of neighbor and primarily defines such love in relation to justice, her work addresses the structural more than it does the intrapersonal. My work seeks to honor and uphold her contributions while expanding the concept of vocation to include aspects of personal character transformation. Whereas Moe-Lobeda's work understands vocation more as a conceptual tool with which to enact justice, I suggest that the very ecology of vocation, namely, the interrelated nature of the callings Christians inhabit, incorporates the structural and intrapersonal at once.

OUTLINE OF THE BOOK

The first chapter of the book, "Surveying the Land: The Shape of Discourse in Christian Ecological Ethics," largely deals with methodology, seeking to address 1) the general historical shape of discourse in Christian ecological ethics, and 2) my particular reading of the ecological ethics landscape inclusive of critique and appreciations. To accomplish the first of these tasks, I speak to the genesis of Christian ecological thought and provide three reasons for the recent burgeoning of the field. I then address the second by noting the plurality of approaches within the Christian community, generally categorized as terreological and practical approaches respectively. The more pervasive approach, the identification of an overarching terreology, is addressed first. Here I outline three major historical approaches to Christian ecological ethics (anthropocentrism, theocentrism, and biocentrism) and survey the ways these approaches deploy deontological and teleological principles, which inform the very types of ethical questions that Christians notice and ask. I then outline major approaches to practical ethical approaches, looking at the pros and cons of natural value theories, constructivism, and ecological subjectivity.

With clear differences and common threads emerging between theoretical and practical approaches and within these categories themselves, the second chapter, "Vocation as Kinship with Clod and Ape: The Planetary Promise of H. Richard Niebuhr's Responsibility Ethic," suggests that a viable Christian ecological ethic be tethered to a radical theocentric terreology while remaining free to manifest in individualized and locally appropriate ways. Using H. Richard Niebuhr's germinal responsibilist framework as a helpful starting place, the chapter begins with an examination of how ecologically-minded behavior (ethics) relates to thinking (epistemology) and relational being in the world (ontology). I suggest that a Christian ethic that honestly and adequately deals with these categories of thought must attend to the concept of calling or vocation, and suggest that vocation is a viable mediating ethical resource for three reasons: 1) the Protestant doctrine of vocation speaks to a three-fold relationship (God, self, and neighbor), and as such, is fundamentally an ethical concept; 2) the passive nature of vocation—namely, that we receive a calling and are faced with the choice to respond—honors classical deontological themes and helps keep an ecological ethic within the realm of theocentricism; and 3) the particular and localized nature of vocation—that each person is individually summoned to serve at a particular time and place in history—speaks to teleology and pushes Christian ecological ethics toward pragmatic virtues that can be measured and practiced.

The latter half of chapter 2 seeks to illuminate the difficulty in clarifying moral agency and pinpointing culpability with regards to contemporary ecological problems. I give a brief appraisal of North American Protestantism's abdication of responsibility in light of salient themes to the contrary in the Scriptures and conclude the chapter with a description of the many factors that lead to ethical complexity and moral paralysis on the part of communities, theological and otherwise. These include the dispersive, aggregate, and intergenerational nature of the problem, the trouble with shifting epistemologies, humans' limited cognitive capacities, and the realities of eco-justice and environmental racism.

Chapter 3, "Writing New Decalogues: Luther, Calvin and the Democratization of Vocation," extends the discussion on vocation as a type of mediated responsibility ethic by excavating the ecological promise of the early Reformers' democratized rendering of calling. I begin by connecting the Reformers' views of vocation to the biblical texts and medieval mystical impulses, arguing that while their conception of vocation was radical it was nonetheless far from novel. I then examine at close view Martin Luther's radicalization of vocation by way of his law and gospel dialectic, noting how vocation as an expression of law binds while yet simultaneously frees the Christian to serve the neighbor. I compare and contrast the ecologically promising and problematic aspects of Luther's *beruf* with John Calvin's emphasis on the spiritual gifts (*kleis*) and demonstrate how both thinkers position vocation as a sort of theological lynchpin between creation and redemption, as a task and a gift. In linking their working understandings of vocation to creation, I highlight the embodied and mundane nature of Christian calling and conclude the chapter by addressing the problems of ascriptivism and individualism respectively.

This book's fourth chapter, "Embodied Work: Ecology and the Protestant Doctrine of Vocation Since the Reformers," traces the ways in which, for better or for worse, the democratization of vocation in sixteenth-century thought was historically received and applied. It begins with a brief discussion of how the Reformers' doctrine of vocation immediately played out in the work of Phillip Melanchthon and William Perkins. I demonstrate how while in theory their emphases on the banal nature of God's calling promoted greater attentiveness to the natural world, in reality their shared soteriological focus led to overly pious and individualized interpretations of vocation.

Through a critical reading of seventeenth- to twentieth-century philosophical and theological thought, I show how these renderings were further fortified by modernism's intellectual landscape and the demands of industry, reducing vocation to either little more than work as characterized by production and consumption or the escape from it. Here I demonstrate how such restricted readings of vocation have and continue to incite social and ecological injustice. Arguing against longstanding theories on Protestantism's supposed contributions to contemporary capitalism and common critiques of the doctrine of vocation, I conclude the chapter by highlighting early voices of resistance and by clarifying how human relationships of injustice and ecological degradation disrupt the fulfillment of vocation, making the Church's return to the Reformers' original sense of calling all the more difficult in contemporary context.

From here I move from historical analysis to contemporary practice by looking at three Christian practitioners in chapter 5, "Voices from the 'Wilderness:' Critical Principles for Contemporary Christian Vocation from the Perspective of a Protestant Priest, Scholar and Poet." This chapter typifies my overall argument, that an ethic grounded in Christian vocation is ecologically adequate and that any ecological ethic depends upon a sense of religious calling, by looking at the work of a Lutheran priest, Paul Santmire, a Reformed academic, Sallie McFague, and a Baptist agrarian poet, Wendell Berry. Seeking to honor each thinker's particular denominational heritage and demonstrating the breadth of community context—congregation, academy and literary/agrarian community respectively—I first identify the method, procedure, and content of each thinker's working ecological ethic. The chapter then connects each to the larger Protestant conversation on vocation by bringing to light implicit and explicit notions of call. I consider how each thinker responds to aforementioned problems of vocation, with particular thought given to the role of eco-justice and highlight key areas of overlap between the three. These result in the chapter's concluding reflections on helpful criteria for a lived Christian ecological vocation, including interrelatedness, wisdom, and restraint.

The sixth namesake chapter, "Ecology of Vocation: The Reclamation and Reformation of a Vital Protestant Doctrine," builds upon previous chapters and explores the theological ramifications and practical implications of a Christian ecological ethic through the lens of a revised Protestant doctrine of vocation. Here I return again to the fractured status of the North American church's ecological ethic and practically consider how one's call to the other-than-human neighbor and the responsibility to endorse work that protects economically and ecologically vulnerable persons and transforms Christian ecological ethics. To do this I consider what ought to be retrieved from the Reformers' initial work and the historical reception and application of their theology and what might be reformed to better speak to the complexity of today's moral landscape. For reclamation I highlight the Reformers' valuation of all callings, a democratizing move that spurs greater authenticity and responsibility, and a clear connection to the doctrine of creation. I also advocate for the retrieval of particular twentieth-century transcendentalist and Social Gospel voices that emphasize the dignity of work and explicitly link social prosperity to ecological justice. The bulk of the chapter, however, attends to the question: "Can contemporary application of the Protestant doctrine lead to complicit participation in structures of evil?" resulting in a discussion of the ways that Protestant vocation must be reconfigured. I discuss what contemporary Protestant renderings of vocation must cast off or clarify to remain faithful to biblical witness. I also consider the potential "elephant in the room" by asking how influential God's call is among Protestants and whether it motivates Christian communities in an increasingly secular context. The chapter concludes with a section on how vocation both is and might more convincingly be a fecund and promising theological resource for the Church today, lifting up exemplary examples of visionary interconnectedness, restraint, wisdom, justice, and hope.

A PERSONAL EXCURSUS

In November of 2013 I presented a working article on ecological vocation as a practical antidote to Nature Deficit Disorder at a national American Academy of Religion Religion and Ecology session. At the time I was trying on and orbiting around the larger research question of how Christian vocation might be a useful ethical construct in our frightful and often disheartening era. The presentation went in a manner that is perhaps predictable for a junior scholar; it was long, rushed in cadence and ultimately far too ambitious. For better or worse I knew this upon giving my concluding statements and braced myself for questions. I remember little of what followed, with the exception of Rev. Dr. Leah Schade's insightful and practical question. As both a scholar working in eco-theology and an ELCA (Evangelical Lutheran Church in America) pastor then serving congregants who earn a living pulling bituminous shale fossils from the earth, she questioned whether my definition of vocation could apply in her rural, low-income Pennsylvanian context. Was I really suggesting that authentic calling had to be decidedly ecological in scope even at the expense of one's livelihood? I fumbled the answer, wrote the question down later that evening, and eventually brought it to my monthly theology writing group. With their help, I realized my interest was not in detailing the methods and practices of a particular ecological vocation. After all, that had been done plenty of times over and wasn't leading the church to greater ecological responsibility or unified resolve. Rather, what charged my curiosity was the very ecology or interrelatedness of the many roles we all inhabit. In what ways do the intersecting points of these roles help or hinder our other-than-human neighbor, and in what ways, be they messy or even paradoxical, might they honor God? These, I have learned, are the questions of pastors and practitioners, teachers and activists, and it is their practical engagement that fuels this project.

NOTES

1. Comparative country and region reports are available on the U.S. Energy Information Administration's website: http://www.eia.gov.

2. Two contemporary peer-reviewed sources in agreement on such forecasts include: Pew Center on Global Climate Change, *Climate Change 101: Understanding and Responding to Global Climate Change*, Arlington, VA: Center for Climate and Energy Solutions, 2011, and IPCC, "2014: Summary for Policymakers" in *Climate Change 2014: Mitigation of Climate Change. Contribution of Working Group III to the Fifth Assessment Report of the Intergovernmental Panel on Climate Change*, edited by Edenhofer et al. (New York: Cambridge University Press, 2014).

3. Bill McKibben, *The End of Nature* (New York: Random House Trade Paperbacks, 2006), xx.

4. Lynn White, "The Historical Roots of Our Ecologic Crisis" in *Machina ex Deo: Essays in the Dynamism of Western Culture* (Cambridge, MA: MIT Press, 1968), 91.

5. Ian Barbour, *Religion in an Age of Science* (San Francisco: Harper & Row, 1990) and *Ethics in an Age of Technology* (San Francisco: Harper & Row, 1993); Alan Padgett, *Science and the Study of God: A Mutuality Model for Theology and Science* (Grand Rapids, MI: Eerdmans, 2003).

6. See, for example, wisdom literature examples where God is personified as the Wisdom who calls to us (Proverbs 8:1–4), or explicit New Testament examples like John 15:16, "You did not choose me, but I chose you" and Matthew 9:13, "I come to call not the righteous but sinners."

7. Classic biblical examples of this include the call and renaming of Abram in Genesis 11, Saul's conversion experience in Acts 9, and the calling of Matthew in Matthew 9.

8. See 1 Corinthians 1 and 7 and Ephesians 4, for example.

9. I primarily draw from the following three works: Richard Bauckham, *The Bible and Ecology* (Waco, TX: Baylor University Press, 2010); David Horrell, *The Bible and the Environment: Towards a Critical Ecological Biblical Theology* (New York: Equinox, 2010); Ellen Davis, *Scripture, Culture and Agriculture: An Agrarian Reading of the Bible* (New York: Cambridge University Press, 2009).

10. For example, Sean McDonagh's work, *Passion for the Earth: The Christian Vocation to Promote Justice, Peace and the Integrity of Creation* (London: Geoffrey Chatman, 1994), wherein he refers to calling in the context of one's work for justice. Mark Allen Torgerson's work on North American churches, *Greening Spaces for Worship and Ministry: Congregations, Their Buildings, and Creation Care* (Herdon, VA: Alban Institute, 2012), uses the term vocation throughout, often with regard to the church's political stance in society. In Mallory McDuff's *Natural Saints* (New York: Oxford University Press, 2010) the theme threads throughout.

11. For example, Larry Rasmussen's recent work, *Earth-honoring Faith: Religious Ethics in a New Key* (New York: Oxford University Press, 2013) touches upon ecological vocation, but is not specific to a Christian audience. Willis Jenkins's *The Future of Ethics* sheds great insight into pragmatic matters related to eco-justice, yet leaves the topic of Christian calling altogether untouched.

Chapter One

Surveying the Land

The Shape of Discourse in Christian Ecological Ethics

In a widely broadcast CBS television interview just months before her death, environmental pioneer Rachel Carson lamented Americans' (read U.S. citizens) subjugation of nature, a nefarious controlling force discussed at length in her 1962 expose of DDT in *Silent Spring*. "We still talk in terms of conquest . . . I think we're challenged as mankind has never been challenged before, to prove our maturity and our mastery, not of nature but of ourselves."[1] Carson, like many naturalists of her day and like those who followed in her wake, was skeptical of organized religion for the ways it emphasized human sovereignty over nature while underemphasizing critical attention to one's own lifestyle. And yet, indebted to her intellectual mentor Albert Schweitzer, a doctor and proto-ecologist who had deep ties to the Christian tradition and championed an ethic that honored the God-given reverence of all life, Carson never disregarded the beneficence of spirituality. Just as the doctrines of religions like Christianity had the potential to bring nature harm, so too these traditions offered the pregnant gifts of wisdom and wonder, therefore proving critical in the preservation of life.[2] If only religion could become more self-critical and embodied, better equipped to listen to and learn from science.

A few Christian contemporaries of Carson *were* listening. An excellent example of such persons is the Lutheran minister Joseph Sittler, who in the 1950s began to speak about the doctrine of creation in innovative ways. Encouraging the Christian community to interpret *creatio imago Dei* as privilege more than entitlement, and interaction with the natural world as responsibility rather than within a framework of utilitarian usefulness, Sittler urged the church to take up what he considered to be the most insistent and delicate task awaiting Christian theology—an articulated theology for the earth. He warned:

> If the Church will not have a theology for nature, then irresponsible but sensitive men will act as midwives for nature's un-silence-able meaningfulness and enunciate a theology for nature. For earth . . . unquenchably sings out her violated wholeness, and in groaning and travailing awaits with man the restoration of all things.[3]

Thinkers like Sittler were marginal in the mid-twentieth century in part because the urgency and gravity of ecological matters was just beginning to become clear in their day. Arguably Christendom's mid-century theological focus was not upon the subjugation of the earth as much as it was upon responding to the evils of genocide in an increasingly secularized post world-war context. With the unity of humanity hanging in the balance the Western church positioned its discussion of values, rights, and justice in largely anthropological terms, marginally attending to the connection between environmental integrity and human well-being.

However, as Indian Aruna Gnanadason has demonstrated, Christians in the East and global South had long been taking up Sittler's task.[4] As is repeatedly the case in religious history, the impact of these groups' creative theological imagineering has been inhibited by the force of colonial empire. At best, the theological innovation within minority Christian communities has been limited to their respective contexts. Case in point: thoughtful Christian theologies of water may prove relevant to Bangladeshis who source their own resources daily, but won't matter much to New Yorkers who pay top dollar for upstate or Great Lakes water. At worst the theological work of such communities has been squelched altogether, perhaps due to longstanding assumptions that places like Tübingen and Yale are the legitimate seats for serious religious reflection. Suffice it to say that Christian reflection on environmental decline isn't novel, even if it's now en vogue in the contemporary North American context. Thus, when related literature marks the late 1960s as a quasi-beginning-point of the Christian environmental movement, as much of it does, it is important to remember that only one part of a larger story is being told, and a later and more localized story at that.

CHRISTIAN ENVIRONMENTAL ETHICS: A BURGEONING FIELD

Why the growing interest in environmental topics among Christian Protestants in North America and specifically the United States these past forty years? What has ushered in or awakened this new consciousness? It seems the answer lies within the convergence of three major factors. First, one could easily characterize the growing movement as an apologetic to the critique launched against Western Christianity. In 1967 Lynn White's "Historical Roots" indicted Christianity for its anti-materialist theology and related ecological crimes. In the famous article, White argues that Western monotheistic traditions, Christianity in particular, have endorsed and promulgated destructive dualisms, which have resulted in the widespread institutional degradation of the natural world. Among his examples are emphasis on heaven as separate from earth, the concept of a sovereign and transcendent God who governs apart from the earth, and the privileging of human life above other life *vis-à-vis* anthropology *creatio imago Dei*. Although often overlooked when referenced, White's thesis included the revision and renewal of religion rather than a rejection of it. "More science and more technology are not going to get us out of the present ecological crisis," White wrote, "until we find a new religion or rethink our old one. . . . Since the roots of our trouble are so largely religious, the remedy must also be essentially religious, whether we call it that or not. We must rethink and refuel our nature and destiny."[5]

Christians have also engaged in conversation about ecology because the scientific community has invited them to do so. Despite religion's mythical and mystical nature as well as its reputation as science's longtime divorcee, many scientists now see religion as critical to the ecological transformation of culture. One of the first scientists to exhibit such hospitality was Aldo Leopold, whose eminent *A Sand Country Almanac* redefined both the object and the objective of environmental ethics. Critical of his scientific peers who attempted to practice conservation apart from the influence of religion he wrote:

> Obligations have no meaning without conscience, and the problem we face is the extension of the social conscience from people to land. No important change in ethics was ever accomplished without an internal change in our intellectual emphasis, loyalties, affections, and convictions. The proof that conservation has not yet touched these foundations of conduct lies in the fact that philosophy and religion have not yet heard of it. In our attempt to make conservation easy, we have made it trivial.[6]

More recently, in a plenary address to the American Association of the Advancement of Science, former President Jane Lubchenco made explicit the connection between knowledge of *how* to manage the planet and explanations as to *why* we've having to manage it in the first place.[7] The humanities, and religion especially, have the apparatuses to address the metaphysics of ecotheological theories and can speak to the moral reflection that occurs within scientific research. So, whereas science may fail to mobilize persons to address and solve moral problems because of its "value-free" identity, religion provides helpful insight into fundamental questions and informs how humans organize and live. Most recently, philosopher of environmental science Dale Jamieson, known to have previously lambasted Christianity for reasons akin to White's, posited that we humans have failed to respond to the challenge of climate change because we lack both charity and imagination. Recognizing the religious foundations of most lived virtues, Jamieson writes, "The challenge is not just to announce our values, as if they were preference for one flavor of ice cream over another, but to mobilize resources of reason, temperament, and shared perspectives to show how we can make progress in resolving our differences."[8]

And finally, a third reason for increased Christian interest in ecological matters relates to Christian witness, or what some communities might call mission and evangelism. Many mainline church communities in North America are experiencing decreased attendance, a symptom that some say corresponds to Christianity's lack of contemporary relevance. Studies like those of the "Religious Landscape Study" conducted by the Pew Research Forum indicate significant decreases among younger populations in recent decades.[9] Many pastors are wondering where the young people have gone. If they're not gathering at church, where are they gathering? Online. Outside. At public rallies and protests. Gallup and Pew Study polls on the preferences of millennials and Generation Z demonstrate great concern for growing social issues, including those related to environmental justice. Teens and young adults care about the earth and equitable access to it. So, as evangelical leaders like A. J. Swoboda have reflected, it follows that the Church ought to also, not only for opportunities to better connect with the youth, but also to lift them up as young Timothys—the leaders—of today.[10]

No matter what Christians' respective motivations for caring and acting, the church's sustained interest in the topic is evident. In the last fifteen years alone, over seven thousand titles related to the Christian tradition and ecology have been produced by major North American publishing houses. Since the formation of The National Religious Partnership for the Environment in 1993, over two hundred societies have emerged for the purposes of hosting eco-religious conversations and promoting ecological advocacy, sixty-one of them decidedly Christian.[11] Throughout the continent, college religion departments and Divinity schools are hiring theologians and ethicists specializing in eco-theology, offering tailored coursework in the area. Surely this spring of concern can and should be viewed in contrast to the anthropocentric Christianity of Sittler and Carson's day, for increased awareness of environmental moral culpability is something to be celebrated. Yet, as already noted, the manner in which the Christian Church's interests have developed vary and often default to a stance of incongruity, division, and lack of shared resolve. So, how and where can Christians come together to put this increased concern for the earth to better practice?

ONE CHURCH, MANY METHODOLOGIES

A great deal of time has been spent defending respective views on Christian ecological ethics rather than on coalescing traditions' various strengths. Deliberating in theoretical and abstract realms, Christianity's short tenure in the department of ecological ethics has largely focused upon the deconstruction and reconstruction of what I call terreologies, or theoretical approaches to ecological ethics. Just as Lynn White vigorously commended religious persons to rethink and refuel their respective spiritual traditions, most ecologically-mindful Christians have sought to reconsider longstanding axioms and beliefs, particularly those promulgating dualisms between the temporal and spiritual. Akin to cognitive behavioral principles of psychotherapy where the focus is on a patient's ability to identify, recognize, and ultimately change thinking on a particular topic, the focus of terreological approaches to Christian eco-ethics has been to reshape belief regarding humanity's relationship to the natural world, trusting that changes in one's ecological behavior and lifestyle will then commence. As we shall see, Christian terreologies greatly vary, ranging from human-centric perspectives to radically organism-centric points of view. Even within a particular shared framework, Christian terreologies employ different metaethical principles. And so, one cannot help but ask, isn't this a problem? In light of contemporary environmental decline, shouldn't Christians be unified in a universal terreological approach to caring for the earth?

Increasingly many are answering no. Pragmatists, agrarians, and social biologists see a plurality of approaches as critical. Among environmental pragmatists the conversation about nature's value (i.e., whether it is innate or functional) is minimized and in most cases abandoned. Environmental pragmatists argue that there will never be consensus on nature's value given the varied ways in which persons experience and understand their relationship to the natural world. Furthermore, such theoretical conversation pays little attention to the practical strategies that moral communities utilize when confronting environmental problems. The more urgent consideration, and indeed the more pragmatic one, relates to nature's political possibility and humans' civic relationship to it.[12]

Similarly, agrarians argue that responsible action occurs as we directly and practically see and feel our connections with each other and the land. Thus, agrarianism stresses the importance of local economies and the uniqueness of ecosystems, keeping one's membership in an agricultural community fairly limited and therefore one's ethic particular to locale. Agrarians with Christian ties such as Wes Jackson, Wendell Berry, and Norman Wirzba posit that if our faith communities better see how our living practices depend upon the land and impact the land they'll be more inclined to choose beneficial practices.[13] So in agrarian perspective eco-ethics are cosmological or universal only insofar as every ethic must honestly ask the questions, "Where am I?" and "How am I to live in this place?"

And along these same lines, social ecologists point out that in addition to the difficulty of nailing down any one terreology, serious thought must be given to the social construction of belief. Building upon Derrida's subjectivism, thinkers like Bron Taylor remind us that views of self, other, and metaphysical realities are in flux and are a direct result of our social experiences.[14] Bruno Latour suggests that the same is true for science. Science seeks to supply the metaphysical in a grammar inclusive of both the speculative and imperative, but in so doing always undergoes a process of interpretation itself. There are no facts that are not also human constructs.[15] Through our actions and interactions we come to know what we think about the world, so what is needed is not a "right" terreology, but rather increased consciousness about the terreology one is employing.

RECONFIGURED TERREOLOGIES

Various metaethical principles manifest in different eco-ethical approaches. In the interest of championing a pluralist approach, it's useful to clearly identify differences between them, as well as common threads. To do so, I utilize Michael Northcott's paradigmatic approach from *Christian Ethics and the Environment*. Northcott suggests that we can easily categorize approaches within three frameworks: anthropocentrism, theocentrism, and biocentrism.[16] Under these headings let us explore the landscape of Christian thought on ecological ethics, noting where along the deontological-teleological spectrum these respective ethical views fall while also recognizing their strengths and weaknesses.

Anthropocentrism

The dominant historical approach to Christian ecological ethics has been anthropocentric, focusing on the active and intentional agency of the human being. This is due in part to longstanding conceptions of how nature relates to human civilization. Prior to the mid-twentieth century it was commonplace to view human power over nature as a derivative of intelligence. "Civilization," the pioneer social philosopher Auguste Comte of the late-nineteenth century wrote, "consists, strictly speaking, on the one hand in the development of the human mind, on the other in the result of this, namely, the increasing power of Man over Nature."[17] As evident in the discussion below, such a focus hasn't been all bad, as anthropological approaches do draw attention to human responsibility. And in this Anthropocene, we humans are growing increasingly aware of the part we play in environmental degradation.[18] Through looking at three particular anthropocentric approaches—godly dominion, stewardship, and priesthood—it's also clear how anthropocentrism's tendency to apply personalized philosophical ethical schemas to nature underestimates natural beings' own agency. With these overarching strengths and weaknesses in mind, I turn now to a closer examination of anthropocentric terreologies.

Godly Dominion

While undoubtedly a minority view in today's theological landscape, the concept of humans exercising dominion over creation in god-honoring ways remains. Older names such as Francis Schaeffer and John Black responded to White's critique in the early 1970s by defending Christian doctrine. In *Pollution and the Death of Man: The Christian View of Ecology*, Schaeffer argues that orthodox Christian theology already holds the answer to our ecological challenges. It does not stand in need of reform; rather, what necessitates change (albeit in large scale) is Christian behavior. Christians, Schaeffer writes, are worse off in the area of ecology than animists, who cautiously and minimally cut down trees due to their belief of spirits residing within the wood. This is not because such nature spiritualists give a greater value to the tree than Christians ought to, but rather due to the church's lack of action on known values.[19] Christians, Schaeffer laments, have focused so heavily upon humankind's separation from "lower forms of creation," a distinction that mirrors the even more significant traverse between humans and God, that they have lost sight of humans' fundamental relationship to creation.[20] What is needed is a reminder of humans' responsibility to use the land as God did in the very act of creation. Turning to the Genesis accounts, Schaeffer recounts how God subdues (*kabash*) and rules over (*radah*) the land. He uses language of higher and lower beings and worship as upward to God rather than downward to creation to flesh out this power dynamic. Calling upon Psalm 8 and Ecclesiastes 3:18–21, Schaeffer asserts that human beings are encouraged, indeed even required, to utilize the land for production and to return human-land relations to their prelapsarian state. Aligning himself with Francis Bacon's thesis in *Novum Organum*—namely that humankind ought to use science, technology, and the arts toward the aim of restituting dominion over the earth—Schaeffer argues that while the land, fecund with interrelated life forms, is valuable within its own "proper sphere of creation," it nevertheless exists in part to serve humankind.[21] Naturally, this is due to the land's utility, as it provides what humans need. But it's also due to the theological destiny of the land, as from Schaeffer's vantage it is already substantially healed and promised to be made whole in the end.

John Black, former professor of forestry and natural resources at the University of Edinburgh and contemporary of Schaeffer's, suggests that the two primary instructions in the Genesis 1 creation narrative, 1) "Be fruitful and multiply and replenish the earth," and 2) "Have dominion over the earth and subdue it," need to be understood not only as direct commands or divine imperatives, but also as projections of what would take place in human history. Calling upon source and redaction criticism and noting the development of the Genesis creation accounts via the ninth-century Yahwist (Genesis 2) and sixth-century Priestly (Genesis 1) documents, Black argues that by the time the texts were composed in written form the Hebrew people could reflect on their increased number and sense of environmental control. In his words,

> With their concept of history as the working-out of the divine purpose, there could be little difference between God's "Do this" and His "This is what will happen": in both ways of expression, man's license is established and it does not really alter if it is put across as command or forecast. Since God knew what was to happen in the future, commands and forecasts were essentially the same thing; hence there is no conflict between the two interpretations.[22]

Dominion, as it were, was inevitable. Black argues that this is true in the texts and true of human nature in general. Even if the dominion of man over nature reaches an absurd state, with the destruction of the habitable earth, no change in attitude will be needed. Rather, limits to dominion are what have always been needed and will continue to prove important. While Black moves beyond Shaeffer in understanding biblical concepts of dominion as a prophesy as much as command, their respective outlooks and desires to defend Christian doctrine are similar. Limits are necessary to enact reasonable control or godly rule. Subjugation of the earth must be held in check with a view toward long-term sustenance of the environment and the well-being of future humans, a view that as we shall see below opens the door for later conversations on creation care as stewardship.[23]

The prosperity of human beings, present and future, is a central aspect of Cal Beisner's contemporary argument for an ethic of godly dominion.[24] A spokesperson for the conservative, evangelical Cornwall Alliance, Beisner builds upon Schaeffer's argument with a renewed focus on the Christian imperative to utilize the land for the sake of free enterprise. The liberal environmental movement, Beiser argues, puts the needs of the planet before the needs of people; animals, trees, and ecosystems may end up thriving as a result of such a perspective, but the poor will not. In response to NASA's 2014 report and President Barack Obama's 2015 State of the Union Address, Beisner reiterates his longstanding thesis, "Spending billions or trillions of dollars fighting perceived global warming will have devastating impacts on the poor. It is an oppressive, rich man's game."[25] Given the centrality of humankind *creatio imago Dei* in his working anthropology, this tradeoff is unacceptable. In the spiritual sense it is dishonorable. Above all, Christians are called and required to protect human life, which will naturally come at the expense of other creaturely life. Beisner associates the privileging of ecosystems above persons with the common failure to distinguish between Adam's call to till (*abad*) and keep (*shamar*) the blessed Eden in Genesis 2:15 with humanity's more general directive to subdue and rule over the entire earth in Genesis 1:28. With Eden being an especially good place, Beisner reasons that Adam's call to godly dominion was to transform the rest of the earth "bit by bit . . . glory to glory," just as contemporary Christians must see the earth as imperfect and in need of transformation.[26] Going one step beyond Black and Schaeffer, he suggests that dominion is not only responsible use of and power over the earth's bounty, but also an act of co-creation itself. The subduing and ruling over the earth should gradually lessen as humankind works to transform through creative acts the earth into God's garden, wherein dominion will metamorphose into the more romantic view of tilling and keeping.[27]

As briefly demonstrated above, proponents for reclaiming dominion differ among themselves, even in their interpretation of subdue and rule. Yet, common among them is a clear delineation between Creator and creation. In this approach to creation care the sovereignty of God proves paramount, with the divinely-inspired law available to humans for the purposes of executing God's will in creation. And in many ways this perspective's deontological form makes possible one of its strengths, a high regard for the aseity of God. Moreover, its deliberations on the unique role of human beings acknowledges the human inclination to assert power over the natural world and can help Christians prioritize responsible production over and above persistent consumption.

As critics of anthropocentric approaches have repeatedly articulated, such strengths do not outweigh the pernicious effects of dominion. To begin, more sacramentally-oriented thinkers claim that the view endorses faulty and misinformed hierarchies with little to no biological grounding. For example, in his recent work, *Earth-honoring Ethics,* Larry Rasmussen gives an overview of the evolutionary science that lends itself to a more modest and even shrunken view of the human. Noting how only 10 percent of the cellular human body is uniquely human, the rest merely a home or host for other forms of life, he suggests that religious persons be wary of any view that ratifies human subjugation of nature and instead recall and remember St. Augustine's fifth-century wisdom: our bodies are the earth we carry.[28] In attempts to highlight the uniqueness of *creatio imago Dei*, proponents of dominion approaches minimize humans' deep interrelatedness with the rest of creation and in so doing tend little to the ways the persons of the Trinity interrelate (or what is often referred to as the immanent Trinity, as opposed to the economic Trinity). Another common critique of godly dominion perspective relates to its rather utopian view of current environmental circumstances, and naïve hope for the future. As Richard Bauckham passionately articulated in his response to Calvin Beisner's presentation at the annual Evangelical Theological Society meeting in 2012, proponents of dominion put too much trust in free-market principles and in human ability to faithfully deploy them while not near enough stock in majority-view scientific findings. Accusing such advocates of "playing silly games with pseudoscience," Bauckham, along with many other contemporary biblical scholars, suggests that such ignorance not only undermines the well-being of the earth and its inhabitants, but also the relevance and authority of the Christian Scriptures for the way in which it mishandles the Genesis narrative and avoids other important texts. "Remember Galileo," Bauckham implored, whose story illustrates the dangers of predicting from Scripture what science must observe.[29] Characterizing most dominion proponents as climate deniers, Willis Jenkins suggests that beyond poor exegesis, this view endorses a Christ-against-culture paradigm which ultimately leads to nihilism. Beisner and others need not use their Christian sensibilities to address the ecology of culture "because ecological problems don't exist."[30] And finally, even those who grant a natural position of human power over nature question human ability to exercise power with sacrificial love. They ask, does not an approach of godly rule over the earth minimize the impact of sin, thereby leaving the earth vulnerable to justified abuse and religiously endorsed oppression?[31] Many theologically conservative thinkers share the latter concern and in response have constructed a more moderate managerial perspective, that of stewardship.

Stewardship

The term "stewardship" finds its origin in the work of the late Matthew Hale, a distinguished seventeenth-century Chief Justice of England. Seeking to prove that the essential truths of religion need not depend upon revelation, but rather could be derived through observation of natural phenomena, Hale describes in *The Primitive Origination of Mankind* that humankind's responsibility is to be the viceroy, steward, or bailiff of this "goodly farm of the lower world."[32] Far from being the dominators of the earth, Hale saw humans as needing to be a tribute of fidelity and obedience, persons who could husband the world while enjoying its fruits with sobriety, moderation, and thankfulness. In relationship to nature, human power should be understood not as power over, but rather in Hale's terms the power to:

> correct and abridge the excesses and cruelties of the fiercer Animals, to give protection and defence to the masuete and useful, to preserve the Species of diverse Vegetables, to improve them and others, to correct the redundance of unprofitable Vegetables, to preserve the face of the Earth in beauty, usefulness, and fruitfulness. And surely, as it was not below the Wisdom and Goodness of God to create the very Vegetable Nature, and render the Earth more beautiful and useful by it, so neither was it unbecoming the same Wisdom to

ordain and constitute such a subordinate Superintendent over it, that might take an immediate care of it.[33]

This metaphor of superintendent has been espoused by many Christian scientists and theologians, who desire to practically acknowledge humankind's historical power in creation on the one hand and great dependence upon it on the other. A Dutch-reformed Christian, professor of environmental studies, and former curator of the University of Wisconsin's arboretum, Cal DeWitt argues that to be a steward is to first remember where human beings come from—Adam from *adamah*—the earth itself and Eve its animating breath of life.[34] As a shepherd attends to and keeps the flock that provides for their very livelihood, so too Christians ought to take care of and advocate for the natural world. However, from this perspective concern for the earth is born not only out of self or human interest, but also out of a divine mandate to serve and keep the land. So, while proponents like DeWitt remain optimistic about human intervention and transformation of the earth, they suggest that any such efforts be siphoned through something akin to Aldo Leopold's land ethic, wherein whatever is right and good is what is right and good for the land.[35] This focus on the Yahwist creation narrative contextualizes the Priestly account in Genesis 1, fundamentally portraying human dominion over the earth as human responsibility to first care for it.

But how? To what end and by what means can this great commission, not of co-creation but rather of keeping, be accomplished? DeWitt suggests that praxis always be considered as integrally related to *scientia* and ethics. *Scientia*, in this case, refers to one's knowledge of how the world works. It includes, "what we have come to call natural science but goes beyond this to include what we learn in social sciences and humanities, and beyond this to whatever other things human beings learn from living in the biosphere."[36] Ethics is the intergenerational body of knowledge about what ought to be with respect to human actions in the biosphere. Related to both, a lived-out contemporary stewardship ethic seeks to do two things: 1) in its serious appraisal of the science behind global environmental change it acknowledges how incompetent and corrupt human custody over the land has been and 2) by retrieving and reviving Scripture's emphasis of service to the land it promotes the transformation of personal and corporate values, opening doors for renewed interest in virtue ethics.

In the past decade Roman Catholics and Protestants, both individually as well as in communion, have colored classical conversations on *arête* green. For example, Roman Catholic Celia Deane-Drummond, a biologist and systematic theologian by training, reads the Aristotelian/Thomist virtue tradition in light of contemporary science, arguing that positive local environmental impact as undertaken by individuals is the most effective way to address the behemoth of climate change. In its primary focus on agents and virtue, she argues, "forces a degree of self-reflection that is not always achievable when the problems are identified as external or alien to ordinary human lives."[37]

It is these very virtues that Reformed theologian Steven Bouma-Prediger builds upon in his virtue-oriented ethic of stewardship. Like DeWitt and Deane-Drummond, Bouma-Prediger argues that humans should enjoy and use creation as needed, while also advocating for the rest it was intended to experience. Therefore, practicing virtue is necessary, lest perceived human needs overtake the innate needs of nature. From Bouma-Prediger's vantage, the translation of classical virtues into ecological and biological terms is an integral part of any stewardship ethic. To enact wisdom, humans must practice temperance in light of creational finitude, patience as trust in nature's rejuvenating fecundity, and respect through mindful relationship to the biodiversity of inhabited ecosystems.[38] Louke van Wensveen's book, *Dirty Virtues,* makes the connection between stewardship and the virtues even more explicit, although proves more critical of the Aristotelian/Thomist model of virtue as endorsed by thinkers like Deane-Drummond. Attempting to situate ecological virtue as an individual's response to God's law more so than one's coming of age (or realization of potential) van Wensveen sees virtue as helpful in the bringing together of emergent praxis and ecological interpretation and expression of Scripture and theology.

The ethical construct of stewardship is one of the most prevalent in the ecumenical Christian eco-ethics conversation. Proponents of earth-keeping employ teleological, deontological, and virtue metaethical principles alike, differing in their response to the question of intent, namely, "Why care to be a caretaker in the first place?" There are many strengths of the stewardship model, one certainly being its applicability in a number of theological traditions. Yet another strength relates to the attention given to humans' radical dependence upon the earth. Far more than something we merely use, this view's anthropology is much more biologically informed than that of the dominion perspective. Even if managers of the land, we remain of the land itself, humans from the humus. A third strength of stewardship is its practicality. Providing a structure for reflection upon the virtues, it offers communities of faith concrete examples of ethical behavior and in so doing puts limits upon human power.

Despite being a widespread perspective on Christian ecological ethics this view has been heavily criticized and remains contested.[39] One of its critiques relates to the reading of Genesis 1–2. Richard Bauckham, in *The Bible and Ecology*, argues that just as dominion advocates tend to overlook the Yahwist creation account, so injuriously stewardship proponents overlook the Priestly account. He suggests that if we understand *kabash* (to subdue) of Genesis 1:28 in proper reference to its object, the land (*eretz*), we can understand the toil of agriculture pursuit. Moreover, if we read *radah* in proper context, including the ways in which it is used elsewhere throughout the prophetic texts, the imperative of "rule over" explicitly connects to human-animal relationship, not the human relationship to the natural world in general. Both of these examples from the Priestly account give us information about *how* we are to communally relate to the land and to the animals, and it isn't a particularly romantic view. To read stewardship as care for and service toward the earth without taking into consideration these harsher realities is to neglect a critical aspect of the larger biblical narrative.

Along with biblical scholars like Bauckham, many scientists and environmental ethicists see stewardship as utopian, noting its soft and naïve interpretation of human/nature relations. As environmental ethicist Holmes Rolston III reminds us, nature is wild, violent, and unpredictable. To claim any semblance of control over it is to totally ignore the realities of biology. Humans, therefore, must shed any pretense of human control. Such critics agree that what is more helpful than a managerial ideal is the acceptance of nature's homeostasis. Remembering to take the long view, humans must see nature as capable, albeit sometimes through violent means, of renewing and restoring itself. Too often stewardship models promote a conservationist attitude toward nature when it is clear that parts of the environment have undergone irrevocable changes; an ethic built upon preservation is unrealistic and sometimes undesirable. Critics argue that in the end this perspective puts too much stock on human awareness and ingenuity and attends too little to human inclination toward abuse and ignorance. And, given the realities of climate change, this critique isn't far off. It isn't that stewardship as a model of preservation is altogether wrong, but more so practically inadequate. At a minimum, this approach to Christian ecological ethics must be supplemented with more active stances, including those endorsing intervention.

Priesthood

Eastern orthodox thinkers like John Chryssavgis, Paulos Gregorios, and John Zizioulas share the above criticisms of stewardship. Positioning humans as managers of the land, even if conscious and grateful ones, undercuts the undeniable, organic connection between humans and nature. Zizioulas argues that eco-ethics is less a conversation about *what to do* and more a conversation about *who to be*. Our concern is ontological, not moral; for if we humans don't love creation we're not only unethical, but in fact cease to be at all![40] What is needed, Gregorious and Zizioulas suggest, is a human-centric ethic wherein people see themselves as priests for all of creation. Theologically speaking, priests are conduits, mediators, or vessels who aim to return unto God what was God's in the first place in order that it might be saved and fulfilled. Just as Christianity's high priest, Jesus, sacrificially loved human beings and laid down his life to make a way for reconciling communion with God, so too humans are to sacrificially love the natural world and seek to preserve it for God's sake. This is humanity's special vocation, according to Gregorios.[41] The orthodox liturgy makes this principle clear, when at the apex of the Eucharist service the priest holds up the bread and wine and together all say in unison, "Thine of thine own we offer unto Thee."

Humans have this special role among beasts due to constitutive ordering, or the *logos*, which comes with being made in God's image. Zizioulas reminds us that neither biology nor rationality renders humans unique from other animals; rather, what sets us apart is the desire to create. *Logos*, although often translated as rationality or one's capacity to reason with the mind, is primarily about human beings' capacity to collect and use fragments within the world to make a unified world (*cosmos*).[42] So while we human beings are inextricably connected to the natural world we "rise above creation and make use of it in a free way, either by creating something new or sometimes by simply destroying what is 'given.'"[43] The distinguishing factor between humans and nature need not be understood as some *thing* placed within humans as much as it is a particular function required of humans, or what Gregory of Nyssa called the *autexousion*—the freedom of the human being. From the dust humans were created and to the dust we shall return, but during the interim of spent life humans carry a mantle of responsibility.

Priesthood views have garnered more attention among Protestants in recent years. This is in part due to Orthodoxy's outspoken "Green Patriarch" Bartholomew, who has called the environmental crisis the greatest challenge yet set before the Church of Christ.[44] Interest in priesthood models has also grown because of the advantages it holds over the aforementioned anthropocentric views. First, priesthood's emphasis on the earthy embodiment of human beings and the sacramentalism of nature dovetails well with modern science. There is room for evolutionary biology within this framework and openness to the beauty and intricate wonder found beyond the boundaries of theology because the world, while neither a phenomenon nor a collection of them, is "the horizon within which phenomena appear."[45] All activity within the world is sacred. Priesthood perspectives are also strong in that they uphold the uniqueness of the human being, a theme that is arguably necessary for any eco-ethic to remain distinctively Christian. As we shall later see by way of comparison, priesthood successfully avoids the pantheistic pitfalls of some biocentric views. And finally, in light of contemporary ecological science, the priesthood view holistically deals with questions of praxis. On a very foundational level this model goes beyond functional methodologies while still including functionality. That is, in asking the question of *who* to be rather than just *what* to do, Christians are encouraged to consider how respective lifestyles impact other life forms. As we shall see below, clear connections emerge between this view's attentiveness to the interconnectedness of all things and a more radically theocentric Trintarian perspective.

There are some significant weaknesses to this perspective, however. To begin, the Bible is full of examples of nature—mountains, trees, river, and birds—returning to and glorifying God with no human intervention. So how is one to understand natural revelation and such texts in light of Zizioulas' argument that nature ultimately dies without some human intervention?[46] Ecological restorationists like Jordan Williams and Dan Spencer remind us that death, a good and critical part of any and all ecosystems, begets life. Trinitarian theologian, Jurgen Moltmann offers a similar perspective in theological terms: "In the life of love, dying is experienced daily and a resurrection every morning. Every act of love is experienced by a man as a little death and every birth is experienced by the woman as a surrender of life. So loving and dying are not antithesis. They are correspondences."[47] What's more is that priesthood views can be hard to swallow historically. When one considers how Christian communities have interacted with nature in the past, and how all communities are implicated in the perfect moral storm of today's Anthropocene it is difficult to make a case for human sacrificial love of the earth. In short, is it appropriate to identify humans as priests when we like no other species in earth's history have wreaked havoc upon the planet? This is a critique of anthropocentric views in general and has led some to endorse a different ethical methodology, theocentrism.

Theocentricism

Since the mid-twentieth century, critics of anthropocentric approaches have cast environmental problems as a perspective problem more than a behavioral one. The issue isn't humans' lack of godly dominion, responsible care, or sacrificial love for the earth; it is the centrality of human beings. Theocentric readings of the Scriptures and ethical approaches highlight God's agency in and through creation, typically espousing a more panentheistic theology. Primarily concerned with divine will, theocentrism often utilizes the deontological ethical framework, situating morality within the scope of Christian worship. A Christian ought to treat the natural world with care not only because the law calls one to, but also because God is present within nature's very own laws. As we shall see with regards to both trinitarian and sacramental forms of eco-ethics, the downside of theocentrism can be its abstraction.

Trinitarianism

In *Summa Contra Gentiles* II.3, Thomas Aquinas famously argued that any error about creation leads to errors about God. Today, many Trinitarian theologians participating in conversations about ecology, ethics, and Christian doctrine are turning Aquinas's phrase, acknowledging that errors regarding one's conception of God can and have led to devastating errors about creation. Trinitarians have attempted to redefine the picture of the creating God through the lens of relationship. Rather than focusing upon the distinctive features of each Trinitarian person, attention is given to the immanence or divine inter-subjectivity of the persons. In the Trinitarian perspective, the space for the wholly other exists in God, as does the space for living with the other. Creator, Redeemer, and Sustainer are with and in each other, just as all of creation is with God and held in God. Therefore, care for creation from this perspective is an acknowledgement of the Triune God's creating and sustaining power and is ultimately an act of hopeful worship.

The influential Trinitarian Karls of the twentieth century, Barth and Rahner, both argued that creation and redemption are but two phases in one larger event. For Barth, all is held collectively in Christ, the cosmic figure. Any lived ecological ethic is therefore merely a response to God's divine presence and command through God's Word. Rahner also cast duty as central, but extended his Trinitarian vision a bit further trusting in the order and purposes of the natural world. From Rahner's perspective humans are to relate to creation equitably not only in response to God's law, but also out of a love for Christ who is the "center of creation" poured out over the cosmos.[48]

While aligned with Barth and Rahner in many ways, Reformed Trinitarian Jürgen Moltmann radicalizes monotheism yet further. Seeing Barth and Rahner as monarchialists for the ways they strove to maintain God's sovereignty above all else (Barth by beginning with self-revelation and Rahner by beginning with self-communication), Moltmann describes the Trinity as vulnerable and open.[49] That is, through the process of *perichoresis*, or mutual interpenetration of each Trinitarian person upon the others, the wholly other exists in God's own being. Adopting Isaac Luria's *zimzum* theory Moltmann argues that even in *creatio originalis* God created a space that is not also God. "The existence of a world outside God is made possible by an inversion of God," Moltmann writes, "This sets free a kind of 'mystical primordial space' into which God—issuing out of himself—can enter and in which he can manifest himself. Where God withdraws himself from himself to himself, he can call something forth which is not divine essence or divine being."[50]

The act of creation, then, also speaks to the paradox of Christian existence. For while God's creative powers testify to the limitless potential and promise within the Godhead, creation can also be seen as the first act in the divine self-humiliation, which reached its profoundest point in the cross of Christ. God remains distinct from creation just as creation remains reliant upon God's creating and sustaining power, but to Moltmann's main point—all due to God's deeply relational motivation.

Part of this created other is the presence of human beings. While often thought of as the apex or pinnacle of creation given their unique status as *creatio imago Dei*, Moltmann submits that Sabbath is in fact the high point of creation and that humans are better understood as *creatio imago Trinitatis*. This is because "the creation of God's image on earth means that in his work God finds, as it were, the mirror in which he recognizes his own countenance—a correspondence which resembles him."[51] Rather than utilizing Dionysian-Thomistic models of *analogia entis*, Moltmann applies his Trinitarian doctrine of God and creation as God's self-limitation to anthropology and argues that understanding the human within the constructs of the divine relations is more biblical, practical, and ethical. So, for him *analogia relationis* becomes the foundation of the human's relationship to the world at large. As mutual subjects with all of nature, humanity is to stand in solidarity with creation in distress just as the Creator and Sustainer stood in solidarity with the self-sacrificing Redeemer, Jesus.[52] And so "the person who protects the earth for God's sake protects it for its own sake . . . and finally for the sake of the human being."[53]

An obvious strength of Trinitarian perspectives is the evasion of anthropocentrism. In placing the natural world within God, Trinitarianism highlights the value of nature apart from its utility to humans and locates the providence of creation beyond the human co-creator. The earth exists both because of and for God's glory. And to this end Trinitarianism brings to bear the strengths of the deontological tradition, wherein human responsibility is understood as a faithful and obedient response to God's purposes and will. Furthermore, by emphasizing the immanent aspects of the Godhead, Trinitarian approaches are naturally poised to address the interconnected nature of our contemporary ecological challenges. The complexity of nature is met and reflected within the complexity of the Godhead itself. So rather than thinly focusing an ethic on prescribed behavior, bound to require perennial adaptation with a dynamically shifting environment, Trinitarianism helpfully draws our attention to the consequences of our relatedness.

There are weaknesses to this view as well, however. For example, how are we to understand theodicy and the devastating ecological realities we face if creation is held in God? If panentheism then why pandemic? Even if one adopts an eschatologically hopeful outlook, wherein *creatio nova* shapes the reality of now, it's difficult to know how to respond to increasingly bad news. Future-focused optimism can fail to activate and motivate believers in the here and now and has the potential to promote complacency as one seeks to rely upon God to make right what we humans, with technology and science, have made so wrong. Additionally, more pragmatic critics view Trinitarianism as overly abstract and ironically under-embodied. It is one thing to have ideas about how the world relates to God and quite another to experience it. What is needed, other theocentric thinkers suggest, is a more radically sacramental view. It is to this view that we now turn.

Sacramentalism

Sacramentality is also a panentheistic perspective, wherein all things have their origin and sustenance in God. Where it differs from Trinitarianism is in its attention to the elements—the water, grapes, and wheat, and every other living thing under the heavens. It is in these sacramental realities that the locus of communion with God is tangibly found; through the gleaming meadows and waters, burning stars and sun one experiences the Divine.[54] Generally speaking, sacramental readings of Scripture align with Dionysian or Bonaventurian emphases on sentimentality and affectivity toward nature, employing an almost biophilic hermeneutic.[55]

This is evident, for example, in the work of James Nash. Espousing a cosmic Christology and, like most Trinitarians, a robust pneumatology, Nash sees God as "intimate with the creation, actively involved, self-revealing, and grace-dispensing, leaving signs and making the divine presence felt in all things—in personal, cultural and natural histories."[56] The biophysical world is critical, not only because it exists for and in God, but also because it plays a critical role in mediating religious experience through the sensate.[57] Through the cosmos all creatures commune with the hidden and real God, who is in, with, and under all the earth. And these embodied holy experiences are morally and spiritually regenerative. The sacramental presence of the Spirit sacralizes nature, calling the human species to live in concord with God's beloved habitat.[58]

Taking the metaphor of habitat a step further, ecofeminist Sallie McFague refers to the world as God's body. Clear about the limitations of the metaphor McFague suggests that God is available to us through the mediation of embodiment alone and in this way all bodies reflect God and collectively constitute God's body as the "backside of glory."[59] A helpful way to think about God's relationship with the natural world, McFague suggests, is to hold in tension agential and organic models, wherein God as the breath of life directs and guides the evolutionary processes of life.[60] For McFague, akin to Nash, it isn't that God is completely embodied by creation, nor is it that God is disembodied. Rather, God is in all finite creatures while not exhausted by them. Thus, what happens to the natural world happens to God. When nature, the "new poor," is overlooked and exploited, God is denounced, and likewise, when creatures great and small are listened to and cared for, God is worshipped.[61]

Roman Catholic ecofeminists Rosemary Radford-Ruether and Ivone Gebara also employ sacramental cosmologies aiming for a mutual and equitable ecological ethic. Critical of Platonism and its legacy of dualisms, Radford-Ruether utilizes Pierre de Chardin's theology of cosmogenesis to argue for the interdependency of all things and the value of the personal in communion. There is no me without the we, no life without death. For, "the material substances of our bodies live on in plants and animals, just as our own bodies are composed from minute to minute of substances that once were parts of other animals and plants . . ."[62] Not only does the physical world help us humans recognize and begin to make sense of God's privileged axis or *telos*, but what's more is that it also aids in our own self-understanding. We are kin with creatures and all living things, linked to God who can only be perceived in and through Gaia, or the interconnected life force of the cosmos. From Gebara's vantage, this is the case because God is not primarily essence or person, but rather relationship. Any knowledge of God, it follows, is experiential and a matter of process.[63] Religion, like ecosystems, is biodiverse. Rather than espousing a universalistic, imperialist theory that can explain the universe and its complex relationships, Gebara urges Christians to notice and reflect upon the material realities of one's own domain, paying special attention to the ways we actually live our lives. Similar to the pragmatists we will hear from below, Gebara suggests that what unites ecologically-minded religious persons is:

> the desire to reconstruct our human relationships and to develop in ourselves the values of sharing and mercy that are so often forgotten by the current system. What unites us is the need to feel, once again, the warmth of bodies around a common table, the need to be persons and not just numbers among so many others. What unites us is the desire to create a common language, to reclaim symbols that are connected to our history and that evoke the noblest things in us.[64]

One of the strengths of sacramentalism is its overt connection of abstract spiritual concepts with the material realm. As Dorothee Soelle suggested at the peak of the nuclear arms race in the early 1980s, any legitimate Christian theology must be examined by the extent to which it seriously addresses our biological realities, or in her words, our lives as "people of the dust."[65] Another strength of this terreology is the approach's coalescence with contemporary science. As the Anglican biochemist Arthur Peacocke observes, patterns of activity in the world of matter not only shed light upon what may be the mind of God, but they might also be the very means by which God's purposes are realized.[66] Therefore, what science reveals is not to be feared or scorned, but rather embraced and celebrated, if not in extension worshipped.

This last point relates to one of sacramentalism's most obvious weaknesses—its proximity to pantheism. Critics ask, are not orthodox standards of distinction between Creator and creation trumped by the criteria of immanent dependence?[67] They suggest that the difference between all things being God and all things sacramentally connecting us to God is a matter of mere semantics. Moreover, critics argue that sacramentalism unnecessarily romanticizes nature, not seriously heeding its innate violence and even chaos. And finally, a critique of sacramentalism that easily applies to Trinitarian thought as well is the approach's failure to practically address the beastly systems partially responsible for environmental decline. Revering nature as the connection with the Triune God doesn't change policy and certainly doesn't address our religiously pluralistic global context. And this is why some Christian lovers of nature suggest a radical cosmological shift, one that centers not upon humans or God, but upon the ecology of life itself.

Biocentrism

Among our three major working categories of reconfigured terreologies, biocentric approaches are least commonplace, known more for their proponents than for any unified methodology. Within biocentricism two major views exist: deep ecology and creation spirituality. Deep ecology is not representative of Christian views per se, although it has greatly influenced the larger conversation on religion and ecology by bringing more attention to marginal and indigenous religious traditions and by questioning the normative categories used in moral evaluation.[68] While one can recognize significant connections between deep ecology and theologies of becoming or process, it is arguable that deep ecologists working around the Christian framework have ceased to become distinctively Christian.[69] Therefore, the focus here shall be upon thinkers like Thomas Berry, John Cobb, and Charles Birch who, whether successfully or not, seek to remain tethered to the Christian tradition and its common beliefs.

Process Theology

Thomas Berry, deeply influenced by Teilhard de Chardin's synthesis, sees the universe as whole and one. To place God above or beside the material world is to piecemeal reality. The universe, he argues, is not some object to be studied or even some object to be cared for and adored. Rather, it is a subject in itself. Having a life of its own, Berry sees the universe to be God made manifest much more than a locale where God dwells or a place that God once created.[70] The earth community, which challenges and forces us like all species to struggle for survival, ultimately reveals itself as "a benign providence."[71]

For Berry, ecological ethics constitute the call for humans to reject cultural pathologies, which enslave us to what he calls an industrial mystique and coding. Instead we humans must re-discover a more shamanistic personality wherein through learning the language of various earth creatures, the mystique of the earth can return to us afresh. And this need not be a retreat to romanticism or idealism. Rather, Berry suggests it is a deep insight into the structure and functioning of the entire earth process, including its rhythms, historical transformations, bioregional diversity, pragmatic functioning, and revelatory communication. After all, in Berry's famous words, the ultimate custody of the earth belongs to the earth. The great work set before humans is to more authentically live into this reality, for "so long as we are under the illusion that we know best what is good for the earth and for ourselves, then we will continue our present course with its devastating consequences on the entire earth community."[72]

Cobb and Birch, who both espouse Whitehead's sense of a universe unfolding, articulate a similar biocentric methodology in their collaborative work, *The Liberation of Life*. In it they argue that God is less of a person, and if personal at all most certainly not a transcendent one. God is better understood as a principle of life, the very force under which creation evolves. This principle is the source of order and the fount of creative-responsive love. Any unique Christian ecological ethic is a manner and way of living that enables the emergence of life and honors the innate value therein.[73]

Christian nature spiritualities clarify the value of life unto itself and awaken human consciousness to the interconnectedness of life's forces. Built upon evolutionary phases of functional cosmology and human development, biocentrism's strength is in its pliability and scientific relevance. Yet if a mutuality model of relating ecological studies to Christian theology is applied biocentric approaches are hard pressed to maintain the autonomy of science and religion respectively. With the earth acting as a mediator of peace over and above the personal Christ, today's Christian may not help but question the integrity of the Gospel from a process point of view. Is Christ the Logos of the Cosmos or simply the enlightened One who has successfully submitted to the curvature of the universe?

ETHICS AS PRACTICED

More pragmatically-minded Christians have tired of such inquiries observing how the questions we ask govern the territory we're able to cover. Willis Jenkins, for example, has convincingly argued that many Christian eco-ethicists and theologians have swallowed the "Lynn White pill."[74] Ironically, in their ardent focus to refute White's claims, many Christians have unconsciously adopted White's discourse-shaping assumptions regarding relations between terreology and environmental problems. The prevailing discussion is that Western Christianity has promoted views of humans as separate from nature; therefore, human domination over it has perpetuated. The ecological solution is the reformation of our religious ideals and worldview, where humans are more explicitly connected to nature.

While moderate pragmatists like Jenkins see value in the reconfiguration of terreologies (or what he calls cosmologies) given the resource they can be toward the invention of new moral capacities and for the way they are called upon in actual practices, they ultimately argue for a more complex pluralist ethic. Contemporary Christian eco-ethics must recognize and honor the myriad eco-ethical approaches—from the moral to the biological, the political to the economic—which have emerged since White's 1967 critique. A failure to do so is to miss "the fertile grounds of lived experience" and to overlook "sites of creative theological production," neither of which can be afforded in our present anthropocenic context.[75]

As with terreological approaches to Christian ecological ethics, there is variance of perspective in practical eco-ethics. There are three primary trains of thought: natural value theory, constructivism, and ecological subjectivity.[76]

Natural Value Theory

Similar in sentiment to Christians endorsing biocentric terreological approaches, natural value theorists begin the conversation with nature itself. Believing that a non-anthropocentric value theory is imperative to inscribe environmental concerns into our everyday lives, Christians espousing this view work from within a deontological framework. Nature, as a law onto itself, must govern our moral standards. And while moral criteria can range from rational agency to emotional fellowship to sentience, this view sees ecological ethics as a matter of accounting for the integrity of the environment.[77]

Respected in theological and secular circles alike, Holmes Rolston III embodies this practical approach. Because human beings can recognize the process of valuation, wherein natural beings value themselves and pursue goods of their own kind, Rolston suggests that human agents attribute intrinsic value to living species, respecting and protecting such life.[78] This isn't to deny the value of passive and inert things, such as dirt, minerals, or air, although neither is it to promote moral responsibility for such inanimate entities.[79] Rather, natural value theory connects these small-scale elements and the larger biotic community, a realm Rolston likens to the sphere of divinity. "We might say that this is praising not so much the dirt as what God can make out of the dirt," Rolston wrote to a group of Christian ethicists months after the first UNCED Summit in 1992, ". . . another way of looking at this is that it is all direct, only we find revealed what dirt can do when it is self-organizing under suitable conditions with water and solar illumination. That is pretty special dirt."[80] Thus, in light of earth's wonders and the vivifying presence behind them said distinctions between duty to God and life in general become ambiguous if not entirely irrelevant. In the earth and therein God we live, move, and have our being; nature *is* grace. Therefore, the Church owes its ultimate moral allegiance to the earth.

A clear strength of this ethical approach is its alignment with a key tenet of nearly all Christian terreologies, namely that creation is valuable because of its relationship to the Creator. Easily baptized, this Leopoldian land-first ethic can give Christian communities clear regulations for life together. Moreover, its attention to valuation of objective, observable phenomena helps Christians contextualize and embody the ethic in a localized and particular fashion. To value the innate life of a creature one must know something about it. This is why Rolston encourages his readers to become competent naturalists every bit as much as sophisticated philosophers.[81]

This last strength can also be reckoned as a weakness insofar as overly localized definitions and descriptions of nature render it normatively obtuse on a more global scale. The onus of this view, therefore, is to demonstrate how nature's moral status bears upon environmental issues, which are specific to creatures and ecosystems on the one hand and complex with regards to policy on the other. Related to this, natural value theories must exhibit motivational "teeth" by which human agents can correlate features of organisms and their systems with concrete forms of moral respect. Some virtue accounts loosely affiliated with this camp suggest that care for the dignity of other-than-human life is a course of pursuing one's own flourishing, and therefore might be better understood as a constructed pragmatic approach, our next examined practical perspective.

Constructivism

Constructivists, who frequently draw upon social ecology, are more interested in moral agency than nature's value and perceive the locus of contemporary environmental problems to be malformed social practices rather than inadequate descriptions of the world. As the postmodern turn has made increasingly clear, not even science can speak to the value of nature since scientific classification has just as much to do with social practices as it does with the description of objects.[82] Because the descriptive and evaluative processes of environmental ethics are always taking place simultaneously, constructivism views the formal object of ethical enterprise as fundamentally political. Our only hope as a people, Christian philosopher of religion Roger Gottlieb argues, is to repair the lifeboat of human culture, which "carries us, as it were, on the sea of life—only as we are sailing it. Because there is no dry land—no life without culture—on which to switch to a totally different boat."[83]

In the Lutheran tradition, which since Sittler has sought to redefine the laws of nature and laws toward nature in a more theocentric light, innovative thinkers like Larry Rasmussen are demonstrating how behavioral changes frequently precede attitudinal ones. Merely greening cosmological models based on varying degrees of consumption will not suffice. Rather, the drag of normalcy must be politically resisted and conventional wisdom doubted. In this ecozoic age where the earth is proving to be a tough new place, what is needed are altogether new wineskins and fresh cloth.[84] From Rasmussen's perspective an authentic ecological ethic must emerge from beyond classical categories of moral theory, to an inclusive moral vision. The "anticipatory communities" that take up this great work should call upon myriad traditions, a matrix of community able to engage what he calls the critical triptych of contemporary affairs—economics, ecology, and religion.[85] Within an economy of communion, small and localized communities are better able to anticipate need. Thus, a globalized and politicized earth-honoring ethic emerges in the accumulation of numerous small-scale efforts and changes. Collectively such efforts come to a tipping point, he argues, which is organic, contextual, and ultimately more productive. The Christian's ethical challenge is clear from this pragmatic perspective—till and keep the very space in which you live, literally and figuratively.

Hailing from the Reformed tradition Gretel Van Wieren offers an approach similar to that of Rassmussen, although she pays less attention to matters of interpersonal justice on the whole. Taken with the environmental pragmatism of Christopher White and heavily influenced by William Jordan's model of ecological restoration, her Christian environmental ethic focuses on action-oriented visions, structural alterations, and concrete practices as appropriate to a context's ecological scale.[86] Van Wieren argues that ecological restoration, as one of many strategies in a pluralist Christian eco-ethic, advances conversations about sustainability by providing the necessary resources to transition from where we are now to where we need to be. By developing vernacular communal values such as cohabitation, sensuousness, and celebration, and by acting as both a symbolic action and also an ecological practice, restoration speaks to sustained action and personal lifestyle. As such it provides an antidote to the long-time separation of theory and action, thereby re-storying earth and our relationship to it.

Constructivism has garnered more attention in recent years due its realist leanings. Seeing the world as already humanized, proponents of this view promote a reformation of anthropocentrism rather than the rejection of it. Since our world for all its troubles has been produced through human practices and is, in Lawrence Buell's words, "a crisis of imagination," constructivism provokes Christians to better utilize our creative cultural resources. After all, Christianity has something to say about the "multivalent character of richer versus impoverished imaginations, greener versus defoliate power arrangements, just versus unjust politics, peaceful verses violent patterns of cultural habitation" and so on.[87]

A downside to constructivism is the potential reduction of life and its systems to social processes. Critics ask, doesn't nature itself play a reciprocal role in the formation of social selves? Connecting the flourishing of the environment with human flourishing by an appeal to the psychology of the ecological self, many evolutionary ecologists answer in the affirmative.[88]

Secondly, more agrarian-minded critics argue that social ecology's emphasis on alternative imagination differs little from natural value theory in its engagement of capitalism's logical structure. While constructivism seeks to radically redefine this cultural force, it nonetheless works within its framework and in so doing maintains a damaging dialectic between humanity and the environment instead of a promising intimacy of interdependence.

Ecological Subjectivity

A third practical strategy, framed in response to the aforementioned views, is ecological subjectivity. Ecological subjectivists value aspects of constructivism and natural value theory but see neither as adequately addressing the ecological character of personhood. Rather than being an autonomous moral agent or not one at all, nature ought to be seen as a reflexive and active participant in the production of self, society, and values. This heightened sense of interdependence, a familiar theme among deep ecologists, agrarians, ecofeminists, and advocates for eco-justice, calls for an ecologically reformed anthropology. The practical moral object is the self, which is fundamentally related to nature and social processes alike. To holistically address the self, this perspective attends to one's environmental experience, seeking to give an account for the ways landscape shapes human beings and human beings shape landscape.

Christian agrarianism exemplifies this approach in its dogged aim to localize ethics. Ecotheologian Norman Wirzba, for example, argues that when we close ourselves off from the manifold riches of spiritual and physical interdependency, we fail philosophically. Although the love of wisdom has historically pertained to otherworldiness—that is the soul's pursuit as set against or beyond the material realm—the very act of thinking is embodied and particular. We humans not only think *about* the world, but also *from* it. "It is only as we are faithful to the particularities and demands of place," Wirzba writes, "and accept responsibility for our actions in those places, that we can claim to be moral beings at all."[89] In the agrarian view, accepting responsibility implies gratefulness and the handing down of intact inheritance, both natural and cultural. Ethically this situates the ecological persona as a caretaker over the things the self did not and cannot make as well as an envisioneer of the cultural resources necessary to recognize and sustain interdependence.

Like agrarianism, contemporary social ecology connects human morality with the realities of landedness. For example, Stephen Kellert's lifetime of work puts forth the thesis that human beings are biocultural creatures, products of biological destiny while also capable of extraordinary cultural construction. His moral imperative of biophilia—defined as persons' inherent inclination to affiliate with the natural world—suggests that we "cannot flourish as individuals or as a species absent a benign and benevolent relationship to the world beyond ourselves, of which we are a part."[90] Critical to this good life is spirituality, and fundamental to spirituality is a sense of connectedness and purpose. These last two resources, kinship with other species and found meaning in life, are readily discovered in nature.[91] In this sense nature supports spiritual query and quest. Of equal importance to the ecological subjectivist, however, are the ways that such spiritual encounters with nature forge the social construction of religion. Nature not only underscores spirituality, but also fosters it. As Mary Evelyn Tucker has identified, Christianity and other major world religions read the circular relationship between nature and religion in one of four ways, with nature being: 1) metaphor, offering a stepping-stone to the Divine; 2) mirror, an expression of the Divine; 3) matrix, a place where people experience the Divine; or 4) material, the means for being in touch with the Divine.[92]

Nature's relationship to identity and the flourishing individual is a theme taken up in racial environmentalism and eco-justice theory. Examining the colonial impulse to conquer and privatize property, eco-justice traces similarities between the subjugation of land and people. A leading figure and scholar in the North American black church, Willie Jennings, skillfully observes how the historical encasement of land has directly related to the encasement of people. To the colonizer, space was (and is) meant to privatized, modified, and developed. The land was valuable to the extent that it brought forth quantifiable product able to be bought and sold. This misplaced desire was in turn applied to the human body and resulted in the ultimate site of commodification—slavery. These ways of seeing ushered in what Jennings calls a "new subjectivity of whiteness," wherein lighter-skinned persons were viewed as heirs of divine supercessionalism and thus the universal aesthetic standard. Jennings and other advocates for racial eco-justice work to show how the brokering of the white universal over the native particular has carried forward patterns of thinking and being, including those which sequester environmental concern to the realm of a few Caucasian elite.[93] And yet, because land has always marked its people and people their land, a revitalized racial imagination must not only retell the narrative and expand functional aesthetics, but more importantly generate greater literacy of our storied place. In contrast to the inconsequential geographical wandering that has become so commonplace, advocates for eco-justice commend the church to define itself topographically. To take seriously the work of expanding our notions of belonging, Jennings reminds us, we must live a life belonging first and foremost to the land.[94]

An obvious strength of ecological subjectivity as we've outlined it in agrarianism, social ecology, and eco-justice is the approach's spaciousness, as it holds in tension the inherent teleology of nature and the coercive power of social structures. In brief, it is a both/and approach or the more mediated ethic. By positioning the biocultural self as the primary interest of ethics, as opposed to natural value theory's emphasis on nature as object and constructivism's attention to social process, ecological subjectivity makes use of the strengths of the other views without risking abstraction or incongruence. It seeks to practically address anthropocentrism, whereas other perspectives seek to dismantle it or reclaim it by heightening the self's relationship both to God and biological other. The result is an embodied and contextualized ethic able to take root in the here and now while yet remaining malleable.

The most common critique of ecological subjectivity relates to its return to the past. While the thriving small farms of agrarianism, regular and refreshing encounters with nature in social ecology, and reimagining of the urban poor's landed heritage are well-intentioned aspirations, critics question their plausibility and efficacy. Being nostalgic isn't helpful, as our environmental challenges prove to be too immense and complex for small-scale responses. Moreover, antiquated retrievals of traditions long since passed can lead to ascriptivism. So, for example, whereas agrarianism often critiques neoliberal capitalism as a type of industrial bondage, critics ask if another sort of bondage is ironically inserted in its stead, that of idyllic neophyte.[95]

NOTES

1. Quoted in Linda Lear, *Rachel Carson: Witness for Nature* (New York: Henry Holt, 1997), 450.

2. One can see Carson's openness to the influences of spirituality in some of her lesser-known writings. For example, while responding to male scientific colleagues who critiqued her for being overly sentimental in her scientific approach, she told a group of journalists, "I am not afraid of being thought a sentimentalist when I stand here tonight and tell you that I believe natural beauty has a necessary place in the spiritual development of any individual or any society. I believe that whenever we destroy beauty, or whenever we substitute something man-made and artificial for a natural feature of the earth, we have retarded some part of man's spiritual growth" (Rachel Carson, *Lost Woods: The Discovered Writing of Rachel Carson*, edited by Linda Lear (Boston: Beacon Press, 1998), 160).

3. Joseph Sittler, "A Theology for the Earth" in *Environmental Stewardship: Critical Perspectives- Past and Present*, edited by R. J. Berry (New York: T & T Clark, 2006), 52.

4. Aruna Gnanadason, *Listen to the Women!: Listen to the Earth!* (Geneva: WCC Publications, 2005), 2–5.

5. Lynn White, "The Historical Roots of our Ecologic Crisis," *Science* 155 (March 10): 1207.

6. Aldo Leopold, *A Sand Country Almanac* (New York: Oxford University Press, 1966), 225.

7. Jane Lubchenco, "Entering the Century of the Environment: A New Social Contract for Science," *Science* 279, no. 5350 (1998): 495. See also J. Lubchenco, et al., "The Sustainable Biosphere Initiative: An Ecological Research Agenda," *Ecology* 72, no. 2 (1991).

8. Dale Jamieson, *Reason in a Dark Time* (New York: Oxford University Press, 2014), 76.

9. For the full report, see "U.S. Public Becoming Less Religious" on the Pew Forum's website: http://www.pewforum.org/files/2015/11/201.11.03_RLS_II_full_report.pdf, last accessed April 14, 2016.

10. See A. J. Swoboda, *The Dusty Ones: Why Wandering Deepens Your Faith* (Grand Rapids, MI: Baker Books, 2016) as well as his edited volume, *Blood Cries Out: Pentecostals,*

Ecology, and the Groans of Creation (Eugene, OR: Wipe & Stock, 2014). This is true among young Christians as well, who are in many cases leading their respective denominations to embrace more environmentally responsible practices. For example, the recently founded Young Evangelicals for Climate Action provides support and resources for students on evangelical college campuses and youth groups (www.yeaction.org).

11. For more information on the NRPE, see: http://www.nrpe.org (last accessed April 14, 2016).

12. Andrew Light, Eric Katz, and Robert Jordan represent this strain of thought. See Light and Katz's edited volume *Environmental Pragmatism* (New York: Routledge, 1995); and Light's "The Case for Practical Pluralism," in *Environmental Ethics: An Anthology*, Andrew Light and Holmes Rolston, eds. (Malden, MA: Blackwell, 2003), 229–248. See also William Jordan, *The Sunflower Forest: Ecological Restoration and the New Communion with Nature* (Berkeley: University of California Press, 2003).

13. Norman Wirzba, *The Essential Agrarian Reader* (Berkeley, CA: Counterpoint, 2003), 8.

14. Bron Taylor, *Deep Green Religion: Nature, Spirituality and the Planetary Future* (Berkeley: University of California Press, 2010).

15. Bruno Latour, *An Inquiry into Modes of Existence: An Anthropology of the Moderns* (Cambridge, MA: Harvard University Press, 2013). Theologically trained scientists, John Polkinghorne and the late Ian Barbour have also demonstrated through research on the intersection between science and religion that values are the foundation of any scientific method.

16. Michael Northcott, *The Environment and Christian Ethics* (Cambridge, UK: Cambridge University Press, 1996), 124. Northcott uses the terms *humancentric, theocentric*, and *ecocentric*. I have modified these terms to better situate the conversation in our contemporary context, but nonetheless adopt his overarching framework.

17. Cited by John Black in *The Dominion of Man: The Search for Ecological Responsibility* (Chicago: Aldine Publishing Company, 1970), 30.

18. P. J. Crutzen and E.F. Stoermer, "The Anthropocene" *Global Change Newsletter* 41 (2002): 1–18.

19. Francis Schaeffer, *Pollution and the Death of Man: The Christian View of Ecology* (Wheaton, IL: Tyndale House, 1970), 58–59.

20. Schaeffer, 53. To this end, he also discusses how the distinction between creature and human being is a qualitative one. Quite outspoken against theories of evolutionary biology, Schaeffer builds his argument upon *creatio imago Dei*. To make clear this point, he goes on to say that just as unbelievers are not true "brothers in Christ" in the way that believers are, likewise, creaturely life is separate from the spiritually alive Christian.

21. Schaeffer, 59. As we shall see below, critics of anthropocentric views fault Francis Bacon for justifying, establishing, and perpetuating a destructive and individualized approach to ecological consideration. Throughout *Pollution and the Death of Man* and *Genesis in Space and Time*, Schaeffer affirms Bacon's views, noting Bacon's distinction between thought and action in the Christian context. Suffice it to say, some of the same critiques charged against Bacon might be equally launched at Schaeffer.

22. Black, *The Dominion of Man*, 36.

23. Black dedicates a chapter in his book to the concept of stewardship, seeing stewardship as a way in which Western civilizations have attempted to solve the problem of corrupt or misused dominion. As we shall see in the discussion on stewardship below, his view of stewardship differs from more contemporary accounts in its conflation of stewardship with the deployment of just dominating practices rather than a divinely nominated managerial role. His working concept is still that humans might use creation with the aim of production over and above humans' call to protect or preserve.

24. It is worth mentioning that in recent years Beisner has begun to use the term stewardship, although his understanding of creation care bears little resemblance to other evangelicals using the term. This will become evident below through a closer look at the work of Calvin DeWitt and Steven Bouma-Prediger's stewardship ethic.

25. E. Calvin Beisner, "Oppressing the Poor in the Name of Fighting Global Warming," from the Cornwall Alliance blog: http://www.cornwallalliance.org/2015/01/27/oppressing-the-poor-in-the-name-of-fighting-global-warming/ (last accessed on March 8, 2015).

26. E. Calvin Beisner, *Where Garden Meets Wilderness: Evangelical Entry into the Environmental Debate* (Grand Rapids, MI: Eerdmans, 1997), 13–18.

27. Ibid., 16–17.

28. Larry Rasmussen, *Earth-honoring Faith: Religious Ethics in a New Key* (New York: Oxford University Press, 2013), 18–23.

29. The content of this critique will be explored in greater detail below, particularly through the exploration of more theocentric approaches to Christian ecological ethics. An archive of the Evangelical Theological Society's panel discussion on global warming can be found at: http://www.livestream.com/zondervanacademic/video?clipId=pla_129295a6-f57e-4459-b6c1-5349ddcb4957&utm_source=lslibrary&utm_medium=ui-thumb (last accessed on March 9, 2015).

30. Willis Jenkins, *The Future of Ethics* (Washington, DC: Georgetown University Press, 2013), 47–48.

31. Jonathan R. Wilson provides an example to this end. In his accessible and popular book *God's Good World: Reclaiming the Doctrine of Creation* (Grand Rapids, MI: Baker Academic, 2013) he situates evangelical anthropology in a creation-redemption dialectic, wherein the ongoing nature of human redemption is just as much a reality as the need for earth's transformation.

32. Matthew Hale, *The Primitive Origination of Mankind*, as cited by John Black in "The Dominion of Man," in *Environmental Stewardship*, edited by R. J. Berry (New York: T & T Clark, 2006), 95.

33. Ibid., 95–96.

34. Calvin DeWitt, *Earthwise: A Guide to Hopeful Creation Care* (Grand Rapids, MI: Faith Alive Christian Resources, 2011). DeWitt has written several books on the topic of Christian stewardship, including: *The Environment and the Christian* (1991), *Missionary Earthkeeping* (1993) and *The Just Stewardship of Land and Creation* (1996). He was also the founding President of the Au Sable Institute of Environmental Studies, a global center and community for Christian environmental studies headquartered in Mancelona, MI.

35. Aldo Leopold, *A Sand Country Almanac and Sketches Here and There* (New York: Oxford University Press, 1966). As we shall see below, Leopold's land ethic is equally applicable to theocentric approaches to Christian ecological ethics. Consequently, a good amount of debate has ensued regarding Christian appropriation of Leopold's transformative work. For example, see Gretel Van Wieren's *Restored to Earth: Christianity, Environmental Ethics and Ecological Restoration* (Washington, DC: Georgetown University Press, 2013).

36. Calvin DeWitt, "Stewardship: Responding Dynamically to the Consequences of Human Action in the World" in *Environmental Stewardship*, edited by R. J. Berry (New York: T & T Clark, 2006), 152.

37. Celia Deane-Drummond, *The Ethics of Nature: New Dimensions to Religious Ethics* (Malden, MA: Blackwell, 2004), 225. See also *A Handbook in Theology and Ecology* (London: SCM Press, 1996).

38. For a helpful chart outlining such ecological virtues see Steven Bouma-Prediger's response to Louke van Wensveen in *Christianity and Ecology: Seeking the Well-Being of Earth and Humans*, edited by Dieter T. Hessel and Rosemary Radford-Ruther (Cambridge, MA: Harvard University Press, 200), 175.

39. For example, the aforementioned book *Environmental Stewardship*, edited by R. J. Berry, exists by and large to question stewardship's viability. See Paul Santmire's insightful article on this matter, "Partnership with Nature According to the Scriptures: Beyond the Theology of Stewardship," *Christian Scholar's Review* 32:4 (Summer 2003): 381–412.

40. John Chryssavgis makes this point in "The World of the Icon and Creation: The Orthodox Perspective on Ecology and Pnuematology," in *Christianity and Ecology*, edited by Dieter T. Hessel and Rosemary Redford Reuther (Boston, MA: Harvard University Press, 2000), 83–96.

41. Paulos Gregorious, *The Human Presence: An Orthodox View of Nature* (Geneva: World Council of Churches, 1978), 82.

42. John Zizioulas, "Proprietors or Priests of Creation," in *Toward an Ecology of Transfiguration*, edited by John Chryssavgis and Bruce C. Foltz (New York: Fordham University Press, 2013), 166–167.

43. Ibid., 166.

44. See, for example, *On Earth as In Heaven: Ecological Vision and Inititiaves of Ecumenical Patriarch Bartholomew* (New York: Fordham University Press, 2011).

45. John Panteleimon Manoussakis, "*Physis* and *Ktisis*: Two Different Ways of Thinking of the World," in *Toward an Ecology of Transfiguration*, edited by John Chryssavgis and Bruce C. Foltz (New York: Fordham University Press, 2013), 204.

46. Zizioulas applies contemporary quantum physics to biblical apocalyptic literature and argues for a finite universe that will someday come into nonbeing. The only way to protect the world from finitude, he argues, is for humans to bring nature into relationship with the infinite One, God (Ibid., 167–168).

47. Jürgen Moltmann, cited on personal blog at http://mammademia.blogspot.com/2012/04/fertile-and-dying-in-me-seed.html (last accessed April 20, 2016).

48. Karl Rahner, *Theology of Death* (New York: Herder & Herder, 1961).

49. Jürgen Moltmann, *Trinity and the Kingdom* (Minneapolis: Fortress Press, 1991), 94–96.

50. Moltmann, *God in Creation* (Minneapolis: Fortress Press, 1993), 87.

51. Ibid., 77.

52. Jürgen Moltmann, *Sun of Righteousness, ARISE!* (Minneapolis: Fortress Press, 2010), 152–153.

53. Jürgen Moltmann, *Ethics of Hope* (Minneapolis: Fortress Press, 2012), 149.

54. These are the words of Roger Gottlieb when reflecting on the work of Hildegard of Bingen in "Transcendence of Justice and the Justice of Transcendence: Mysticism, Deep Ecology and Political Life," *Journal of the American Academy of Religion* 67, no. 1 (1999): 149–166.

55. I am referencing E.O. Wilson's biophilia hypothesis here, which suggested that human beings have an instinctive desire and need to connect with other living systems. See Wilson, *Biophilia* (Cambridge, MA: Harvard University Press, 1984). With reference to Pseudo-Dionysian and Bonaventurian readings I am referencing the ladder of ascent and the role of contemplation on the visible things of the world. In Bonaventure's *The Mind's Road to God*, for example, the way up to God begins with reflection upon God's most humble creatures.

56. James Nash, *Loving Nature* (Nashville: Abingdon, 1991), 111.

57. Nash, 111. Nash sees experience as equally valid to tradition, with Scripture ultimately informing both. Of course, many Protestants would hold to a four-fold methodology akin to John Wesley's Quadrilateral, where reason makes these three sources rational and defensible.

58. "Beloved habitat" is Nash's preferred phrase, as he thinks metaphors relating to God's body or divine *oikos* border too closely on pantheism. Habitat, he argues, preserves the otherness of the world and God while prioritizing God's immanence.

59. Sallie McFague, *The Body of God* (Minneapolis: Augsburg Fortress, 1993), 134.

60. McFague builds upon Teilhard de Chardin's synthesis to this end, suggesting that process theology must be supplemented with a metaphysic of some kind. Referring to this tenuous relationship between God and world as process ontology, she claims that "all things are being transformed through their processes of natural growth toward the divine source and goal of their existence" (*Body of God*, 141).

61 McFague, *The Body of* God, 179.

62. Rosemary Radford-Ruether, *Gaia & God: A Ecofeminist Theology of Earth Healing* (San Francisco: Harper Collins, 1992), 252.

63. Ivone Gebara, *Longing for Running Water: Ecofeminism and Liberation* (Minneapolis: Fortress Press, 1999), 22. To this end, she argues, "Our knowing is conditioned by those who hold the cards, that is, by those who possess the power both to know and to decide within a given social order" (37).

64. Gebara, *Longing for Running Water*, 208.

65. Dorothee Soelle, *To Work and to Love* (Minneapolis: Fortress Press, 1984), 32.

66. Arthur Peacocke, *Creation and the World of Science* (Oxford: Clarendon Press, 1979), 291.

67. I am calling to mind four basic, classical constituents of a viable doctrine of creation: distinction, dependence, decision, and duration. See Bernard McGinn, "Do Christian Platonists Really Believe in Creation?," in *God and Creation,* ed. David Burrell and Bernard McGinn (Notre Dame, IN: University of Notre Dame Press, 1991), 208–209.

68. For example, see Bron Taylor's *Deep Green Religion* on indigenous religions. John Cobb discusses the philosophical benefits of deep ecology in *Sustainability: Economics, Ecology and Justice* (New York: Orbis, 1992), 102–103. Interestingly Arne Naess, who coined the term *deep ecology,* claims to have been influenced by Christianity.

69. Matthew Foxe's work is a good example of this. In his efforts to extricate Christianity of original sin, the doctrine of atonement is eliminated and the concept of a creation made entirely finite (see *The Coming of the Cosmic Christ: The Healing of Mother Earth and the Birth of a Global Renaissance* (San Fransisco: Harper Collins, 1988). John Cobb, by way of contrast, argues that deep ecology cannot be blindly adopted by Christians for two reasons. First, the Scriptures testify to the uniqueness of humanity. We are not simply one species among others, but rather, an especially responsible specifies with profound abilities to impact the earth for better or worse. Secondly, the Scriptures do not advocate for a return to pre-lapsarian Eden. Rather, Christianity seeks a "future wholeness, a new synthesis of what has come into being since the fall as well as elements of what existed before." See *Sustainability: Economics, Ecology and Justice* (Eugene, OR: Wipf & Stock, 1992*)* 111).

70. In many ways, Berry's earth theology sacramentalizes longstanding ideas regarding cosmic totalization, as seen as early as the early seventeenth century with Spinoza. James Lovelock and Lynn Margulis were among the first in the past century to present the idea that the universe is an organism, having its own soul, or *anima mundi.*

71. Thomas Berry, *The Dream of the Earth* (San Francisco: Sierra Club Books, 1988), 11.

72. Berry, *The Dream of the Earth,* 35.

73. Cobb notes the variance among Christians who hold this biocentric view, ranging from animal-rights advocates to land ethicists to Gaia proponents. See chapter 6 of *Sustainability: Economics, Ecology and Justice.* Interestingly, in this chapter, Cobb rebrands the term dominion, suggesting that it can be useful within a biocentric perspective. He sees dominion has the position to make ethical decisions with respect to the preservation of species and the treatment of animals." "To refuse to assume responsibility on the grounds that taking responsibility is the problem," Cobb argues, "leaves the field to the irresponsible. We *have* dominion whether we want it or not" (112–113).

74. Willis Jenkins, "After Lynn White: Religious Ethics and Environmental Problems," *Journal of Religious Ethics* 37, no. 2 (June 2009): 284.

75. Jenkins, "After Lynn White," 289.

76. In format and in name, I am calling upon Willis Jenkins' categories of environmental pragmatism in chapter two of *Ecologies of Grace* (New York: Oxford University Press, 2008).

77. Even secular natural value theorists are skeptical of nature's innate value and focus more upon its cultural value. They regard animals and plants as moral subjects, therefore to be regarded with nonmalificence at a minimum. See, for example, Eric Katz's theory of noninterference in *Nature as Subject* (Lanham, MD: Rowman & Littlefield Publishers, 1996) and Peter Singer's sentient utilitarianism in *Animal Liberation* (New York: Harper Collins, 2002) *and Practical Ethics* (New York: Cambridge University, 2011).

78. Holmes Rolston III, *Conserving Natural Value* (New York: Columbia University Press, 1994), 168–180. See also "Value in Nature and the Nature of Value," in *Philosophy and the Natural Environment,* eds. Robin Attfield and Andrew Belsey (New York: Cambridge University Press, 1994), 13–30.

79. Rolston's view differs from deep ecology views in how it articulates subjectivity and personality. Nature on a whole is not personal, just as ecosystems are not subjects. Strictly speaking, ecosystems most accurately define the combination of living subjects. For Rolston, a viable ethic practically prioritizes the value of observable living things and ascribes duty to them.

80. Holmes Rolston III, "Environmental Ethics: Some Challenges for Christians," *The Annual Society of Christian Ethics* (Washington, D.C: Georgetown University Press, 1993), 183.

81. Rolston, *Conserving Natural Value,* 161–163.

82. For example, see Foucault's *The Order of Things: An Archeology of the Human Sciences* (New York: Random House, 1994).

83. Roger Gottlieb, *A Greener Faith: Religious Environmentalism and Our Planet's Future* (New York: Oxford University Press, 2006), 21. It is worth mentioning that while Gottlieb is a proponent for religious political environmental action, his overriding approach to religious environmentalism is terreological in nature. So while ecotheology should always have practical application, it is important because "before we can act, we must think, and before religion can act in response to the environmental crisis, it must learn to think religiously about it" (21).

84. I am using Larry Rasmussen's phrase here, which he gleans from the parable in Luke 5:36–39 (see *Earth-honoring Faith*, 71–73).

85. Rasmussen, *Earth-Honoring* Faith, 223–224.

86. Gretel Van Wieren, *Restored to Earth: Christianity, Environmental Ethics, and Ecological Restoration* (Washington, DC: Georgetown University Press, 2013), 27.

87. Jenkins, *Ecologies of Grace*, 51.

88. For example, see E. O. Wilson's *Biophilia* (Boston, MA: Harvard University Press, 1984) and Stephen Kellert's *Birthright: People and Nature in the Modern World* (New Haven, CT: Yale University Press, 2012).

89. Norman Wirzba, "Placing the Soul: An Agrarian Philosphical Principle," in *The Essential Agrarian Reader*, edited by Norman Wirzba (Berkeley: Counterpoint, 2003), 95.

90. Stephen Kellert, *Birthright* (New Haven, CT: Yale University Press, 2012), xiv.

91. Ibid., 99.

92. Mary Evelyn Tucker, "Religion and Ecology: The Interaction of Cosmology and Cultivation," in *The Good in Nature and Humanity: Connecting Science, Religion, and Spirituality with the Natural World*, eds. S. Kellert and T. Farnham (Washington, DC: Island, 2002).

93. Secular philosopher Rob Nixon makes this same argument in *Slow Violence and the Environmentalism of the Poor* (Cambridge, MA: Harvard University Press, 2011).

94. Taken from Willie Jennings' plenary address to Upper Midwest AAR group on April 17, 2015. He covers much of this material in *The Christian Imagination: Theology and the Origins of Race* (New Haven, CT: Yale University Press, 2010).

95. If we take Wendell Berry's work as an example of North American agrarianism, we find two primary critiques, the technological and the feminist. The technological critique is straightforward, finding fault in Berry's suspicion of society's increased use of and reliance upon technology. The feminist critique attends to Berry's working sense of home economics and the role of heterosexual marriage in society. On both accounts critics argue that Berry seeks to merely reinforce status quo roles, and provides little to no room for social change. A good rebuttal to such criticisms is found in Berry's article, "Feminism, the Body, and the Machine," initially published in *What Are People For?* (New York: North Point Press, 1990), 178–196.

Chapter Two

Vocation as Kinship with Clod and Ape

The Planetary Promise of H. Richard Niebuhr's Responsibility Ethic

Having a broad and multivalent understanding of how Christian theology and its ethicists have sought to reconfigure terreologies and put to practice strategies, we return to the question posed at the beginning—by what ecological ethic should the church live into our future? What parameters, constructs, and practices will help us become more responsible agents in the many interconnected aspects of our vocation, in the ecology of our vocation? As evident in the analysis of aforementioned approaches, our environment is in turmoil due to the combined factors of badly-adapted worldviews, inadequate knowledge, and poor political structures, or as ecofeminist Val Plumwood shortlisted them—illusion, ignorance, and interest.[1] Our Church *is* culpable for the present environmental crisis in the ways that it has underwritten ideologies of dominion and anthropocentrism. It *has* perennially scorned the marvels of science, not least of all ecology and the burgeoning field of climate science in defense of a *sapientia* unhindered by the confines of the here and now. And the church *will remain* responsible for its lack of macro sociopolitical structural engagement as well as its misappropriation of such structures. In light of this we must ask, what is Christian ethics if not an honest corporate reckoning of our intentional and tacit participation in the problem at hand and an equal vulnerability in the quest for a responsible response?

H. Richard Niebuhr was dealing with very similar tensions when sketching out his working ethics in the mid-twentieth century. While not explicitly addressing ecological matters, but more so the rising threat of nuclear world war, Niebuhr utilized his guiding questions of "What is happening here?" and "How shall we respond?" to begin articulating a mediated relational ethic capable of speaking to theory and praxis equally well. For Niebuhr, ethics was the stuff of vocation in the ways that ethics articulated the content of right relationship, and likewise vocation was the foundation of Christian ethics for the meaning and purpose it provided. Christian ethics speaks to terreology because it finds its source in the Gospel and directly speaks to one's relationship with the Divine. Unlike his liberal predecessors, Niebuhr saw ethics as a matter of relationship rather than an external system to which Christian principles could be added. Like his contemporary Karl Barth, he upheld Christ as the object of faith and the embodiment of ethics. Christ was and is the center of value and Christ is sovereign.

Yet this value can be and in fact *is* accessed beyond revelation, as life's deepest questions are always at once religious and moral. Seeking to approach ethics *en media res* Niebuhr argued that moral thinking is particular and universal at once, inhabiting a rich space between the objectivity of Christ and the subjectivity of lived experience. Here Niebuhr's practical approach to ethics and his appreciation for the complexity and plurality of cultural context comes through. Influenced by thinkers such as Troeltsch, Rauchenbusch, Whitehead, and the pragmatist William James, who on variant scales and to different ends relied upon disciplines like sociology, psychology, and history to uncover the good, Niebuhr viewed ethics as taking place among real persons in actual time. These extra-biblical disciplines speak to the many forces acting and reacting, attracting and repelling upon persons, with ethics being the response to such actions. Therefore, to consider ethical questions only in the realm of terreology, or theory, would be to relegate ethics to the realm of abstraction. We don't undergo ethical reflection by attempting to get our theology right, Niebuhr insisted, but rather we begin from right where we are. We know things, including that which is good, true, and beautiful, because we first value them in the context of relationship—a relationship with ourselves, God and the other (or to my preference, neighbor). While extra-biblical resources fail to be handmaidens of theology, as Troeltsch and other twentieth-century liberal Protestants suggested, Niebuhr found them helpful to communities in locating their lived values.

This mediated realism, which Niebuhr called objective relationalism, seeks to uphold the objectiveness of God on the one hand while acknowledging the interrelated nature of human subjectivity on the other hand. More than an ethics of one being in the making (in Niebuhr's terms, *homo faber* and in many others' teleology), or ethics of one coming under some certain constraint of rule (*homo politicus*, or what might be more commonly understood as deontology), Niebuhr understood Christian ethics as fitting relations (*homo dialogicus*). Three relations exist in community: 1) God and self; 2) neighbor and self; and 3) self acting upon God and neighbor. From this vantage, being and value are held in tension. Ultimately, a person's being is determined by the relationship one shares with another more than one's potential to become (as is typically articulated in the case of *homo faber*) or one's enactment or embodiment of any said standard (as in ethics *homo politicus*). In the first of the threefold relations, personal being is predicated upon God's being. Vis-à-vis *creatio imago Dei*, the qualified potential of self is realized because God was, is, and is to come. The relationship here is primarily one of human responding to God's action upon the self. Albeit influenced by Whiteheadian thought, Niebuhr never leveled the theological ground to suggest that God is somehow obligated to respond to human action, but suggests that in all things and at all times God is acting within the world and through the world.

Naturally this ontological reality differs in the neighbor-self relationship, wherein the acting upon one another is shared. In the neighbor-self relationship, the self is defined in the apophatic sense; the neighbor constitutes what I am by embodying what I am not. Yet beyond the apophatic ways God and neighbor determine the self, the condition of *ontos* is not merely reactive or even responsive, but also intentional and willed. In a qualified sense, we are how we relate to God and neighbor.

For Niebuhr, when a person consciously reacts to the action brought upon them, recognizing God's sovereignty in the process, and takes corporate responsibility for their action in return, responsible ethical reflection is taking place. And it is here, at the nexus of relationship, that Niebuhr's proposal proves ecologically promising for the ways it brings together a radical theocentric terreology and an interdependent rendering of self. Such a view promotes a pluralist ecological ethic without relativizing the particulars of Christian faith or arresting helpful practices.

Moral value, then, speaks to the reciprocal nature of said responses and actions. As Niebuhr's student James Gustafson helpfully summarizes, such a relational theory is concerned with the great multidimensionality of value, which is not the multidimensionality of an abstract realm of essential values, but rather the multidimensionality of beings in their relations to each other."[2] All beings are sources of value, so value never comes from simply the essence of something. Instead, value emerges in one's relationship to others. This working methodology allowed Niebuhr to pay less attention to the ideal nature of the church and more attention to how the Christian community exists before God and in responsible companionship with the world.

Here connections between Niebuhr's working ethic and Protestant renderings of vocation can be made with relative ease. The democratization of vocation in early Protestant thought released the doctrine from the trappings of ethical privatization so prevalent in late medieval thought, ensuring that a well sought-after vocation always tended to the relationship shared between self, God and neighbor. To move into one's calling was to move into greater relationship. These connections will be explored more fully in chapter 3.

RADICAL THEOCENTRISM AS A MEDIATING TERREOLOGY

In relation to the various metaethical perspectives surveyed in chapter 1, Niebuhr most assuredly promotes a form of theocentrism, but of a radical sort, for he argues the revelation of God involves a change in the moral law so that *all* creatures and things are within the network of moral relations. "When the Creator is revealed," he writes:

> it is no longer necessary to defend man's place by a reading of history which establishes his superiority to all other creatures. To be a man does not now mean to be a lord of the beasts but a child of God. To know the person [Christ] is to lose all sense of shame because of kinship with the clod and the ape.[3]

From a radically theocentric point of view whatever has being is valuable and worthy of affection because God is its relational source. Although like Carson, Niebuhr was greatly indebted to Albert Schweitzer, who argued for a reverence ethic wherein humans feel a compulsion to give to every will-to-live creature the same reverence for life that one gives to their own, Niebuhr extended being beyond the constructs of the will to include all of life, including life yet to come.[4] Ecologically speaking, this is an especially important insight, as the welfare of the unborn remains an important consideration. Theocentrism, or radical monotheism as Niebuhr called it, must dethrone absolutes in the principle of being itself while giving reverence to all things. It must heed two biblical imperatives: "I am the Lord thy God; though shalt have no other gods before me," and "Whatever is, is good."[5]

Such radical theocentrism presents a third theological path beyond polytheism and henotheism. Similar to aforementioned biocentric terreologies, polytheism as Niebuhr labels it, equivocates culture with God, connecting divine movement with socio-historical forces or natural processes. To Niebuhr's eye such perspectives compromise the potency of the Gospel by universalizing it, ultimately undermining the sovereignty of God. On the other hand, henotheism, a social faith upholding one object of devotion among many, mimics many anthropocentric terreologies in the way it endorses loyalty to a particular community (in the case of ecological ethics, the human community) and promotes the continued brokerage of dominant power.[6]

What is most faithful and realistic is an approach where God is understood as the One beyond the many, or "the principle of being and value that transforms all of our thinking and theological construction."[7] In radical monotheism the value center is neither closed to certain individuals (henotheism) nor the principle of a society loosely bound together by many views (polytheism); rather, it *is* the principle of being and value itself. As Niebuhr sees it there is a reality beyond all, in which everything exists and participates. "It is not a relation to any finite, natural or supernatural value-center that confers value on self and some of its companions in being," Niebuhr claims, "but it is value in relation to the One to whom all being is related."[8]

This third theological way most closely resembles theocentric approaches to Christian ecological ethics in the way it highlights the supremacy and centrality of God and the interrelations of life in community. However, Niebuhr's radical monotheism is also a critique of many theocentric terreologies for the way it receives and appropriates information about the Divine from myriad sources. For Niebuhr, Christian ethics and universal human ethics are convertible due to the immanence of the Triune persons. That is, all morality can be said to be Christian; environmental ethics is creation ethics. This does not mean, however, that philosophical ethics require religion. The field of environmental ethics can speak to the value of nature without Christian terreology. Here, for example, we see how theocentric models of sacramentalism too readily baptize natural processes by Niebuhr's standards. The primary goal of an ecological terreology isn't to assert or prove God's mysterious presence in with and under the earth's elements, but more so to radicalize our view of God that faith can more fully incorporate the insights of science.

ECOLOGICAL SUBJECTIVITY AS A MEDIATING PRACTICE

The liability of theocentrism—namely the potential for abstraction—is mitigated by Niebuhr's proposal, for rather than the relational aspects of objective relationalism eclipsing the objective, they in fact define it. The object of ethics, Niebuhr asserts, is not the human encounter with God, but God in godself. Ontology and ethics are distinguishable, but inseparable from Niebuhr's perspective.[9] In our lived experience we don't parse out knowledge of being from knowledge of value; we don't need a "right" view of God before valuing God's creation. "It is not at all evident," Niebuhr writes,

> that the One beyond the many, whether made known in revelation or always present to man in hiddenness, is principle of being before it is principle of value. Believing man does not say first, "I believe in a creative principle," and then, "I believe that the principle is gracious, that is, good toward what issues from it.' He rather says, "I believe in God the Father, Almighty Maker of heaven and earth." This is a primary statement, a point of departure and not a deduction. In it the principle of being is identified with the principle of value and the principle of value with the principle of being.[10]

So, like practical perspectives on ecological subjectivity, which hold in tension the innate value of nature on the one hand and the social construction of value on the other, Niebuhr's responsibility ethic proves more casuistic in nature. It values experience alongside the big questions, practical proposals in addition to analyses. And because experience is always an individual's encounter within the context of community, Niebuhr's ethic denies a distinction between personal and social ethics. Much like agrarian perspectives on ecological ethics, his germinal eco-ethic brings together the importance of a localized, personal morality that emphasizes lifestyle transformation and the attainment of ecological virtues and appropriate participation in macro-structures that mindfully attend to economic and political justice. As such, Niebuhr's mediated and practical ethic successfully straddles distinctions often made between teleological ethics and deontological ethics, offering an approach uniquely suited to address the complexities of our anthropocenic age.

TWO CRITICAL QUESTIONS AND TRUTH-TELLING IN THE ANTHROPOCENE

Thus far, I've provided a panoramic view of Christian ecological ethics by examining strengths and weaknesses of terreologies and practical approaches alike. I have argued for a pluralistic ecological ethic capable of incorporating myriad theological perspectives and resources and turned to H. Richard Niebuhr's promising responsibility ethic as fine an example of such a multivalent approach. I've shown how within Niebuhr's ethic the merits of theocentrism and practical concerns of ecological subjectivity are held in tension, mimicking the very three-fold form of vocation; relatedness between God, self, and neighbor.

But before offering anything resembling a normative ethic Niebuhr always took care to address the descriptive. That is, before asking of any ethical quandary, "How should the Christian faithfully respond?" he argued the Christian must first seek answers to, "What is going on here?" Niebuhr's intuition was right in his day and remains true today. We will not be able to achieve right relatedness between the various vocational roles we occupy, including our relationship to our other-than-human neighbors, without interrogating the nature of those relationships as they stand. Protestants must honestly assess the state of humans' (and particularly the church's) relationship with the natural world and evaluate the factors that both indict and limit human agency, particularly in the North American context.

The Abdication of Responsibility in Protestant Communities

To speak honestly about ecological calling, and indeed the very ecology of Christian vocation, the church must first acknowledge and repent of its corporate failure to honor and protect the natural world. While good and important work has been done on exceptions to the rule, the fact remains that in comparison to many other world religions and alternative Christian sectarian groups, Protestantism has been late to the ecological game.[11] Despite its prevalence within affluent and resourced contexts, the church has not used its power to impact change. It seems Rachel Carson's intuitions in the mid-twentieth century were well-founded and perhaps even prophetic when held up against Protestantism's recent track record: as an institution Christianity presents great ecological promise, if only its adherents weren't so consistently lacking the courage to enact such hope.

The ecological promise about which Carson speaks is arguably most accessible in the Hebrew Bible's accounts of creation, although ironically critics of the Christian tradition have and continue to point to these texts as indicative of Christianity's environmental problem. In the Yahwist text, Adam (literally named as the one from the earth, or the *adamah*) is mandated to till and keep the earth. This agrarian narrative, a picture of care more than intervention, underscores humankind's responsibility to serve and protect creation. The Priestly account in Genesis 1 calls human beings to subdue the land and to exercise authority over it. Here again, a deeper reading of such verbs paints an ethically challenging ecological picture, wherein humans are to creatively and resourcefully foster the fecundity of the land and to take responsibility for creation.[12]

Yet, to date Protestant communities, particularly those in North America, have neglected to serve and protect creation by repeatedly abdicating the responsibility to thoughtfully and resourcefully utilize the fruits of the earth. This is evidenced, for example in Torgerson's study *Greening Spaces for Worship and Ministry: Congregations, Their Buildings, and Creation Care*, which uncovers the consuming habits of U.S. Protestant churches.[13] Ironically such abdication is also evident in attempts some Protestant churches *are* making. For example, Torgerson's work highlights religious communities seeking to reform their architectural residences and vision. Many of the Protestant communities he highlights have invested hundreds of thousands of dollars and years and years of time to intentionally remodel or design green worship and community spaces. However, as he points out, very few of these communities are also revisiting practices such as their overarching consumption habits, their liturgies, educational emphases, or investment commitments. In other words, they have merely made "green" old habits and old ways rather than radically reconsidering the interrelationality of God's call to love the earth.[14]

Participation in the Problem

Now, to be fair, such radical reconsideration is harder than meets the eye, for the variables surrounding our contemporary environmental challenges are myriad and complex. Thus, the second aspect of telling the truth about Christian ecological vocation requires a naming of the ways many of us Protestants participate in the problem, overtly and inadvertently, and an exploration of how such participation indicts or inhibits our moral vision and action.

In his groundbreaking book *The Perfect Moral Storm: The Ethical Tragedy of Climate Change*, philosopher Stephen Gardiner observes that global, intergenerational, and theoretical storms distort our interpretation of environmental problems while also corrupting our abilities to take responsibility for them, thus accounting for a "perfect moral storm."[15] He suggests human agency in environmental matters is complicated for three primary reasons. First, the problem is dispersive: its origins, often difficult to identify, make culpability nebulous and elusive. Secondly, environmental problems are largely the result of unintentional harm. So while most of us don't think our lifestyles particularly unjust, implication is virtually universal, and particularly in consumptive contexts like the United States.[16] And finally Gardiner cites intergenerationality as a third major factor in our modern moral storm. Presently we are inheriting the ecological wake of industry undertaken before our time, just as we are also sowing formidably infertile seeds to be reaped in vain by future generations.[17]

For these reasons, it remains difficult to clarify the Christian's call to love and serve creation, in ways that it was not in sixteenth-century Protestantism wherein Christian conceptions of vocation were democratized. How can the Christian respond to a problem she herself caused, and continues to cause? How can the Christian address the quandary he cannot see, or evade participation in a dilemma he's unable to imagine?

Contemporary environmental problems also prove complex because of human theoretical ineptitude. We simply lack the ability to see things like climate change as they really are due in part to shifting views on knowledge and neurological limitation. Add to this the role of sin, or in some traditions depravity, and even the Christian can be said to "know" the truth without knowing the truth. We deceive ourselves. Accompanying postmodernity's incredulous posture toward metanarratives has been the celebration of experience and an altogether new way of knowing. In this context *scientia* no longer wins the day over *sapientia*, the latter being a form of wisdom perennially championed by religion. As fact/value divides have been steadily dismantled, the role of value in the scientific process has been highlighted like never before. And, as contemporary ecofeminists have helped us see, to distance an external philosophical epistemological construct from contextualized communities, including those of faith, is to endorse and propel standing hierarchical, anthropocentric, and androcentric biases and structures of power. Longstanding essentialist epistemologies, even those characterizing liberationist movements, often fail to take seriously the priority of experience. The meaning of truth is easily lost if knowledge is not made one's own by way of experience. In Ivone Gebara's words, "To the degree in which we distance these truths from their origins and from ourselves, we act as if they had some hidden power over us."[18] Instead, an interdependent, relational epistemology has real power, for the truth is found in the relatedness between subject and object, individual and collective, the Transcendent and the Immanent, making the knowledge about God, self, and neighbor (including the other-than-human other) a process.[19] So climate change, for example, is not only empirically true, but also true because it finds its partial origin in us, that is in human behavior. Climate change is also "real" in the way it impacts and will continue to impact our very lives. While more modern epistemologies may be enticing, especially to those hailing from more analytical philosophical camps, our ways of knowing what is and what is to come are far more nuanced.

And not only that, but science itself has demonstrated that our cognitive capacity is biologically limited; our brains are not well adapted to problems with abstract causation, inherent uncertainty, and extensive scales of time and space.[20] As a result, some deny the problem of climate change exists, while most hold discussion forums on environmental challenges and set forth solutions that pale in comparison to the problem's actual immensity and intricacy.[21] As environmental philosopher Dale Jamieson notes, we humans

> have a strong bias toward dramatic movements of middle-sized objects that can be visually perceived, and climate change does not typically present in this way ... Climate Change must be thought rather than sensed, and we are not very good at thinking. Even if we succeed in thinking that something is a threat, we are less reactive than if we sense that it is a threat. Consider the difference between touching a hot stove and being told that the stove is hot. Scientists are telling us that the world is warming, but we do not sense it and so we do not act.[22]

Jamieson's concerns regarding humans' impaired judgment are shared by the eco-literary scholar Rob Nixon, who raises the question, "How are we to respond to that which extends before us in time and space?"[23] Bruno Latour, a leading sociologist undertaking work on the new climatic regime, suggests that we cannot, for whereas the idea of human agency once distinguished the human from nature, contemporary humanity finds itself acted upon. The consequence is that "people are not equipped with the mental and emotional repertoire to deal with such a vast scale of events ... they have difficulty submitting to such a rapid acceleration for which, in addition, they are supposed to feel responsible."[24]

This is where religious creativity plays a critical role, as it can help us transcend biological limitations, or, at the very least, make us more aware of them. As Christian ethicist Willis Jenkins argues in agreement with Gardiner, it isn't that we need new theories or better approaches, but more so that we make our inherited concepts do new things.[25] As we shall see, Protestantism has a valuable resource in the doctrine of vocation given the historical democratization of the concept and its widespread use, but this doctrine must be put to work in new and relevant ways. For example, by conceiving of vocation as the development and practice of virtue as much or more than obedience, the doctrine might prove ecologically promising in many contemporary communities, Protestant and otherwise. And by redefining neighbor to include the other-than-human other-than-humans, the notion of calling is expanded.

Eco-Justice and Environmental Racism

Doesn't this distinction have the potential to feed yet another complicating factor in the moral storm of climate change, mounting injustices? Some conservative, and even climate-denying entities, have rightly observed that too much emphasis on other-than-human neighbors can eclipse urgent human need.[26] In particular, more theologically conservative Protestants suggest that the creation of humankind *imago Dei* elevates human concerns over ecological ones and must therefore attend to aiding the poor first and foremost. Yet, pitting economics against ecology proves far from helpful, as the two together play a critical role in the homeostasis of our global *oikos*, or household. The vulnerable global poor will live at greater risk if our ecological habits and structures remain. Rather, what's necessary is a clear assessment of responsibility, for not all members of the household have equally violated the rights of the other-than-human neighbor. By and large those who have and are causing climate change are not the communities most impacted by it, yet another truth-telling complication. For example, a study assessing data gathered between 1961–2000 published in the *Proceedings of the National Academy of Sciences*, found that

> Climate change and ozone depletion impacts predicted for low-income nations have been overwhelmingly driven by emissions from [high-income and middle-income nations], a pattern also observed for overfishing damages indirectly driven by the consumption of fishery products. Indeed, through disproportionate emissions of greenhouse gases alone, the rich group may have imposed climate damages on the poor group greater than the latter's current foreign debt.[27]

As environmental law professor Amy Sinden remarks, the crisis of climate change "divides us both in terms of culpability and vulnerability."[28]

It divides not just across continents, but also within national borders according to socio-economic and racial lines. The science of climate change might be without prejudice, but the factors leading to it and the fallout from it are anything but colorblind. Take the recent example of Flint, Michigan, for example, where widespread contamination of waters due to washed-up industry endangers hundreds of thousands of residents.[29] Certainly Flint residents aren't the only U.S. citizens perpetually exposed to lead-ridden waters; exposure to toxins is increasingly pervasive throughout the United States; however, the flow of such toxins *is* unequal because such ecological realities are and have been shaped by social power.[30] As majority-world ecofeminists have been telling us for years, environmental catastrophes are social disasters and ecological relations ultimately political ones.[31]

Hence, for the Protestant doctrine of vocation to be practically useful today, the Reformers' early political impulses and the doctrine's bridging of the personal and political must be reclaimed. To be sure, this will be difficult in much of North American Protestantism given the prevalence of white privilege in such communities. As Larry Rasmussen reflects, the field of religion and ecology has been so white in demographic because it has been so white in method.[32] Emilie Townes and the late James Cone agree, noting how much of ecotheology begins with idealized views of creation rather than genuine experiences of oppression.[33] Yet, the "yoking of civil and environmental rights is crucial to ontological wholeness," Townes argues, and necessary to undo what she calls "the collective lynching" of earth and people.[34] Preferred norms of eco-justice in predominately Caucasian scholarship differ greatly from environmental justice, which has organically emerged from within communities of color, because each calls upon a different construction of justice.[35] The challenge for predominately Caucasian Protestant communities, therefore, will be to listen, learn of the ecologies of racism, and to redefine calling to include the responsibility to evacuate ecological ethics of white privilege.

With these challenges in mind, the remaining chapters speak to how vocation has and might function as an ethical response in both form and language. While an increasing number of Christian eco-ethical works are employing terminology of calling, very few have shed light on what it might mean for a Christian to be called, just as one might be to say work or domestic life, to care for the environment and even less has been said about what the fulfillment of ecological vocation practically entails. To begin unpacking these questions and to demonstrate how vocation incorporates a radical theocentrism capable of addressing pragmatic concerns we turn to the Reformers who initially democratized the doctrine.

NOTES

1. Val Plumwood, *Environmental Culture* (London: Routledge, 2002), 237.
2. James Gustafson, *Sense of the Divine* (Cleveland, OH: Pilgrim Press, 1996), 63.
3. H. Richard Niebuhr, *The Meaning of Revelation* (New York: Macmillan, 1962), 173.
4. Albert Schweitzer, *Out of My Life and Thoughts* (New York: Henry Holt and Company, 1933), 186.
5. H. Richard Niebuhr, *Radical Monotheism and Western Culture* (Louisville, KY: Westminster/John Knox Press, 1970), 37.
6. Interestingly, Niebuhr categorizes atheism as a form of henotheism. Scientific naturalism as an example of popular atheism holds confidence in some center of value, namely the value of loyalty to objective belief and the suspicion of all things supernatural. Niebuhr points out that it isn't the rejection of the supernatural that makes atheism incoherent, for there may be many reasons for questioning the supernatural. Rather, what makes atheism irrelevant is the impossibility of actually living it out. Even the staunchest of atheists maintain a closed-off social system and an ethical imperative of loyalty where allegiance to one cause over another is upheld (*Radical Monotheism and Western Culture*, 25).
7. Niebuhr, *Radical Monotheism and Western Culture*, 112.
8. Ibid., 32.
9. H. Richard Niebuhr's student James Gustafson makes this relationship between theological ontology and ethics abundantly clear in *Ethics from a Theocentric Perspective* (Chicago: University of Chicago Press, 1981), where he writes, "Theology is reflection on the action and nature of God; ethics is reflection of the response of man to the action and nature of God." (*Ethics from a Theocentric Perspective*, Vol. 1, 68).
10. Niebuhr, *Radical Monotheism and Western Culture*, 32–33.
11. Evidence of this exists in Roger Gottlieb's compendium, *Religion and Ecology*, for example, which dedicates chapters to many other religious traditions (New York: Oxford University Press, 2006). Naturally a spectrum of perspective exists within each respective religion, just as they do within Protestantism. Among Hindus, for example, variant views on the value of the material world exist, creating varying beliefs on environmental matters. Here, as in Christianity, one can see discrepancies between theory and praxis.
12. Richard Bauckham's reading is particularly helpful. In *The Bible and Ecology: Rediscovering the Community of Creation* (Waco, TX: Baylor University Press, 2010), 10–32, Bauckham notes how the use of *kabash* (subdue) is specific to the land (*eretz*), not necessarily to animal life or other forms of life. Paul Santmire's critique of typical stewardship models also gets at this differentiation, noting how both creation accounts focus on different things, the first (Gen. 2) on care and the second (Gen. 1) on intervention ("Partnership with Nature According to the Scriptures: Beyond the Theology of Stewardship," in *Christian Scholar's Review* 32, no. 4 (Summer 2003): 381–412).
13. Mark A. Torgerson, *Greening Spaces for Worship and Ministry: Congregations, Their Buildings, and Creation Care* (Herndon, VA: The Alban Institute, 2012).
14. Bron Taylor refers to this as a form of "greening religion," which is decidedly different from deep and dark green religions. His typology, in *Dark Green Religion* (2009) is a helpful one when teasing out such applications
15. Prior to the publication of his book (New York: Oxford University Press, 2011) Gardiner published the article, "A Perfect Moral Storm: Climate Change, Intergenerational ethics and the Problem of Moral Corruption" in *Environmental Values* 15 (2005): 397–413. In it he says, "Climate change is a perfect moral storm, like the three storms that converged in the North Atlantic to doom the fishing vessel *Andrea Gail*, it involves the convergence of a number of factors that threaten our ability to behave ethically . . . . Their interaction helps to exacerbate and obscure a lurking problem of moral corruption that may be of greater practical importance than any of them" (399).
16. Dale Jamieson makes a helpful distinction here, noting the difference between causal responsibility and moral responsibility. One can be causally at fault for climate-changing GHG's without being morally responsible for them. A case in point might be the parent who drives an SUV to pick up their kids from soccer practice. By contributing to the environmental

problem, this parent could be accused of morally effective behavior, except for the fact that his/her thinking doesn't fall under prevailing concepts of negligence, recklessness, etc. (see Jamieson, *Reason in a Dark Time* (New York: Oxford University Press, 2014), 151–152 for more on fault liability).

17. Building upon Stephen Gardiner's work, Dale Jamieson also marks this as a perplexing factor in the moral storm of climate change. He writes, "Since every generation benefits from its own emissions by the costs are deferred to future generations, they have an incentive not to control their emissions. Moreover, since each generation (except the first) suffers from the emissions of previous generations, benefitting from their own present emissions may even appear to be just compensation for what they have suffered. But of course, this reasoning leads to the continuous buildup of GHG's in the atmosphere over time" (*Reason in a Dark* Time, 100).

18. Ivone Gebara, *Longing for Running Water* (Minneapolis: Fortress Press, 1999), 49.

19. Cynthia Moe-Lobeda also notes how ways of knowing in modernity now come up short, as we have learned to prioritize the voices of those who experience injustice, and there are many voices that we cannot perceive at all (waters, critters, winds, etc). However, it isn't that we need to return to a pre-modern mode of knowing, which was uncritically appropriated, and hence, quite deadly. She says, "Epistemology for the ecological era will incorporate and go beyond both; we will learn to learn from other-than-human parts of creation. We will seek to glimpse reality as experienced by otherkind" (*Resisting Structural Evil*, 198–199).

20. E. M. Markowitz and A. F. Shariff, "Climate Change and Moral Judgement," *Nature Climate Change* 2, no. 4 (2012).

21. Naomi Klein uncovers organized climate change denial well in the first chapter of her bestselling book *This Changes Everything: Capitalism vs. the Climate* (New York: Simon & Schuster, 2014), noting how the "Right is right" to worry about the revolutionary economic changes climate realities now require.

22. Jamieson, *Reason in a Dark Time*, 102–103.

23. Nixon, *Slow Violence*, 14.

24. Bruno Latour, "Agency at the Time of the Anthropocene," *New Literary History* 45 (2014): 1.

25. Jenkins, *The Future of Ethics*, 43.

26. This is a major argument of the Cornwall Alliance, for example, which has clear financial and relational ties to one of the most influential climate denying political entities, the Heritage Foundation.

27. U. Thara Srinivasan, et al. "The Debt of Nations and the Distribution of Ecological Impacts from Human Activities," *Proceedings of the National Academy of Science* 105:5 (February 5, 2008): 1763–1773.

28. Amy Sinden, "Climate Change and Human Rights," *Journal of Land, Resources, and Environmental Law* 27 (2007): 255.

29. And this crisis isn't unique to Flint, Michigan. See, for example, the Washington Post's January 2016 article, "It's Not Just Flint": https://www.washingtonpost.com/news/energy-environment/wp/2016/01/27/its-not-just-flint-poor-communities-across-the-country-live-with-extreme-polluters/, last accessed on April 19, 2016. In the summer of 2015, a documentary, *I Do Mind Dying: Stories from Detroit about Water*, shed light on very similar problems in Detroit, MI.

30. For example, in April 2015, a study was published noting that half of Minnesota rivers and streams are unclean: http://www.startribune.com/half-of-s-minn-waters-found-too-polluted-for-safe-swimming-fishing/301702651/, last accessed on April 19, 2016.

31. It is important to note that not all ecofeminism has championed this perspective. As Tovis Page has demonstrated, the connection between environment and justice has lagged in much of ecofeminist scholarship due to sustained evaluation of worldviews rather than practices ("Feminist, Gender and Sexuality Studies in Religion and Ecology: Where We Have Been, Where We Are Now, and Where We Might Go" in *Inherited Land: The Changing Grounds of Religion and Ecology*, Whitney Bauman, Richard Bohanon, and Kevin O'Brien, eds. (Eugene, OR: Wipf and Stock, 2011), 102–124). Dorceta Taylor concurs, connecting the dots between abstraction within North American ecofeminism and a focus on white women's

experiences. She argues that environmental justice projects are predominately led by women of color because these leaders understand their struggles for justice in ways at once more concrete and more complex ("Women of Color, Environmental Justice, and Ecofeminism," in *Ecofeminism: Women, Nature and Culture*, Karen Warren, ed. (Indianapolis: Indiana University Press, 1997).

32. Rasmussen, "Environmental Racism and Environmental Justice: Moral Theory in the Making?," *Journal of the Society of Christian Ethics* 24, no.1 (2004): 4–23.

33. James Cone, "Whose Earth Is It Anyway?" in *Earth Habitat: Eco-Injustice and the Church's Response*, Dieter Hessel and Larry Rasmussen, eds. (Minneapolis: Fortress Press, 2007), 30.

34. Emilie Townes, *In a Blaze of Glory: Womanist Spirituality as Social Witness* (Nashville, TN: Abingdon Press, 1995), 60.

35. Karen Baker-Fletcher has a great discussion of this in the second portion of her book, *Sisters of Dust, Sisters of Spirit: Womanist Wordings on God and Creation* (Minneapolis: Fortress Press, 1998).

Chapter Three

New Decalogues

Luther, Calvin, and the Democratization of Vocation

Inhabiting a theological space open to multiple sources of reflection is not a modern pursuit or endeavor. Indeed, the seeds of a mediated Christian ethic like that of H. Richard Niebuhr's germinated centuries prior to the publication of his unfinished ethic. Contemporary questions on how one might appropriately relate to God and fittingly relate to neighbor, while taking the objective realities of life into account are perennial. In Protestant circles the ethical fusion of theory and practice has long been construed as vocation, so much so that in some Protestant contexts ethical terminology has been eclipsed by semantics of calling.[1]

But why? Why tie moral behavior to call and response? Have not the liabilities of vocation been made plain by Troeltsch, Weber, and others in recent decades?[2] Can something as allusive, subjective, and qualitative as vocation really help Christians address the concrete challenges of our anthropocenic era? These questions uncover the burden of this chapter, as well as those that follow.

In the immediate query I turn to two pillars of the Protestant Reformation, Martin Luther and John Calvin, to demonstrate the democratization of the doctrine of vocation and its related ecological promise. By excavating their working dialectics—creation and redemption, law and gospel—I will show how vocation, when stripped of the trappings of production and consumption that have plagued its application since the mid-seventeenth century, provides necessary form and language to the above proposed mediated responsibility ethic. As a theological resource, an expansive theology of vocation deals with all three aspects of a responsibility ethic. First, it speaks to the relationship between God and self, ultimately serving as a form of the law, given by

God. It also addresses the practical relations between neighbor and self, always proving dynamic in nature, fluxing according to the perceived and real needs of the other. And finally, as a way of life vocation embodies the ethics of response that H. Richard Niebuhr and others identified as critical for life in the twentieth century and beyond. Because the realization of calling requires not only radical dependence on a monotheistic God, nor merely an interdependent rendering of self, but also attention to the spaces between the three poles of relationship (God, self, and other), it serves as a bridge between theoretical and practical ethical models without relativizing the particulars of Christian faith or arresting helpful practices.

Three areas of emphasis demonstrate the relational ethical quality of vocation, or "ecology of vocation." First, I outline the impact of Luther and Calvin's democratization of the doctrine, noting the influence of medieval mysticism on Luther's thought in particular. I then demonstrate how both Reformers' views of vocation explicitly connected human life to creation and its laws and in so doing attributed vocation to all Christians as a way of life more than a duty or working out of God's law. And finally, I outline and address some of the problems with Luther and Calvin's working sense of vocation, namely ascriptivism and personalism.[3]

THE SOWN SEEDS OF VOCATION RADICALIZED

Contrary to inferences from contemporary literature on the Protestant doctrine of vocation, Luther and Calvin's democratization of the doctrine further propelled reform set forth before their time. Their working theologies of vocation were radical, yes, but not necessarily innovative. The Reformers never saw themselves as inventors, but more so as bulwarks of God's Word. To them, the extension of vocation to the realm of the mundane and necessary was biblical, and the link between the well-being of creation and calling a primitive Christian truth.[4] Making clean and tidy distinctions between sacred and secular callings didn't occur to early Christians like Paul, nor did the elevation of some vocations over others. Instead, practical and religious duties were held in tandem when a person placed themself at the service of Christ.[5] Honoring God and growing in Christ's likeness had just as much to do with building tents, milking cows, and raising children as it did with prayer and spiritual practices.[6] Seeking to reiterate the eschatological urgency of the Greek Scriptures and what they thought to be the practical conduct of the early Church, Luther, Calvin, and their early followers focused on vocation as a way of life between the event of *creatio orginalis* (original creation) on the one hand and the *parousia* (earthly return of Christ) on the other. More prescriptive renderings of vocation didn't emerge until the second century and were not commonplace until the end of the fifth century.[7]

Gradually the doctrine became restricted, referring either to a person's spiritual calling or a particular call to a religious role/order.

By the late Middle Ages feudal agrarianism was sufficiently replaced by a less economically-stratified urban community, resulting in a larger bourgeois class eager to have more philosophically sophisticated answers to longstanding religious questions.[8] Not least among these questions was whether the contemplative life (*vita contemplativa*) was more valuable than the active life (*vita activa*).

The great scholastic doctor of the Church, Thomas Aquinas, addressed this question head on. Working from a fundamentally Ptolemaic model of the universe, he argued that calling is one's designated function in the context of God's designed whole.[9] "A person's state," as Aquinas referred to it, "denotes a kind of position, whereby a thing is despised with a certain immobility in a manner according to its nature . . . that alone seemingly pertains to a man's state which regards an obligation binding his person."[10] All men are obligated and summoned to labor, but by nature some are to labor primarily in their love of God and others in a love of neighbors.[11] The more active, material, and manual labors in society—inclusive of the embodied calling to care for the natural world—were performed by what Aquinas referred to as the "lower orders," or those less fitted by nature to rule.[12] Collectively those in higher states and lower states come together under mutual and varying obligations to society at large. This social solidarity, built upon a corporate sense of identity quite foreign to the individualism that reigns in the North American context today, was a "cosmos of callings," or God's larger ecology of vocation.[13]

Naturally, not all late medievalists happily acknowledged their bound state, nor stayed content within it. Seeds for dissent existed before Aquinas's day. In the twelfth century, for example, Peter Waldo and the Waldensians began arguing for the "priesthood of all believers," demonstrating how every station in life was a possible gateway to God, thereby making more ambiguous distinctions between the contemplative and active life. Later third-order mystics like Meister Eckhart (1260–1328), a contemporary of Aquinas, sought to lead contemplative lives while active in addressing the needs of society, encouraging others to do the same in the contexts of their families and occupations.[14] And it was through these mystics and fringe movements that the German *ruf* passed into theological vernacular. By the mid-fifteenth century *beruf* was used by the Reformers' older contemporaries, such as Erasmus of Rotterdam. In his teachings on prayer, Erasmus wrote at length about the dignity of common craftsmen and peasants. Rather than viewing persons of simple means with seemingly trivial callings as beneath those with explicit religious or political vocations, he saw the proletariat as the "backbone supporting the structures of aristocracy."[15] This is not to say that Erasmus advocated for the dissolution of societal hierarchies, for like the majority of mystics, he was content to stay within a prescribed system of ecclesial and sacramental piety and power. However, thinkers like Waldo, Eckhart, and Erasmus probed the status quo enough to put in motion a larger reformation of the doctrine of vocation.

LUTHER, CALVIN, AND THE DEMOCRATIZATION OF VOCATION

One of the impacts of such late medieval thought was a more explicit connection between vocation and creation. Luther, who in Augustine's footsteps, situated everything in double perspective—law and gospel, spiritual and temporal—saw vocation not only as the shared call to faith and the reception of baptism, that is vocation as Gospel, but also as the distinctive and embodied social station(s) one inhabits, or vocation as law. Luther was thoroughly premodern in endorsing this binary conception. Like other medievalists he separated the *saeculum*, or "age," from the eternal. As Charles Taylor reflects,

> People who are in the *saeculum* are embedded in ordinary time, they are living the life of ordinary time; as against those who have turned away from this in order to live closer to eternity. . . . One is concerned with things in ordinary time, the other with the affairs of eternity.[16]

What is unique to Luther's conception of calling is the fusion of the now and not-yet in the life of one person. Calling, Gustaf Wingren argues, was Luther's dialectical lynchpin, bridging the theological gap between creation and redemption.[17] Another effect of medieval mysticism's influence upon the Reformers was the flat-lining of the doctrine and a renewed focus upon Pauline metaphors of gift and body. And thirdly, progressive medieval thought began to expand the doctrine of vocation as a way of life, inclusive of, but beyond mere obligation or responsibility. Collectively these three paradigmatic shifts amounted to the radical democratization of vocation, so much so that one might view the Reformers' teaching on vocation as equal to justification in terms of its significance.[18]

Ironically, the historical Protestant doctrine of justification, for all its emphasis on freedom, has done little to raise ecological awareness among Christians. This was, after all, central to Lynn White's famous criticism and has been taken up by many Christian ecotheologians since. Old hymns remade and broadcast today illustrate this problem well: "All I know is I'm not home yet. This is not where I belong. Take this world and give me Jesus. This is not where I belong."[19] Who needs creation, even a creation restored, when one has Jesus? Since the sixteenth century the Christian doctrine of vocation, on the other hand, has been defined and understood in light of material realities and yields great ecological promise today when viewed from the aforementioned threefold perspective. To better understand why and how, a more thorough examination of each is warranted.

Vocation as the Lynchpin Between Creation and Redemption

For Luther and Calvin the realm of the world, of creation, is also the realm of the law. In the Spirit creation governs itself, demonstrating principles of natural law that are in turn reflected in the Scriptures. As I have argued elsewhere, Luther (and I would now add Calvin) inherited the scholastic traditions of natural law and, with significant revisions and their own appropriation of the tradition, embraced it.[20] Working from the second chapter of Romans, Luther underscored how the universal negative law is "written with the finger of God, on [persons'] hearts. By nature and indelibly the law of nature is imprinted on [persons'] minds." Whereas biblical law is a form of positive law situated within the context of divinely mandated civil law, and therefore specific to particular people at a particular time, the basic principles of practical reason found within the Law of Moses apply to all persons at all times. The temporary callings one inhabits in this life are discerned and acted upon according to this universal law and the respondent's related sense of duty. In this sense, vocation is best understood as task.

Yet, because the needs of vocation's object, namely the neighbor, are dynamic, the application of such law fluctuates and evolves. So while calling is necessarily bound by the law, it is never limited to it.[21] This is all the more true when one recalls the Reformers' emphasis on the passivity of vocation. Like faith, a calling is ultimately given and then received, making vocation more about conformation to Christ and His will than the imitation of Christ. Here a theology of ascent is replaced with a theology of consent.[22] "New decalogues" are perennially constructed as the needs of the neighbor emerge, evidence that Luther's hidden God and Calvin's sovereign God creates anew yet today.[23] Both Reformers argued that the Gospel is implied in the law, just as the law is included in the Gospel by being fulfilled rather than abolished. So for Luther vocation depends upon *Stundelein*, or the opportune right time and place for action.[24] Karl Barth later riffs on this, observing how obedience in vocation necessarily leads to freedom in one's own "sphere of responsibility."[25] And when focusing on the Reformers' promissory side of vocation, which prioritized redemption and renewal, calling is cast as more of a gift than a task.

Vocation, together as both task and gift, spans the gap between the doctrinal categories of creation and redemption. Calling becomes the lynchpin between what is sometimes thought of as the vertical and horizontal endeavors, or the love of God and neighbor respectively.[26] In this way, vocation represents a third ethical space, one beyond the polarities of theory and praxis discussed in chapter one. To pursue one's vocation, including one's ecological calling to live as participant of creation, is not just to honor God, nor is it to primarily care for the other, but rather to do both simultaneously. H. Richard Niebuhr regards this space as cathecontic,[27] I will refer to it as the ecology of vocation, due to the ways one's love of God and love of neighbor interrelate. Either way, it should be understood as the manner in which called-out-ones (*ekklesia*) move in a mediated existence that upholds God's laws on the one hand and allows Christians to live into God's promises on the other.

Naturally the idea of living into God's promises is enticing, and indeed it should be! Yet, as we shall see in the following chapter, viewing vocation solely from the perspective of redemption is problematic. The result can be a pious, individualistic rendering of calling with the potential to devolve into little more than a health and wealth theology, where faithfulness is cast as production, and blessing as opportunities to consume. Surely Luther and Calvin depict calling in light of the Good News, but do so *vis-à-vis* a very nitty gritty doctrine of creation. To each of them vocation is discovered and pursued in the mundane, through the necessary happenings of life and by thoroughly embodied means.

The Reformers' doctrine of vocation developed in a polemic with contemporary Catholic and, to a lesser degree, Anabaptist views of calling. As a former priest and Augustinian monk, Luther had intimate knowledge of the Catholic context. Likewise, Calvin, born into a family with responsibilities at ecclesial court and later employed as a clerk to the local Bishop, was well acquainted with Catholic teachings. Catholic teaching restricted vocation to clerical life. Priests, monks, and nuns were society's chosen few to live out the counsels of perfection, summed up in vows of poverty, chastity, and obedience. In contrast, early Anabaptist theology made such counsels possible for all and went so far as to require them. Despite the considerable differences between these traditions both modes of thought prized the religious or spiritually pious life over other lifestyles. Luther was one of the first to invert such approaches to vocation. Rather than separating the law from the counsels of perfection he joined them, arguing that vocation wasn't something to be sought in isolation and contemplation, but instead constituted the tasks of daily life in an earth-bound community. "It does happen," Luther wrote in his Sermon on the Third Sunday of Advent, 1522, "that the farmer does better with his plow before God than the nun with her chastity"[28] In his mundane tasks the farmer is equally able, if not better positioned, to honor God and serve the neighbor because of the ways God is sacramentally at work in the world and, ironically, often absent amongst clergy.[29] If God's will is manifest in the germination of a seed and the splendor of a lightning bolt just as it is in the Eucharist and the healings of Jesus, as Luther argued it was, then calling in the Christian life can be relegated to the necessities of the everyday as much as it is to the spiritual.[30]

Calvin, too, emphasizes vocation in and through the mundane, although his doctrine of creation stopped short of Luther's sacramentalism. Rather than centering his theological schema on *theologia crucis* (a theology of the cross), Calvin focused upon the sovereignty of God. For him, the reality and promise of God's ongoing creative action was the starting place for the doctrines of creation and vocation. Why contemplate the abstract essence of God's nature when it is recognizable in the activity of creation itself? And why over-spiritualize calling when one's gifts exist for the sake of the world?[31] This is not to say that creation is capable of holding God, or that the Church will ever perfectly model God's love for the world, for Calvin parted ways with Lutheran teachings on the finite having a limited capacity to contain the infinite, and like Luther proved quite sober in his estimation of humankind's proclivities and abilities.[32] However, it *is* to stress Calvin's pragmatic and even embodied sense of vocation. "No task will be so sordid and base," he writes, "provided you obey your calling in it, that it will not shine and be reckoned very precious in God's sight."[33]

While it's Luther who is most frequently accused of ascriptivism, a critique addressed below, one can certainly see its latent form in thoughts like this from Calvin. Indeed, both Reformers endorsed an ethic of staying-the-course.[34] If one sought to imitate the saints it should be to resemble the faithfulness with which they worked, not their work itself. Each person has their own God-given tasks and is to be faithful to such responsibilities.[35] In this way, vocation is manifest in the necessary just as it is in the mundane in the sense that certain things of life must simply be done. Vocation need not be glorious, interesting, or even fulfilling in the modern sense of the word. It is, rather, a response to material needs, and not just the needs of the human neighbor at that. The fields have to be plowed and livestock tended and husbanded.[36] "For if we are to live," Calvin writes, "we have also to use those helps [gifts] necessary for living. And we also cannot avoid these things which seem to serve delight more than necessity. Therefore, we must hold to a measure so as to use them with a clear conscience, whether for necessity or for delight."[37] Luther saw those who were malcontent in their callings as lacking not just conscientiousness, but also faith. "Where there is no faith," he writes, "and one judges according to his own feelings, thoughts, and experiences, then boredom begins, for he feels only the complaints of his own life and not that of his neighbor. He does not see the advantage of his life nor the suffering of his neighbor."[38] In faith, however, the soul is free, the conscience happy and the body bound to the estate it was intended for. "Christ," Luther reminds his parishioners, "did not redeem our hands from work, our persons from our office, our bodies from our estate, but [He redeemed] our souls from a false delusion and our consciences from a false faith. He is a Redeemer of consciences and a 'Bishop of souls' as St. Peter says (1 Peter 2:25). Yet, He lets our hands remain in our work, our persons in our offices, and our bodies in our estates."[39]

Here we see the third way vocation is integrally connected to creation—it is always embodied. As Wingren suggests through his study of Luther, in the early Protestant era vocation belonged to the world, not to heaven; it was a "bending toward the world more than a reaching up to God."[40] And because of this vocation had everything to do with one's earthly realities and the material needs of the neighbor. Once again, Luther's own words make this clear:

> Just as the spiritual realm of responsibility shows how people should act properly in relationship to God, so the earthly realm shows how people should live in relationship to each other and how they do it in such a way that body, possessions, wife, child, home, land, and material goods remain in peace and security, and how they can fare well on this earth.[41]

As a lynchpin between creation and redemption, vocation addresses the entire *oikos* of communal life. An authentic and legitimized calling, therefore, takes on flesh while simultaneously honoring flesh; it is born out of place just as it seeks to preserve place. As Calvin observes in his commentary on Genesis, in no way can human beings—literally enlivened earth in the coming together of Adam (*adamah*, or earth) and Eve (*ev*, or breath/life)—be separated from the physical realm. To forget one's fundamental attachment to the dust and clay is in his words "excessively stupid" and does "not hence learn humility."[42]

The Problem of Ascriptivism

And yet, many in recent decades have argued that not only *can* human vocation be construed apart from the realm of creation, but that it *ought* to be.[43] For example, a contemporary of Gustaf Wingren, Einar Billing, emphasized the freedom of vocation by primarily linking the doctrine to justification. When forgiveness is a mere opiate, vocation is nothing more than a job and is therefore defined by the temporal. However, in true faith vocation is more of a gift than a task, a *charisma* to use the Pauline language in 1 Corinthians 7. And as a gift, vocation has more to do with finding than seeking, resting than pursuing.[44] Rest in this sense is not to be equivocated with a static outlook or posture toward life, but speaks more so to the assurances of vocation, which are limited to believers.[45] Critics of Luther read the biblical concept of calling as dynamic, not only for the ways the neighbor's needs change, but also for the prospect of social mobility. While the promises of the gospel are not yet fully realized, they exist in part in the here and now. Luther's doctrine of vocation, such critics argue, doesn't leave room for such dynamism, as he puts too much distance between believers and the *parousia*, leaving eschatological ends as realized in the realm of the conscience over and above societal structures. The result is a stifling of vocation wherein change to one's given place, particularly as it relates to socio-economic realities, in society is altogether unwarranted, or at best postponed.[46]

Yet, as already noted, Luther's doctrine of vocation cannot be defined by law alone; it is equally informed by Gospel, spanning the gap between task (duty) and gift. What's more is that Calvin, often thought to have successfully avoided the pitfalls of Luther's ascriptivism, endorses a strikingly similar view.[47] To his eye, each individual has been given his or her own "sentry post" so that even "a man of obscure station will lead a private life ungrudgingly so as not to leave the rank in which he has been placed by God."[48] As thoroughly pre-modern in their social conceptions, both Luther and Calvin were able to hold profound tensions in equilibrium. The giftedness of an individual, the personalization of a calling, mattered, but not at the expense of the community at large. Premoderns bound up common zeal in collective rites, devotions, and allegiances. If an individual broke rank it wasn't their business alone, and even less so were they to blaspheme or desecrate a rite. In such cases there was an immense shared motivation to bring the individual back into line.[49] In this respect the critique of ascriptivism risks anachronism, bringing more modern individualistic sensibilities to a doctrine that was in its initial democratization fundamentally relational. Though Luther and Calvin rejected the claims of the papacy and the overt spiritualization of vocation, they also worked from within a Medieval system that viewed human community as an organic whole, a living body of diverse members. In their context, feudal emphases of social solidarity and a need for civil order naturally bridled personalism and individualism, thereby qualifying Christian freedom.[50] Beyond this, to reject the tenets of Luther's (and Calvin's) doctrine of vocation on the grounds of ascriptivism is to forfeit vocation's ecologically promising aspects. As outlined above, casting calling by way of the mundane, the necessary, and the embodied clarifies the needs of our immediate neighbors and challenges us to see God at work in our actualized surroundings.

Vocation for All People

With a view of God's activity in the simple and trivial matters of life, Luther and Calvin also democratized calling by extending it to everyone. All Christians are called and all have duties, making a whole variety of vocations legitimate and each vocation multifaceted.[51] This, a more familiar trademark of Reformation thought given parallel theological emphases on the "priesthood of all believers," was a type of fear reversal in its time.[52] Rather than paying indulgences and homage to clerics, fortifying the vocational distinction between clergy and laity, the Reformers challenged perpetual anxiety among the masses and transmuted it into an accessible confidence. As a part of the church, God's body on earth, every Christian has a station, and while they are undoubtedly distinct, they are inseparable from others. Just as one person inhabits many different callings, an *oikos* of vocation, likewise there is an interrelationality between the various callings held and pursued in community. In reference to the Pauline body analogy, Luther writes, "What a fine thing it would be if it were to happen that each attended to his own affairs and yet served others with them, and thus traveled together with one another on the right road to heaven."[53] For Luther, the purpose of vocation is service to neighbor because the Christian ultimately lives not in themself, but in Christ through faith and in their neighbor through love.

Calvin flat-lines vocation in a similar manner to Luther, although he takes more care to distinguish between gifts within the Body of Christ. For Calvin there is a difference, and an important one, between the post of cobbler and that of preacher. The distinction isn't spiritual, nor particularly substantive. Rather, it's doctrinal, as Calvin vocation deals primarily with living out sound dogma and secondarily with loving the neighbor. Were the called preacher to willfully take on the role of cobbler he [or she] would be disregarding God's instruction, which is "in everything the beginning and foundation of well-doing."[54] In addition to and yet beyond the neighbor's needs, Calvin urges Christians to follow the Creator's lead out of reverent worship. "Let this be our principle," he writes, "that the use of God's gifts is not wrongly directed when it is referred to that end to which the Author himself created and destined them for us, since he created them for our good, not for our ruin."[55]

Vocation as a Way of Life

In addition to linking vocation to creation and extending it to all, the Reformers also democratized vocation by framing its pursuit as lifestyle rather than a categorical aspect of one's life. A response to God's call was more about becoming the person who Christ says we are and less about perfection in the here and now. Here again, as before, we see vocation as a means of conformation to Christ rather than of imitation. This insinuates vocation's durative and ongoing nature. Much like the patterns of life surrounding and supporting us, vocation is conceived of and realized as something unfolding with time.

For Luther, viewing vocation as a way of life centralized the cross and gave Christians opportunities to be what he called "little Christs."[56] Christ, who simultaneously embodied perfection while arduously fighting an inherited, foreign sin, is the one who calls. As such, calling as life is characterized by freedom and struggle alike (a riff of sorts on Luther's *simul*, from the

Pauline idea that a Christian is simultaneously sinner and saint).[57] Rejecting concepts of holiness, or what his Medieval predecessors referred to as the art of perfection, Luther understood vocation to be a lifestyle that seeks first and foremost to die to self.[58] The moral life, then, is always enabled by the Spirit rather than individually sought after. Lest one be deceived by the "filthy rags" of works righteousness, vocation as an ethic is more about being willing to become a vessel of God's work than the sanctified will of any one person. This helps explain why many in contemporary Lutheran contexts understand practical or applied ethics in terms of vocation, often using the terms interchangeably, even to the extent of minimizing or dismissing sanctification as an explicit doctrine.

Naturally, Calvin's view on the third use of the law puts different parameters on vocation. For him, the process of sanctification runs between two poles, the forgiveness of sins, which continually restores us to our intended calling, and our calling itself, which reflexively references the forgiveness of sins. As a way of life, vocation draws us closer to God because in our work we are reminded of God's presence and power. In the pursuit of calling one necessarily becomes more interested in internal matters, or what Calvin understood to be personal character, over and above external affirmation. This isn't to say that Calvin endorses a virtue ethic per se, but rather a lifestyle characterized by the fruit of restraint and temperance, which he saw as proof of the indwelling of the Holy Spirit.[59] A frequently cited passage to this end illustrates this point well:

> Therefore, even though the freedom of believers in external matters is not to be restricted to a fixed formula, yet it is surely subject to this law: to indulge oneself as little as possible: but, on the contrary, with unflagging effort of mind to insist upon cutting off all show of superfluous wealth, not to mention licentiousness, and diligently to guard against turning helps into hindrances.[60]

For Calvin, even service to the neighbor can potentially become a hindrance if it is done in vain attempt. In fact, he discusses the dilemma of serving one's family before the stranger as a case in point.[61] Beyond the love of neighbor he saw the purpose and goal of vocation as holiness, "which we must ever look at if we would answer God when He calls [Isaiah 35:8]. For to what purpose are we rescued from the wickedness and pollution of the world in which we were submerged if we allow ourselves throughout life to wallow in these?"[62]

The Problem of Individualism

Calvin's reference to the pollution of the world is ironic in contemporary perspective, for emphases on personal holiness can and have led many Christians down a road of sanctification that cares little for the sanctity of the earth. In short, they can amount to a form of desecration born out of the avoidance of the secular, a pollution from the seemingly glimmering clean. This enigma discloses another major critique of the Protestant doctrine of vocation, especially in its Reformed manifestations—the problem of individualism. Can an emphasis on vocation as a way of life foster attentiveness to one's close and critical connection to others, particularly life forms within the natural world? And furthermore, in its promotion of fruits and virtues like Christ-like love, restraint, and temperance does vocation steer clear of the liabilities of anthropocentrism as discussed in chapter 1?

There is no question that both Luther and Calvin's working anthropologies were more anthropocentric than theocentric or biocentric in nature. Each, for example, in their respective Commentaries on Genesis regards creation as a provision given for human use and enjoyment. In their sermons, reference to the created world via themes of godly dominion and mindful stewardship abound. Yet again, to dismiss the Reformers' working theology of vocation on this account alone would be to overlook and underestimate the radical trajectory of their views. Situating vocation as lifestyle rather than a partitioned section of life brings responsibility to the fore, and in all realms of one's life. From this purview, it isn't enough to claim faithfulness in the workplace, for example, if the work itself undermines God's more universal calling. This is why Luther and Calvin agreed on a shortlist of jobs that cannot constitute vocation in any biblical sense of the word. It is also why the contemporary church should be equally critical of many lines of work, including those systemically violating the integrity of the earth and subjugating the world's most vulnerable persons.[63]

Additionally, the focus on vocation as unfolding underscores God's role in *creatio continua*. As Luther notes, while it is God who preserves what has been created, humans play a significant adaptive role as mutable persons themselves. We have been "created so that we can be changed," he wrote in his rebuttal to Erasmus, which makes pitting the way of love against a life of faith *non sequitor*.[64] Both Reformers saw faith and works as fundamentally connected to creation and together integrally connected in the Christian life. While the latter can never grant or merit the former, it is love that will remain eternally, well after faith has served us in this life.[65] And so understanding vocation as a lifestyle of kenotic love, capable of bearing many related fruits, need not be individualistic in outlook, but rather deeply personal and practical.

NOTES

1. Paul Althaus's reading of Luther is a classic example of this (see chapter 3 of *The Ethics of Martin Luther* (Minneapolis: Fortress, 2007).

2. I will discuss these critiques at greater length in chapter four. Weber's well-known thesis connects the Protestant notion of calling to the rise of capitalism, demonstrating how Calvinist-sect theological views of calling have condoned and legitimized meaningless and inhumane work for the sake of production. As I will argue in chapter 4, I don't think Christian vocation promoted capitalism as much as capitalism changed the face of Christian calling. To this end, Ernst Troeltsch's work is helpful. While he too charts potential liabilities of vocation, these being an openness if not affinity for unfettered economic growth and ascriptivism respectively, he is quick to note Calvinism's tempering of economic growth by charitable love and a strong sense of the common good.

3. Naturally anthropocentrism presents as another problem, one I will address in brief at the end of this chapter and in greater detail near the end of the book. In short, there's no question that by contemporary standards Luther and Calvin's respective doctrines of vocation smack of anthropocentrism. Neither thinker reflects deeply on the calling of other-than-human neighbors. However, in their working doctrines of creation both lift up the dignity of other-than-human life and our dependence upon it.

4. Ruth Douglas See, *The Protestant Doctrine of Vocation in the Presbyterian Thought of Nineteenth-Century America* (New York: New York University Press, 1952), chapter 2. See also John Calvin's "Dedication to Francis I," in volume I of *The Institutes of Christian Religion.*

5. As New Testament scholar Ernest F. Scott remarks, "Paul was at once a craftsman, a missionary and a theologian, and it never occurred to him that these were separate callings. It was he, indeed, who gave us the world 'calling' and it meant for him that each man is called by Christ, to perform in his name whatever duty is laid to his hands. The practical and religious duties, as he saw them, were all of a piece, in so far as in both of them a man placed himself at the service of Christ" (*Man and Society in the New Testament* (New York: Charles Scribner's Sons, 1946), 160–161).

6. An interesting illustration of this can be found in Luther's sermon on Luke 2:33–40, where he notes that Anna, the widow and prophetess who prayed night and day in the temple, must have been a childless widow and without parents, " . . . otherwise she would have been serving the devil, not God, by not departing from the temple and neglecting her divine duty of governing her household." Demonstrating the equality of vocations before God, Luther goes on to say, "It is, therefore, a very dangerous thing to look at only the works and look neither at the person nor at the estate or calling. It is very intolerable for God when anyone neglects the works of his calling or estate and wants [instead] to undertake the works of the saints. . . . This would be the same as walking on your ears, putting a veil on your feet and a boot on your head, and turning all things upside down" (*LW* 75, 416).

7. This insight comes from Ruth Douglas See's aforementioned dissertation on Protestant vocation. See suggests that distinctions between the sacred and secular emerge more clearly during Augustine's lifetime, as neoplatonism offered "a new rationalization of world experience and the idea of a present reality and life in an eternal setting" (*The Protestant Doctrine of Vocation in the Presbyterian Thought of Nineteenth-Century America*, 31). In Augustine's work, monasticism was held in high regard, and distinguished from other vocations, while never being regarded as higher than another calling. In chapter 19 of *City of God*, Augustine writes, "No man has a right to lead such a life of contemplation as to forget in his own as the service due to his neighbor; nor has he any right to be so immersed in active life as to neglect the contemplation of God."

8. Charles Taylor explains elements of this shift well in the first chapter of *A Secular Age* (Cambridge, MA: Harvard University Press, 2007) where he charts the slow move from an enchanted world, where lines between the spiritual and material were porous, to a disenchanted one, where religious superstition and belief began to be challenged.

9. The description of Aquinas's schema as techtetonic comes from Ernst Troeltsch's famous commentary on vocation and work on the social development of Christianity. In *The Social Teaching of the Christian Churches*, translated by Olive Wyon (New York: The Macmillan Company, 1931). Troeltsch suggests that natural law is so critical to Aquinas's schema that even something like vocation was seen as a matter of natural causation, a product of natural forces itself (Vol. 1, 275).

10. Thomas Aquinas, *Summa Theologica*, translated by Fathers of the English Dominican Province, 17 volumes, second and revised edition (London: Burnes Gates and Washbourne, Ltd., n.d.), II-II, 183.1.

11. Aquinas, *Summa*, II-II, 182.2.

12. Aquinas, *Contra Gentiles*, III.81.

13. Troeltsch coined the phrase "cosmos of callings" (*The Social Teaching of the Christian Churches*, Vol 1, 143–144).

14. Not all Eckhart scholars consider the medievalist to be a mystic in the tradition sense of the word. As Jeremiah Hackett outlines in the introduction of his recent work, *A Companion to Meister Eckhart* (London: Brill, 2012), some contemporaries place Eckhart in the tradition of philosophical mysticism, to which neo-platonists like Plotinus, Porphyry, and Proclus belong. Others argue that Eckhart ought not to be associated with mysticism at all, but rather, be viewed merely an innovative hermeneutical thinker located firmly within in the medieval philosophical tradition. Here I follow Bernard McGinn's work on Eckhart, which firmly locates him in the Beguine mystical movement, most active in the thirteenth to sixteenth centuries (see *The Presence of God: A History of Christian Mysticism* (New York: Crossroad Publishing, 1992) or his edited volume, *Meister Eckhart and the Beguine Mystics: Hadewijch of Brabant, Mechthild of Magdeburg, and Marguerite Porete* (New York: The Continuum Publishing Company, 1994)).

15. Hackett, *A Companion to Meister Eckhart*, 44.

16. Charles Taylor, *A Secular Age*, 55.

17. Gustaf Wingren, *Luther on Vocation* (Eugene, OR: Wipf & Stock, 1957), 180. To this end, Luther adopts and develops the insights of the late mystics while ultimately moving beyond them. As Robert Calhoun observes, Luther deliberately attached divine sanction to any sort of serviceable status in society ("Work and Vocation in Christian History," in *Work and Vocation*, edited by John Oliver Nelson (New York: Harper & Brothers Publishers, 1954), 107–108).

18. In his numerous articles on Luther and vocation, Robert Kolb has suggested this, as has Douglas Schuurman in *Vocation: Discerning Our Callings in Life* (Grand Rapids, MI: Eerdmans, 2004).

19. This is the stanza of Building 429's 2011 hit song, "Where I Belong." There are notable exceptions to such popularized conceptions of justification. For example, Vitor Westhelle conceives of justification less as a doctrine and more as a "habit of learning" wherein the Christian learns to continually receive what is given in real time within the actual enactment of creation. See *Transfiguring Luther: The Planetary Promise of Luther's Theology* (Eugene, OR: Cascade Books, 2016).

20. See "The Option for Life," *Dialog: A Journal of Theology* Vol 54, no. 2 (Summer 2015). In it, I call upon Gary Simpson's exploration of Luther's working natural law, "Written on Their Hearts: Thinking with Luther on Scripture, Natural Law and the Moral life," *Word and World* 30, no. 4 (Fall 2010): 420. The extent to which Calvin endorsed and adapted the natural law tradition is debated. For a helpful brief overview of twentieth-century scholarship addressing Calvin's natural law teaching, see J. Todd Billings, *Calvin, Participation, and the Gift* (Oxford, UK: Oxford University Press, 2008), 152. Stephen J. Grabill's published dissertation sets forth one of the most coherent arguments for reading Calvin within the natural law tradition. Grabill laments the captivity of Calvin's teaching on natural law to the Barth-Brunner debates of the early twentieth century, arguing generally that "when evaluated by its treatment of Calvin's understanding of the natural knowledge of God. . . . points to serious problems in semantic ambiguity, *vorverstandis* [preconception], and the misuse of passages to fortify the disputants' predetermined conclusions" (*Rediscovering the Natural Law in Reformed Theological Ethics* (Grand Rapids, MI: Eerdmans, 2006), 79).

21. By "bound," I mean that principles of natural law carry more weight than particular applications of biblical law in matters of civic morality. Luther asserts that biblical law speaks specifically to matters of salvation, whereas natural law complements biblical law by addressing civil matters. So while reason is "the Devil's whore," having no place in the spiritual kingdom on the one hand, reason can also be regarded as a handmaiden of God in the earthly kingdom.

22. There are some important differences between Luther and Calvin on this point, as will be explored in the "Body of Christ" section below. Some read a budding theology of ascent into Calvin's doctrine of vocation because of his third use of the law. For example, see Julie Canlis's *Calvin's Ladder: A Spiritual Theology of Ascent and Ascension* (Grand Rapids, MI: Eerdmans, 2010) and Paul Santmire's *Before Nature* (Minneapolis: Fortress Press, 2014), 139. I read Calvin's doctrine of sanctification as similar to Luther's concept of freedom and see neither thinker defining vocation by way of maturation or holiness. For Luther, the Christian is to be hidden in Christ and his cross, by faith receiving God's unmerited grace and through the power of the Holy Spirit empowered to love and serve the neighbor. For Calvin, the Christian is to glorify God in all things, by faith sacrificing the desires of the will, being made free to focus on the needs of the neighbor. In both cases, conformation to Christ is the dominant theme, leaving the active life as privileged above the contemplative one.

23. *LW* 34:112. When speaking about "new decalogues," Luther is referring to Paul's work in the epistles. Paul, Luther suggests, understood that any law constructed in light of contemporary challenges must always hold in sight the gospel.

24. Luther writes more about this expression "of the time" and "of the hour" in his expository of Ecclesiastes in 1523. *WA* 20:61.

25. For Barth, there are three primary questions related to Christian vocation: 1) What gifts/aptitudes does one have? 2) What place is a person in his/her life cycle? and 3) What place is a person in history? *Church Dogmatics (CD)* 3/4, 607–647.

26. Twentieth-century missiologist John Stott popularized these concepts. By "vertical," he was referring to a love of God and by "horizontal," a love of neighbor (*Christian Mission in the Modern World* (Downers Grove, IL: InterVarsity Press, 1975).

27. H. Richard Niebuhr suggests that human beings are always in the midst of a "field of natural and social forces, acted upon and reacting, attracted and repelling" *The Responsible Self* (New York: Harper Row, 1963), 56. We are, by nature, answerers to the action that is upon us. Ethics, then, is always a response to such action, which involves both interpretation and a fitting response. Therefore, the moral life must go beyond classical categories of teleology and deontology, respectively. In his words, "The approach to our moral existence as selves, and to our existence as Christians in particular, with the aid of this idea makes some aspects of our life as agents intelligible in a way that the teleology and deontology of traditional thought cannot do" (67).

28. *LW* 75:131.

29. For more on Luther's sacramentalism, see Santmire's, *Before Nature*, 141. To read more of Luther on the "secularization of the clergy," see LW 75:133.

30. While Luther's doctrine of creation is expansive and open, it is important to note how his working sacramentalism differs from modern-day panentheism. In good Medieval stead, Luther condemns the *Deus sive natura* tradition. God is not straw in a sack (*WA* 26:339), nor can God be known spatially in any way, save God's revelation in the incarnation. Rather, "God wants us to respect and acknowledge them [creation] as His creatures, which are a necessity for this life. But He does not want us to attribute divinity to them, that is, to fear and respect them in such a way that we trust them and forget Him. . . . Thus God has given all His creatures that they may serve us and we may use them, not that we may serve and worship them. Therefore, let us make use of bread, wine, clothing, possessions, gold, etc.; but let us not trust or glorify them. For we are to glorify and trust in God alone; He is to be loved, feared, and honored" (*LW* 26:95–96).

31. John Calvin, *Commentary on II Thessalonians*, translated by John Pringle (Edinburgh: Calvin Translation Society, 1855) 3:6–10.

32. Calvin is undeniably more cautious in his delineation between Creator and creation. Nowhere in the *Institutes* or in his *Commentary on Genesis* do we see an equivalent to Luther's "masks of God." In his doctrine of God, transcendence is prioritized over immanence. Nonetheless, Calvin's doctrine of creation is radically theocentric, not in the sense of sacramental presence, but in a revelatory sense. It is through the natural world, and most notably, the Incarnation, that we're able to reflect upon God.

33. John Calvin, *Institutes of the Christian Religion*, edited by John T. McNeill and translated by Ford Lewis Battles (Philadelphia: Westminster Press, 1960), 3:10:6.

34. In "Against the Fantastic and Furious Sect of the Libertines Who Are Called 'Spirituals'" Calvin condemns those who see vocation as the inclination of one's own nature or the pleasure of one's own heart. Such "wretches" as he calls them, forget that a great many vocations directly contradict God's laws, propel evil, and foster bad habits. What is needed is the Christian who orders life according to the Scriptures, adopting what God approves. In this sense Christians do not choose their estate, but discern it and faithfully serve within it.

35. The 1522 Church Postils illuminate this point well. See for example, *WA* 10, 1, 306–308, or 311–312 and even more clearly, 412–414. See also Luther's *Commentary on Romans*, 1515, *WA* 56, 418.

36. Luther cites the Virgin Mary as a prime example of this. She doubtlessly went on with her necessary housework after the Annunciation: "See how purely she bears all things in God, that she claims no works, no honor, and no fame. She acts as she did before, when she had none of this. She does not ask for more honor than before. She does not plume herself, nor vaunt herself, nor proclaim that she has become the Mother of God. She demands no glory, but goes on working in the house as before. She milks the cows, cooks, washes the dishes, cleans, performing the work of a housemaid or housewife in lowly and despised tasks. . . . She is esteemed among other women and her neighbors no more highly than before, nor did she desire to be. She remained a poor townswoman, among the lowly crow" (*WA* 7.575).

37. Calvin, *Institutes* 3.10.1.

38. *LW* 75:358.

39. *LW* 76:30–31.

40. Wingren, *Luther on Vocation* (Philadelphia: Muhlenburg Press, 1957), 180. Wingren's reading of Luther's doctrine of vocation is decidedly different from that of his contemporary, Einar Billing. Like his teacher Max Weber, Billing emphasized the social aspects of vocation, but did so by focusing on Luther's doctrine of justification. In his short work *Our Calling* (Philadelphia: Fortress Press, 1964), he writes, "Whoever knows Luther, even partially, knows that his various thoughts do not lie alongside each other, like pearls on a string, held together only by common authority or perchance by a line of logical argument, but that they all, as tightly as the petals of a rosebud, adhere to a common center, and radiate out like the rays of the sun from one glowing core, namely, the Gospel of the forgiveness of sins" (4). From this theological center, vocation is freedom, not duty. Calling is the form life takes as God organizes it through grace (8), and so it includes both God's forgiveness and providence, or what Reinhold Niebuhr would later identify as pardon and power. Justification was the rosebud or common center of Luther's theology, by which he argued that the gifts of vocation be read in the context of the Great Commandment.

41. *LW* 13:197.

42. John Calvin, *Commentaries on the First Book of Moses Called Genesis* (Grand Rapids, MI: Eerdmans, 1948), 111. Charles Taylor convincingly argues meaning in pre-modern times resided in things as much as it did in the mind. From the perspective of enchanted world meaning can exist in the external and influence us from the outside in *A Secular Age*, 34.

43. Karl Barth, Jacques Ellul, Miroslav Volf, and Stanley Hauerwas all argue for this. I will take up their concerns in some detail in the final chapter, "Ecology of Vocation."

44. Gilbert Meilander emphasizes this aspect of vocation in chapter six of his very practical work *The Freedom of a Christian: Grace, Vocation and the Meaning of Our Humanity* (Grand Rapids, MI: Brazos Press, 2006).

45. Perhaps more vehemently than his aforementioned colleagues, Stanley Hauerwas places vocation firmly within the realm of the Christian community. As linked to justification, he argues that vocation does not apply to all persons at all times. Orders of creation don't dictate the various stations of life; only the Holy Spirit provides this direction. Therefore, to speak about vocation in any temporal sense is nonsensical to Hauerwas. Like election, the doctrine pertains to the Church alone. For example, see chapters 3–6 of *The Peaceable Kingdom: A Primer in Christian Ethics* (Notre Dame, IN: Notre Dame University Press, 1983).

46. A classic proof text to this end can be found in Luther's famous "Freedom of a Christian" treatise, where he writes, "Each one should do the works of his progression and station, not that by them he may strive after righteousness, but that through them he may keep his body under control, be an example to others who also need to keep their bodies under control, and

finally that by such works he may subject his will to that of others in the freedom of love" *Martin Luther: Selections from His Writings*, edited by John Dillenberger (New York: Anchor Books, 1962), 78.

47. Jeffrey Scholes' recent work, *Vocation and the Politics of Work: Popular Theology in a Consumer Culture* (New York: Lexington Books, 2013), makes this claim. In the tradition of Weber and Troeltsch, Scholes distinguishes between Luther's external accent to vocation and Calvin's internal emphasis. He writes, "Despite the rather harsh sentence that Calvin orders of a human life lived within a calling, obstacles to social mobility are diminished when compared to Luther's sentence. Room is left in Calvin's theology of vocation for Christians to change from one job to another as long as productive work is sought that contributes to the common good" (213). Troeltsch's reading of Calvin went so far as to suggest that such mobility safeguards individuals from what Calvin deemed the most destructive vice, laziness. See *The Social Teachings of the Christian Churches*, vol. 2, 611.

48. Calvin, *Institutes* 3.10.6. Here, Calvin seems to be directly working from Cicero's *On Old Age*. In it, Cicero writes, "Pythagoras forbids us to desert our fort and station in life unbidden by God, our commander."

49. Taylor, *A Secular Age*, 42.

50. Robert Calhoun has a good discussion on this in his chapter in *Work and Vocation*, 109–110. Marc Kolden also discusses the critique of ascriptivism and demonstrates the centrality of obedience to God in Luther's thought. On many occasions, Luther, and the later 1550 Magdeburg Confession, present a theology of resistance to that which is contrary to the authority of God. Kolden suggests that obedience to God morphed into a more blind obedience to authority throughout the seventeenth- and eighteenth-century Lutheranism because of the receding role of creation. The tradition of vocation lost its connection to God's ongoing work and "became merely reactionary and often oppressive" ("Christian Vocation in Light of Feminist Critiques," *Lutheran Quarterly* Vol. X (1996): 74).

51. For example, in Luther's *Commentary on Galatians*, he writes, "Therefore all duties of Christians, such as loving one's wife, rearing one's children, governing one's family, honoring one's parents, obeying the magistrate, etc. which they regard as secular and fleshly, are fruits of the Spirit" (*LW* 26.217).

52. I am using Charles Taylor's working concept here. See *A Secular Age*, 77.

53. *LW* 75, 355.

54. Calvin, *Institutes* 3.10.5.

55. Calvin, *Institutes* 3.10.2.

56. In the John Commentary, Luther speaks about Christians being *of* Christ (as in the genitive), just as they *are* Christs (nominative plural).

57. Luther sees sin as a reality until the Eschaton, wherein sin will be entirely extinguished at last. In *Bondage of the Will*, for example, he directly cites *On Marriage and Concupiscence*, where Augustine states, "Sin is forgiven not so much that it does not exist, but so that it is not imputed" (*LW* 33, 430).

58. Thomas Aquinas never depicted clerics as perfect, but rather uniquely poised in "the state of perfection," as those "intending to become perfect" (See *Summa* 2–2, q. 185, art. 5). Luther saw this framework as "pernicious and poisonous doctrine." He writes, "Who does not know that a monk can wear a cowl, tonsure and yet be a rogue inside?" (See *LW* 76, 34).

59. Regarding virtue, Calvin makes clear its efficient cause: "When we hear mention of our union with God, let us remember that holiness must be its bond; not because we come into the communion with him by virtue of our holiness! Rather, we ought first to cleave unto him so that, infused with his holiness, we may follow whither he calls" (*Institutes* 3.14; 16–17). On virtues being evidence of regeneration, see *Institutes* 3.14.19.

60. Calvin, *Institutes* 3.10.4.

61. Calvin, *Institutes* 2.8.55.

62. Calvin, *Institutes* 3.14.19.

63. Both Reformers condemned usury, prostitution, unlawful management, etc. As we will briefly explore in the final chapter, many contemporary jobs violate these principles (i.e., unfair-wage textile markets, the pornographic industry, parts of the fossil fuel industry, etc.).

64. Luther, *Martin Luther: Selections from His Writings*, edited by John Dillenberger, 177. Luther's sentiment here resembles that of Augustine's, whom he references in "Bondage of the Will." In *Sermon 170* Augustine writes, "He who created you with you will not save you without you."

65. See Luther on this in *LW* 34:195–196.

Chapter Four

Embodied Work

Ecology and the Protestant Doctrine of Vocation Since the Reformers

It is one thing to make a case for the democratization of Luther and Calvin's working doctrines of vocation and quite another to demonstrate the existence of such principles in the work of their successors. In less than the span of either Reformer's lifetime, the radically democratized doctrine of vocation, including an intentional linking of calling to the material world, had begun to be reduced to little more than a theology of work, which by the mid-to-late seventeenth century was generally characterized by production and consumption more than neighborly love and embodied presence.[1] While many students of Christian thought have causally linked Protestant renderings of vocation to the rise of industrialism and capitalism, a closer reading of the history of the doctrine uncovers a gradual cooptation of the doctrine due to the pervasive influence of such forces.[2] Calling began to be changed by modernism's intellectual landscape and eventually compromised by the demands of industry, thereby restructuring work relationships around increasingly systemic patterns of injustice, ecological and otherwise. The contemporary result is the Protestant community's bifurcated sense of vocation wherein one might profess Christ crucified while "make a living," even accumulating wealth, with little to no moral regard for the real ecological and social cost of work.

Three matters pertaining to the historical reception of the Protestant doctrine of vocation are relevant. First, through a close and selective reading of Luther and Calvin's earliest progeny, I highlight germinal doctrinal emphases that made possible the reduction of vocation to the particular aim of work. Second, I explore how restricted renderings of vocation led to increased injustice in the workplace, propelling what remain today misdirected and anachronistic critiques of the Reformers' working doctrine. And finally, I show how human relationships of injustice and ecological degradation disrupt the fulfillment of vocation, making our return to the Reformers' original sense of calling all the more difficult in contemporary context.

VOCATION IN EARLY PROTESTANTISM

The first of these tasks takes up the work of Philip Melanchthon and William Perkins, both intellectual peers and fellow conspirators in the transformation of the church. In most ways, these academics and churchmen carried forth the Reformers' tradition of calling, describing vocation as enacted faith and materially-bound worship. However, the manner in which Melanchthon and Perkins situated such embodied vocation in relationship to the doctrine of justification opened the door for later siphoning of the doctrine, ultimately leading scholars like Max Weber and Ernst Troeltsch to connect the Protestant doctrine of vocation to the rise of industrialism and capitalism and prompting some twentieth-century and contemporary thinkers to altogether distance vocation from the doctrine of creation.[3]

Philip Melanchthon and Vocation as Enacted Faith

Luther's younger colleague has long been considered the Reformer's perfect companion for, among other things, his disciplined and organized habits in contrast to Luther's brilliant, but sometimes fiery, impulsive thinking. For example, immediately after Luther's 1519 debate with Johann Eck at Leipzig, Melanchthon corresponded with Eck, putting to print the heart of the emergent Evangelical theology, earning himself the reputation as principal spokesman for the Evangelical position. Two years after the correspondence, Melanchthon further fleshed out such theological differences in his lectures on the book of Romans. The *Loci Communes Rerum Theologicarum*, as they were entitled, became the first systematic statement of Evangelical theology and wildly popular in its day.[4] Accustomed to rising early in the morning to pray and write, Melanchthon produced prolific works at an early age. Also in 1521, he produced a series of lectures on the Epistle to the Corinthians, and two years later, lectures on the Gospel of St. John. Impressed by the young scholar's aptitudes, Luther stole both manuscripts and sent them off to the printer, despite Melanchthon's known tendency to perpetually edit and revise his own work. And it is in these early works, in addition to the famous *Augsburg Confession*, that we have greatest exposure to Melanchthon's views on vocation.

Like Luther, Melanchthon understood vocation in a dual sense; one has both a spiritual and temporal calling, with the former informing the latter, although, as Reformation scholar Robert Kolb has noted, Melanchthon often approached the question of calling from a different vantage than Luther. Heavily influenced by his study of Greek philosophy, Kolb suggests that Melanchthon had a more difficult time shaking off preferences for the spiritual over the material.[5] This is evident, for example, in his short 1522 Treatise on "The Difference between Worldly and Christian Piety." In it, Melanchthon never explicitly connects piety and external discipline or habit in the same manner as Calvin, although he certainly makes more room for the role of reason than his collegial teacher, Luther. To the extent that reason helps us discern our offices, which are in turn used to respond to God's gifts, reason can be said to produce piety.[6] Piety, in this sense, is not to be read as perfection, for perfection is definitively unattainable in this life.[7] Rather, it is better understood as the quest for perfection: "All people, whatever their calling, should seek perfection, that is, growth in the fear of God, in faith, in the love for their neighbor, and in similar spiritual virtues."[8] Here, as in Luther, vocation is described as a kind of lynchpin between law and gospel. In a section on love in *The Loci Communes* Melanchthon illustrates this bridging of theological concepts well: "For he who comprehends mercy by faith cannot help but love God in return, and thus love is the fruit of faith. From the love of God arises also the love of one's neighbor when we desire to serve God in all creatures."[9]

Does this passing statement suggest a larger view of the neighbor? Was Melanchthon insinuating responsibility toward the human and other-than-human neighbor alike? In his commentary on Paul's letter to the Colossians he makes explicit the connection between God, creation, and human works. Realities were not made to exist without God's help, he argues: "He is not like a carpenter, who hands the ship he has built over to the crew and goes away." Rather, God is the one in whom we live, move, and have our being. "That realities endure, that we breathe, that we live, that we eat, that we speak, that we perform our natural capabilities, are all works of God," Melanchthon continues.[10] Hidden in the form and function of nature, God animates and moves nature in such a way "as belongs to each part of nature. He moves trees in one way, beasts in another, and men in yet another. In this way He grants to men a certain reason and power of choice. God does not take away this power to choose. He imparts life and motion, while we choose and do."[11] And because this general activity of God is hidden, Melanchthon sees no point in trying to determine *how* God sustains and moves nature; to his mind the Scholastics wasted a great deal of energy and ink on such matters. What is more relevant and urgent is human restraint, that God's will might be done for all creatures. The object of calling, in this sense, isn't necessarily nature as much as it is a letting be within the natural world.

In this sense, Melanchthon clearly underscores Luther's theology by linking vocation to the doctrine of creation through embodied service to the neighbor. He goes a step further than Luther, however, in the way he connects vocation to redemption. It isn't that justification merely makes possible the receipt of a calling, but that it also promotes the cultivation and practice of spiritual virtues. And where might these virtues be fostered if not in one's daily work? By emphasizing the spiritual or internal aspects of calling, Melanchthon, and what would later be termed the "Philipists," highlighted Lutheranism's shared theological territory with Calvinism and subjected the doctrine of vocation to emergent cultural definitions of work, which by the mid-seventeenth century were increasingly industrialized. Staunch and rigid Lutheran Confessionalism (*Verkonfessionalisierung*) also configured vocation in terms of work, although more so in keeping with the wedding of church-state relations. In this case, the quality of lived vocation became nominal, in doctrine and practice alike. For example, Nicholas Amsdorf, a sixteenth century Lutheran theologian, went so far as to suggest that good works hindered the Christian life by prizing sanctification above justification.[12] Practically speaking, Confessionalists began exclusively regarding *beruf* as station, or one's place of duty within Christendom, which by the seventeenth century was more readily defined by conformation to society than by the transformation of it. As Einar Billing observed, "Almost every strong religious revival which has visited Luther's church since his day has resulted in an undermining of this teaching about the call rather than in a strengthening and deepening of it. . . . " for ". . . . the measure in which the forgiveness of sins degenerates into an opiate, the call shrinks into a job."[13] This gradual secularization led early German Lutheran pietists to conceive of vocation differently; they argued that calling had less to do with assent (*assensus*) and more to do with personal faith (*fiducia*); faithfulness in one's work was regarded as more valuable than the fulfillment of any said role.[14] Here Lutheran pietism closely resembles Anabaptist lines of thinking within Calvinism, the primary sectarian focus of Max Weber's famous study in the ways it personalized and privatized vocation.

William Perkins and Vocation as Worship

In his 1605 *Treatise of the Vocations*, dedicated to an exchequer in the court of Queen Elizabeth I, William Perkins discusses vocation in a fashion similar to that of his contemporary Melanchthon. Perkins also distinguishes between a spiritual vocation (what he calls *general*), and a secular vocation (*particular*). And like all three of the aforementioned Reformers, he situates this bifurcated sense of vocation in the midst of a Christian dialectic, wherein one is both free and slave at once.[15] In principle, the Lutheran and Reformed voices agree—because of the work of Christ one is free according to their general calling, and yet obligated to the neighbor according to their particular callings.

For the Reformers, this boundedness explains why vocation is necessarily pursued in the context of community and why thinkers like Perkins were so critical of clerics and monastics, which he brazenly referred to as "popish votaries."[16] Because they have historically viewed their calling as extraordinary and undertaken it in a separatist fashion, they are "justly condemned from ancient times as thieves and robbers," for in living apart from the common societies of men "they are neither the members of any body, nor maintainers of any of the three states (church, family, state)."[17] In Perkins's work, akin to the others, vocation is democratized in a threefold sense: all callings are deemed equally valuable under God; all persons "of every degree, state, sex, or condition, without exception, must have some personal and particular calling to walk in;" and every person truly discerns his/her calling by seeking advice and the help of others.[18]

What makes Perkins's perspective on vocation decidedly Reformed, distinct from Luther and his successors, is its Christocentrism and explicit focus upon the glorification of God beyond the beneficial human impact of calling. Perkins outlines at great length characteristics of the honest, lawful, and good calling, underscoring the need for one's work to profit the common good. However, he nevertheless emphasizes a more individualized goal of vocation, that being worship. Perkins makes clear: humankind, "despite having fallen from that integrity in which he was created," is designed to serve God and has been "set in order" by God to bring Him (sic) glory.[19] For Perkins, work can function as a type of worship when undertaken in the right spirit, a spirit of *Deo gloria*. Moreover, it is the faith that Christ confers upon people that makes the discernment of calling possible in the first place. Whereas in Luther and Melanchthon there is a greater focus on vocation as the Spirit-led response to the needs of the neighbor and the presence of the invisible God, in Perkins' view vocation comes primarily through one's irresistible encounter with the living Word.

Perkins differs from the Lutherans, and to an extent even Calvin himself, in his prioritization of holiness. For all of his commentary on vices—sloth and idleness, vain ambition and greed—as well as virtue—wisdom and humility, perseverance and frugality—it is easy to see why pietists and Puritans like Richard Baxter, George Fox, and Jonathan Edwards called upon Perkins's *Treatise* in their meditations on the Christian life. To his eye it was one thing to affirm the Lutheran paradox of slave-yet-free, but quite another to embrace the Lutheran tradition of *simul justus et peccator*. In his earlier work, *The Foundation of the Christian Religion Gathered in Six Principles*, Perkins describes the fruit of repentance, which includes things such as a zeal to love God, a craving for pardon, and a legitimate fear of one's own sin.[20] The believer's plaguing beast of uncertainty is not satiated by justification alone, but rather also by sanctification. Growth toward Christ in His likeness makes greater joy possible, equating in the direct relationship between happiness in one's calling and righteous living.[21]

The troubles of holiness traditions, and debate regarding the third use of the law among Reformers have been well articulated elsewhere, and need not be rehashed here. Suffice it to say, this angle of Perkins's views on vocation runs the same risk of over-personalization discussed in chapter three, if not a more egregious form of individualism. Those who applied Perkins's teachings stifled vocation to a form of legalism rather than enlarging it as a Spirit-filled response to God's invitation, as evidenced in the well-known work of Richard Baxter. In his 1657 *The Whole Duty of Man* and later *A Christian Directory*, Baxter writes of the "right choices" for calling and ordinary labor, appealing the Christian to pursue what is appropriate and fittingly, not solely most desirable. Baxter believed that through virtue, particularly that of restraint, the will of God and the will of God's child could be reconciled.[22] And so while Perkins himself renders holiness as more of a gift than an earned blessing, the trajectory of his personalized reading of vocation lends itself to what Max Weber later called the "Protestant work ethic."

THE GRADUAL COOPTATION OF VOCATION TO THE PARTICULAR AIM OF WORK

As previously noted, to locate the underlying force of industrial capitalism within the Protestant doctrine of vocation, even later renditions of it in the form of Phillipist Lutheranism or modified Calvinism, is to underestimate the influence of culture upon theology. As early readings of Luther and Calvin's doctrines of vocation were interpreted through Humanism's heightened sense of individualism and the shapeshifting of knowledge, calling became conflated with work, and increasingly unjust models of work at that.[23]

Cultural Revolution and Vocation as Knowledge

From the time of Luther's death in 1542 to the onset of the Industrial Revolution roughly between 1750–1760, a scientific and cultural revolution ensued, wherein vocation became explicitly connected to knowledge. The Revolution championed having more knowledge with the particular aim of applying it toward mastery of the natural world, rather than simply knowledge of nature. In what historians of science regard as the first phase of the Scientific Revolution, Nicolaus Copernicus (1473–1543) called into question the relationship of objects to persons, be they divine or human, as well as consciousness. In doing so he induced a five-hundred-year journey to empty the cosmos of agency, all the while ironically recasting humanity as the technical controller of and intervener in earth's habitat.[24] Building upon Copernicus, Galileo Galilei (1564–1642) famously risked apostasy by highlighting the mathematical nature of the laws of nature, championing heliocentrism over geocentrism. A good Jesuit, Galileo never intended to violate the Council of Trent or challenge the authority of the Papacy, and yet saw continuity between the biblical texts and heliocentrism, ultimately proposing methods of observation over speculation. Such movement forced philosophers like Francis Bacon (1561–1626) to reimagine the world of the interior, or the realm of the Spirit. Was spiritual meaning in history really the locus of rational purpose? By formally introducing the inductive method of inquiry, Bacon provided a resounding "No!" to such a question and proposed spiritual significance in humanity's rational reordering of material earth. In his watershed *Novum Organum*, Bacon argues that only humans who are engaged in controlling nature qualify as fully human. As spirits themselves, such humans bring meaning and purpose to the morally empty and inert earth.[25] Their true vocation, in Bacon's estimation, was to exhibit and practice knowledge over creation.

In short, over the course of little less than a century the universe as humans knew and understood it was radically altered. Human experience no longer proved paramount; what became critical, rather, was human mastery of and over the laws of nature. As these paradigmatic shifts took place, religious definitions of calling gradually shifted from embodied, corporate responses to God's initiative in the needs of the neighbor to individualized quests for knowledge, of self and world alike. In this sense, it wasn't that the Reformers' sense of vocation was stripped of anything in particular (although as will be discussed in subsequent chapters loss of some kind is undeniably present in the unfettering of vocation to the doctrine of creation), but rather that a great deal was *added to* the Protestant doctrine of vocation, molding the concept in new and different directions.[26] This is evident in what is often deemed the second phase of the Scientific Revolution, or the "Age of Reflection."

Renes Descartes (1596–1650), a contemporary of Galileo and Bacon, saw such evacuation of cosmic agency as promoting the alienation of mind from matter and ultimately an instrumentalist and domineering attitude toward nature. Contrary to fundamental tenets of longstanding Scholasticism, Descartes saw no distinction between substance and form. The bodily form, our only access to actual space or place, cannot know the essence (*ousia*) of external forces; it has knowledge of the mind and body (*res cognitans* and *res extensa*) only. In the Cartesian framework, calling was not about discerning the divine mind, responding to neighborly need, or about co-participating in creation; it was, rather, to know oneself, that is to become a thoroughly reflective person. In this sense, the intimate, spiritual nature of vocation, which began with Luther and Calvin, was abstracted from society. Rather than drawing its power from the expressed command of God, calling became a duty and obligation founded upon necessity. And while this necessity might be grounded in something resembling divine providence, its origin in the will of the Creator was tenuous at best. The need to act in the unknown web of history made very different demands than God's inward call or textual command. "A Christian could act on a calling, but the secularist could join in action based upon necessity. The grounds of obligation had become natural, and the duties of a calling had now become natural law and natural right. It became possible to speak of callings without speaking of God, or indeed of any caller whatsoever."[27] With regards to the doctrine of vocation, Jean-Luc Marion's reading of Descartes remains true, namely, that the inauguration of a split between physics and metaphysics was taken up by Sir Isaac Newton in *Philosophiae Naturalis Principia Mathematica* (1687) and Immanuel Kant, who later clarified it through discourse on the distinct realms of science and ethics in *Critique of Practical Reason* (1788) and *Metaphysics of Morals* (1797).[28]

The unfolding search for autonomous reason and conscience colored philosophical and theological interpretations of vocation among later seventeenth-century Christians. John Locke (1632–1704), for example, whom regarded Christianity as "the most modest and peaceable religion that ever was," understood particular callings as that "which embraced the diligently industrious pursuit of a particular profession or trade" and general calling the duty of all, regardless of position, to pray, study, and engage in other pious activities.[29] It wasn't that vocation was limited to a job for Locke; he speaks at length about the range of responsibilities facing a gentleman in any particular station.[30] However, Locke does suggest that labor, more than any other aspect of vocation, is evidence of God's call in the ways it discloses God's fruitfulness on earth as well as in heaven. So, while Locke regarded vocation as obedience to God in a similar manner to Luther and Calvin, he spoke of it principally as the responsibility to create and generate wealth. It is in Locke that the Christian concept of calling becomes most obviously reduced to work, with work generally functioning as another word for employment or economic transaction. As historian Paul Marshall notes, Locke bridged the gap between moral and technical economic theories in his day, the former of which prized justice, charity, and stewardship over and above efficacy, gain, and growth, and the latter which saw self-interest as an unredeemable core to all economic transactions and as such an incontrovertible good. Locke was "obsessed with comfortable hopes of a future life," and the common good, but was equally concerned with a "quiet and prosperous passage through this life."[31] Calling, therefore, could not be discerned and measured under the rubric of sanctification alone, as pietist and puritan Protestants had long argued. Instead, for Locke calling was primarily interpreted through the lens of production, which in the forms of private wealth and the growth of trade could potentially lead to the moral good of public wealth. Here, vocation as a response to the needs of the neighbor takes on a much more passive tack than in the sixteenth century and demonstrates what some have described as modernism's anthropological optimism (or naïveté), wherein one's work to satiate individual need and participation in the larger commercial community are thought to collectively work to meet the needs of all. If everyone takes care of themselves and their own families, society will be better for it.

Adam Smith (1723–1790), the West's celebrated "Father of Modern Economics," followed Locke's lead on relating vocation to production. Although he was less tethered to Christian doctrine than the aforementioned thinkers, having been greatly influenced by the utilitarian, David Hume among others, Smith viewed work as something with eternal purpose. Real work was fixed in a localized reality at a particular time and provided a tangible good for society at large. "Man," he wrote in *An Inquiry into the Nature and Causes of the Wealth of Nations*, "was made for action and to promote by the exertion of his faculties such changes in the external circumstances both of himself and others, as may seem most favourable to the happiness of all."[32] The "work" of pastors, philosophers, and politicians was therefore regarded as unproductive for the way it "perished in the very instance of [its] performance."[33] This is not to say that human vocation was reduced to the production of wealth alone, as many of Smith's critics may like to believe, but *is* to say that Smith saw the venture of work as the very fabric of society.[34] Work leads human beings to the primary ambition, which for Smith was individual happiness within the masses. In this sense, vocation proves a mere means, not the *telos* itself. This is why work didn't need to embody anything particularly moral or existential for Smith and need not concern itself with matters of human dignity, or ecological integrity for that matter. Each and every one is called to work of some kind by compulsion and necessity, and out of self-interest seeks to obtain wealth to "avoid irksome labour and impose it on others."[35] As Miroslav Volf helpfully summarizes Smith's thought, it is the ultimate goal of each person to avoid working. Yet, "on the other hand, the goal is also to increase the quantity and quality of work because on the whole the progress of society depends upon economic development."[36]

Adam Smith's thought was publically received and applied as the early stages of the Industrial Revolution were unfolding. Steam power required one-tenth of the fuel of former production practices, and increased mining led to the greater affordability and accessibility of metals, forever changing production and transportation. Many Protestants located themselves and their functional sense of calling within this burgeoning industrialism and its related ideological shift.[37] For them, vocation was defined primarily in terms of production, resulting in the yet familiar question, "What do you do for a living?" In oppositional response to this pervasive view, some Romantics retreated from work and in so doing defined vocation in terms of privilege, embodying the question "What do you wish to be?" The following sections address the issue that neither of these responses resembles the democratized, interrelational, or ecological nature of the early Reformers' doctrine of vocation, which brought to bear alternative questions like "What is the appropriate way to relate to my neighbor?" and "How am I to use my gifts and talents where I am?" Both vocation as production and vocation as the escape from it drew upon the cultural milieu of the day more than biblical or historical theologies. Furthermore, in their respective restrictions of vocation, both perspectives fostered injustice in the workplace, an *oikos* that included persons and the natural world alike. I now turn to explore these modern reflections on vocation by engaging some of the theological conversation partners on the Protestant understanding of work, including Richard Baxter, Max Weber, Ernst Troeltsch, Jonathan Edwards, Ralph Waldo Emerson, Frederic Henry Hedge, and Walter Rauschenbusch.

Industriousness and Vocation as Production (1760–1840)

Many historians link coal with the emergence of the textile industry and the invention of the steam engine, both critical markers in the rise of industrialism. Coal was easily mined, practically pouring out of riverbeds in some regions like Northumbria, UK and the Ruhr River Valley of Germany. Mined on a private agrarian basis, the mining of coal initially fostered equality within Medieval craft guilds. For example, in early sixteenth century, the regions encompassing modern-day Germany shared ownership and the use of rights in mines led to a coded system of morality wherein certificates were issued to participants of large mine collectives and clerks recorded sales within shared accounts.[38] Such mutualism dissipated, however, as mining gradually required deeper digging and more capital investment, often resulting in bitter conflicts between workers (miners) and owners, as was the case with the infamous Peasants Revolt of 1525. Over time, guilds for the organization of mining gave way to characteristic capitalist forms of corporate shared ownership and waged work, setting new patterns for vocation as production or labor, which have dominated both capitalist and communist forms of mercantilism up until the present day.[39]

Historian Lewis Mumford is less intrigued by the role of coal-powered machines and more interested in the force of the clock. Strategies of time-keeping, initiated in tenth-century monasteries, passed into time-serving, time-accounting and time-rationing, and as this took place, "Eternity ceased gradually to serve as the measure and focus of human actions."[40] By dissociating time from human events, clocks helped fortify belief in an independent world of mathematically measurable sequences, or what Mumford calls "the special world of science."[41] It was this device above all others that made possible the standardization of production, the measurement of space and time, and hence the reliable navigation of the whole earth, in ways that had not been possible before and are characteristically modern.

Whether the clamoring for coal or the clicking of the clock better illustrate the industrial spirit, theological reflection in the late eighteenth and nineteenth centuries was undeniably influenced by modernism's fury for production. Evidence of this is easily uncovered in the work of Puritan Pastor, Richard Baxter, for example. In his 1825 *A Christian Directory*, production is considered to be the reason "God maintaineth us and our abilities: work is the moral as well as the natural end of power. It is the act by the power that is commanded us. It is action that God is most served and honoured by: not so much by our being able to do good, but by our doing it."[42] For good reason, Baxter is a primary subject of interest in Max Weber's famous study, *The Protestant Ethic and the Spirit of Capitalism*. Yet, perhaps one of the most thorough studies on the influence of industrial capitalism upon theology lies not in Weber, but in the work of his lesser-known contemporary, sociologist Ernst Troeltsch.

Troeltsch's Reading of the Protestant Doctrine of Vocation

When it comes to vocation, Troeltsch's work is often overlooked, particularly in comparison to the work Weber. Like Weber, Troeltsch exhibited keen interest in the Protestant doctrine of vocation, with particular regard for the social implications of vocation as work. Mistakenly, his views are frequently insinuated within Weber's working thesis, so much so that some history of the doctrine classifies the two as sociologists in tandem.[43] Yet, Troeltsch, a theologically trained historian, sought to understand the relationship between capitalism and Protestant vocation on terms far different from Weber. Whereas Weber's primary interest was the development of global capitalism, the exploration of religion's role in the generation of and establishment of social patterns and the religious nature of calling therefore rather tertiary, Troeltsch sought to make clear the significance of capitalism in the theological development of the Calvinist sect-type.[44] His inquiries on vocation and the Protestant work ethic were decidedly theological. When comparing his own work to that of Weber he simply states, "Behind our researches the points of view are very different."[45]

Contrary to many contemporary readings of Weber, Troeltsch didn't see *The Protestant Ethic and the Spirit of Capitalism* as directly correlating capitalism with the Protestant concept of calling. The relationship between the two isn't causal. Rather, he read the trajectory of Weber's thesis as capitalism further strengthened by some renditions of Protestant vocation. The relationship between capitalism and vocation was symbiotic, in Troeltch's view; the conjunction of these two elements a "historic accident," whereby accident means no immanent development between the two, "not that these things have happened *sine Deo*" (915–916). To his eye it wasn't that Protestantism, and particularly Calvinist ideas on vocation, produced capitalism, but that both possessed an affinity for each other.[46] Vocation, as an applicable Christian ethic, gained importance in the modern age when supported by an accident of this kind, for "the Calvinistic ethic of the 'calling' and of work, which clears that the earning of one with certain precautions is allowable, was able to give [capitalism] an intellectual and ethical backbone, and that, therefore, thus organized and inwardly supported it vigorously developed, even though within the limits of anti-mammon."[47]

However, because Troeltsch's primary interests related to the social implications of Christian doctrine it isn't enough to examine why and how Protestant vocation changed the functional face of eighteenth- and nineteenth-century capitalism. Imperative to Troeltsch's work was an investigation of how Calvinism changed as a result of capitalism. Troeltsch asserts that if Geneva had been a large commercial town, on par with a locale like Venice, perhaps Calvin would have held capitalism with greater reproach. Geneva, however, was a small territory surrounded by hostile and rival neighbors, its conditions narrow and provincial. And it was in this form that Calvin found capitalism acceptable, as

> a calling which suited the existing conditions in the city, and which was capable of being combined with loyalty, seriousness, honesty, thrift, and consideration for one's neighbour. It was just because the economic conditions at Geneva were so bourgeois, and on such a small scale, that Capitalism was able to steal into the Calvinist ethic, while it was rejected by the Catholic and Lutheran ethic.[48]

As discussed in chapter 3, both Luther and Calvin grounded their working concepts of vocation between the doctrines of creation and redemption, and so to staunchly differentiate the Calvinist ethic from the Lutheran one seems simplistic if not altogether inaccurate. While Troeltsch may be correct in observing that the economic practices within Geneva were different from those in Wittenberg, it remains true that later Protestant renderings of vocation went far beyond the interests of Calvin and the city of Geneva. As Troeltsch himself states,

> Once capitalism had been accepted, even with many precautions, given the right milieu, everywhere it led to results which increased its power; while the specifically Calvinistic habits of piety and industry justified its existence and helped to increase its strength, which give it in the Calvinistic communities a special character and a peculiar intensity. The exhortation to a continual industry in labour combined with the limitation of consumption and of luxury, produced a tendency to pile up capital, which for its part—in the necessity of its further utilization in work and not in enjoyment—necessitated an ever-increasing turnover. The duty of labour, coupled with the ban on luxury, worked out "economically as the impulse to save," and the impulse to save had the effect of building up capital."[49]

And due to this dance, work became increasingly objectified, and vocation limited to the economic realm. However, as Troeltsch notes far more than Weber, this was not without some limitation. The Calvinist espousal of modern economic theory was always tempered by the Christian idea of love, for labor and profit must never be viewed as personal interest alone. "The capitalist is always a steward of the gifts of God," Troeltsch writes, "whose duty it is to increase his capital and utilize it for the good of Society as a whole, retaining for himself only that amount which is necessary to provide for his own needs. All surplus wealth should be used for work of public utility, and especially for purposes of ecclesiastical philanthropy."[50]

Mass Production and the Injustice of Work

Yet, as vocation became steadily reduced to work, and work gradually limited to the economic realm increases in capital were used for anything but public works and the common good. Money fueled further trade and a form of production that became increasingly disconnected from channels of direct use to those of remote trade toward the acquisition of larger profits. All of this made for "a larger margin for new capital expenditures for wars, foreign conquests, mines, productive enterprises . . . more money and more power," making some "powerful to the extent that they neglected the real world of wheat and wool, food and clothes, and centered their attention on the purely quantitative representation of it in tokens and symbols."[51] Naturally the social price of such economies, of such a recast vision of vocation, was high. For the majority, modernism's quest for autonomy and independence led to an ironic, crippling dependence as command of production fell time and again to those with the most capital. Capitalism, Lewis Mumford argues, utilized emergent machines, not to further social welfare, but to

> increase private profit: mechanical instruments were used for the aggrandizement of the ruling classes. It was because of capitalism that the handicraft industries in both Europe and other parts of the world were recklessly destroyed by machine products, even when the latter were inferior to the thing they replaced: for the prestige of improvement and success and power was with the machine, even when it improved nothing, even when technically speaking it was a failure. It was because of the possibilities of profit that the place of the machine was overemphasized and the degree of regimentation pushed beyond what was necessary to harmony or efficiency. It was because of certain traits in private capitalism that the machine—which was a neutral agent—has often seemed, and in fact has sometimes been, a malicious element in society, careless of human life, indifferent to human interests.[52]

With the increased mechanization of production, the banality and inhumanity of work became more pronounced, as did related ecological degradation. The worker and the natural resources used to work were perpetually subordinated to profit. Work had meaning for what it contributed to the end product, meaning that the worker and their environment had meaning only as productivity was enhanced. Here the inciting voice of Charles Dickens—who did extensive research on England's nineteenth-century workhouses and was publically critical of financial chicanery, the callous mistreatment of the poor, and the inhuman pursuit of profit—beautifully illustrates the arrogance and ecological disregard characteristic of many nineteenth-century capitalists. They, like Dickens's wealthy maritime mercantilist Paul Dombey, believed "the earth was made to trade in, and the sun and moon were made to give them light. Rivers and seas were formed to float their ships, rainbows gave them promise of fair weather, winds blew for or against their enterprises, stars and planets circled in their orbits, to preserve inviolate a system of which they were the centre."[53]

NATURE, RETREAT, AND VOCATION AS PRIVILEGE (1780–1850)

What Ernst Troeltsch and Max Weber didn't address in their respective tomes was the other response to modernism's heightened individualism—Romanticism, a movement that with regards to vocation largely prized retreat from the banality of daily work. Concurrent with Industrialism, Romanticism aimed at inclusiveness and a willingness to open oneself to the realm of experience. While manifest in many variant regional forms the movement generally valued such personal sentiment over reason, particularly affective experiences within nature. In the words of Rousseau, often regarded as the prototypical Romantic, it was a "force to free reason from its isolation."[54] No longer conceived after the model of the great cosmic machine, to be mastered and managed, nature was regarded by Romantics as a creative process with great diversity. Human vocation was to find kinship with nature and be unified with the infinite, whole Spirit at work in the world. As church historian James Livingston notes:

> The God of this creative process was conceived of, once again, as the Platonic Demiurge, the creative Eros who makes for the actualization of all creative potentials and who values creative diversity above all else. Life and art should, in turn be a copy of Nature's insatiate creativity and the God who is the very soul of Nature's impulsing multiform life.[55]

This new appraisal of Platonism expanded on Calvin's (and Perkins's) radical prudence and set the stage for philosophically more complex modes of thinking about God's presence in nature.

Cambridge Platonism, which reached its peak at Harvard and Yale by the early eighteenth century, drew upon Neo-Platonism to portray the world as an immediate, ongoing creation of the Holy Spirit, an organic unity in its diversity. We see evidence of this mindset in the work of a particularly well-known Yale graduate, Jonathan Edwards (1703–1758), who frequently reflected about the shadows or images of divine things in creation, so much so that he kept an ongoing journal from the time of his marriage, posthumously entitled, "A Dissertation on the End for Which God Created the World."[56] For Edwards, the goodness of God emanates in creation, flowing "like an overflowing fountain or luminary." Like the sun, a favorite Edwardian image, God "is abundantly communicative; he is a fountain of goodness continually scattering abroad himself and diffusing of his bounty plentifully and abundantly as the sun diffuses his rays; as the light of the sun fills the world, so does God's goodness."[57] Edwards knew that in a materially-driven world it no longer sufficed to say that God merely created the world to manifest glory, as Thomists and early Calvinists had argued, for rationalists claimed that divine glory is readily manifested in things like mathematics and mechanics. Rather than disputing such claims Edwards saw empirical facts and law as an actual organism, "alive and resplendent with the omnific glory of God."[58] To Edwards, God was identical with what God communicated. "The corporeal world," he argued, "is to no advantage but to the spiritual."[59] And given that God communicates in and through creation, hearing and responding to God's call requires great attentiveness to the natural world, often to the exclusion or sanctioning of modern life. While a man deeply knowledgeable in the ways of the world, Edwards ultimately warranted some semblance of withdrawal in the pursuit of what he called "authentically holy affections," and as such participated in what had by his time become a larger revival of Protestant awakening.[60]

North American Transcendentalism's Impact on Protestant Vocation

Jonathan Edwards's radicalized theocentrism and focus on internal spiritual transformation had tremendous influence on many North American transcendentalists of the early-to-mid nineteenth century such as Margaret Fuller, Amos Bronson Alcott, and the more widely known Ralph Waldo Emerson, Henry David Thoreau, and Walt Whitman. To varying degrees and for divergent reasons, such thinkers recast vocation as retreat from modern production. Exalting nonconformity and the higher purpose of art and poetry in harmony with nature, the pursuit of calling became an even more elite quest to individually perceive the Spirit and its moral laws within nature.

For example, in what has since been famed as the founding text of North American Transcendentalism, Emerson adopted Calvin and Edwards's notion of God's radical presence in nature while rejecting biblical literalism and the theological concept of predestination. Behind and throughout nature the Spirit creates, Emerson argued, making the world itself an expositor of the divine mind.[61] Hence, the more persons can perceive that Spirit, the closer humanity will come to redemption. "Then," Emerson wrote, "will God go forth anew into creation."[62]

Such a vocation was, of course, a privilege quite foreign to the average working-class family, not to mention a stark impossibility for indigenous communities and formerly-enslaved persons who were in most cases forcibly removed from their beloved land and required to work new land they could never own or profit by.[63] For them, work was far from an ideal and often embodied in taxing and physically grueling ways. Indeed, Emerson's vision, not unlike much of early North American religious environmentalism, was the product of a more liberal coastal branch of puritan civilization, which consistently prized contemplation over activity. So, while it might be argued that Emerson and his transcendentalist counterparts released the genius of reformed Protestantism from its theological cage, clothing it in the glittering, seductive color of individual potential, it can also be said that in so doing the sobering realities of life within the community at large were overlooked, if not altogether lost.[64] As environmental historian Mark Stoll remarks, the transcendental seeker, much like the good puritan, communed alone in the woods with God, needing to be free from society's conventions for the sake of personal transformation.[65] "Why," Emerson questions, "should we grope among the dry bones of the past, or put the living generation into the masquerade out of its faded wardrobe? The sun shines today also. There is more wool and flax in the fields. There are new lands, new men, new thoughts. Let us demand our own works and laws and worship."[66]

Individual Retreat and the Social Injustices of Work

Such optimism, while extraordinarily popular in early- to mid-nineteenth-century intellectual circles, quickly came under critique by progressive Christian transcendentalists like Frederic Henry Hedge (1805–1890) and socially-minded ministers such as Walter Rauschenbusch (1861–1918). Noting the growing disparity between the generationally wealthy and the working poor, they argued that such a view of vocation was idealistic in its disregard for the invisible work of unnoticed people, who with virtually no agency of their own, support and make possible such pioneering lifestyles.[67] Even more egregious than such naïve optimism was transcendentalism's unscrupulous push toward the future. Surely those who were left among the dead could do little more than grope among the very "bones" Emerson so longingly desired to leave behind. After all, someone had to. It was they, the nineteenth-century working poor, who worked the overharvested "fields" and "old lands" while elites looked for a novel aesthetic education in the retreat from work and enjoyment of luxury. Thinkers like Hedge and Rauschenbusch rejected the equivocation of vocation with luxury. For them, to hear and respond to God's call was to perceive it in the most unexpected and ordinary of places, and work, which is dignified and concretely connected to material reality, is a consequential cultural necessity for everyone.

Frederic Henry Hedge (1805–1890)

Hedge, a Unitarian pastor and professor at Harvard Divinity School, was a thoroughgoing transcendentalist in his concern for self-consciousness and belief in human progress. He saw his own denomination as the last and fullest development of Protestantism, largely for its inclusion of modern science and proclivity for religious tolerance. Religion, and particularly Christianity, is more about spiritual attraction than compulsion, "in which the individual abandons his own desire in order to worship divine truth and exhibit divine love."[68] Hedge deemed Christianity "a grace, a charm, a beauty, a happy privilege," where self-abasement could be replaced with self-surrender to the winning power of love. And by love, Hedge meant not charity or any single affection, but rather the "principle in human nature which draws us out of ourselves and makes us forget self in the service of our kind."[69]

Christian vocation, therefore, could never simply be the pursuit of personal enlightenment, a retreat to nature and the confines of one's own mind. It must be, rather, a force that values and possesses the material world. For Hedge, vocation was attendance to the present, to the actual needs of the neighbor and the world not just a place to be punished or in which to simply wait, but as a place to work. It is in present work that "spiritual athletes are to be trained, to start from barriers, unencumbered and eager, on the endless race toward the goal of the Divinity."[70] Therefore, everything in religion which denounces nature and insults human life must be abandoned for principles which show the present worth of nature and the dignity of men. In Hedge's words, to "fill the moment worthily is everlasting life."[71]

Having lived through the period leading up to and through the Civil War, Hedge witnessed many principles worth abandoning. While evidence is lacking to prove Hedge's active role in penal civil rights reform, his long-term service with the Sanitary Commission of the Red Cross and outspoken critiques of U.S. labor and education practices demonstrate a prophetic departure from romantic and early transcendentalist philosophies. "My prophecy," says Hedge, "is that the coming man will be a working man. . . . for the course of history ever since [humankind's beginning] has been a growing recognition of the rights of labor."[72] To Hedge's eye, elites, like most of his intellectual and social peers, were losing sight of the value of work, for labor in the way of production was comparatively scarce, and in mercantile life was rather redundant.

> Let the public prints advertise for a clerk in a counting room and straightaway a hundred applicants present themselves as candidates for the vacant office. Had these waiters on the chances of trade been instructed in some useful handicraft, they might have been profitably employed in the needful service instead of suing for crumbs which fall from the table of commercial prosperity.[73]

For Hedge it was better to produce a good pair of shoes than to produce something "doubtful and ephemeral" with one's brain, quite a bold sentiment for a high-ranking academic to hold.[74] For example, he was critical of his own beloved Harvard for endorsing such social stratification by training the brain without training the hands, or employing what he called principles of coercion over those of operation. Students, he wrote in an address to Harvard alumni, often do little more than passively move knowledge from one vessel to another, making professors mere taskmasters and college presidents virtual chiefs of police.[75] And yet, it is precisely these elites who criticize the morals of the lower class and reprimand the ecological practices within such sectors of society. They speak about the value of work, having worked little themselves, and advocate for the conservation of nature without connecting the dots between their own wealth and the systemic degradation of the natural world. On both accounts, Hedge saw the privileged as contributing to the social ills within his day, thereby undervaluing the truly democratic nature of calling.

Walter Rauschenbusch (1861–1918)

While Christianity's Social Gospel Movement is generally marked after Hedge's lifetime, its impulses are easily identifiable in this form of progressive transcendentalism.[76] It was voices like those of Hedge that led theologians like Walter Rauschenbusch to move beyond the nineteenth century's religious individualism and the reigning theological focus upon a "personal savior."[77] In *Christianity and the Social Crisis in the 21st Century* Rauschenbusch wrote, "Religious individualism was a triumph of faith under abnormal conditions and not a normal type of religious life."[78] On the contrary, Christianity, a religion that Rauschenbusch regularly reminds his reader initially focused on the present reality of God's kingdom on earth, values all aspects of human life, not just the spiritual.

> If now we could have faith enough to believe that all human life can be filled with divine purpose; that God saves not only the soul, but the whole of human life; that anything which serves to make men healthy, intelligent, happy, and good is a service to the Father of men; that the kingdom of God is not bounded by the Church, but includes all human relations—then all professions would be hallowed and receive religious dignity. A man making a shoe or arguing a law case or planting potatoes or teaching school could feel that this was itself a

contribution to the welfare of mankind, and indeed his main contribution to it.[79]

For Rauschenbusch, work is a good and necessary component of Christian vocation. It is a doctrine that should be preached to all for the morale it can provide and creativity it can generate.[80] Beyond what one's work produces or what reprieve and financial freedom it might provide, work is an expression of self. It is "the output of [a person's] energy and [one's] main contribution to the common life of mankind. The pride which an artist or professional man takes in his work, the pleasure which a housewife takes in adorning her home, afford satisfaction that ranks next to human love in delightesomeness."[81]

And yet, Rauschenbusch's primary concern did not center upon the evasion of work, but rather the unscrupulous and earnest way in which industrial capitalism stripped humanity of this fundamental joy.

> One of the gravest accusations against our industrial system is that it does not produce in the common man the pride and joy of good work. In many cases the surroundings are ugly, depressing, and coarsening. Much of the stuff manufactured is dishonest in quality, made to sell and not to serve, and the making of such cotton or wooden lies must react on the morals of every man that handles them. There is little opportunity for a man to put his personal stamp on this work. The medieval craftsman could rise to be an artist by working well at his craft. The modern factory hand is not likely to develop artistic gifts as he tends his machine. It is a common and true complaint of employers that their men take no interest in their work. But why should they? What motive have they for putting love and care into their work? It is not theirs. Christ spoke of the difference between the hireling shepherd who flees and the owner who loves the sheep. Our system has made the immense majority of industrial workers mere hirelings.[82]

In this context, work as an aspect of vocation not only ceased to provide meaning and purpose, but also ceased to provide security, unity, and a sense of ecological relatedness. Before the rise of the machine and its partnering philosophy, capitalism, Rauschenbusch argues that workers had a good amount of independence, hope, and vocational autonomy. While "they had no hope of millions to lure them" and "lacked many of the luxuries accessible even to the poor today," poverty was less insidious. Arguably, they did not have the insurmountable structural realities of poverty to haunt them. And, as Rauschenbusch candidly reminds the reader, "man liveth not by cake alone."[83] Yet as the wealthy gradually glutted the market by monopolizing production and consumption alike, all in the name of gaining an elite status that would permit them like longstanding aristocrats to retreat from work, the owners and masters of small enterprises became themselves owned and mastered. The result was a bifurcated class system wherein one was either the employer, "whose hands were typically white and whose power was great" or the wage-earner, who only in rare instances could hope to own the machinery which replaced the knowledge he once had of his trade.[84] And within this system a worker had little to no say about the type or quality of his or her work, and even less to say about his/her compensation for it.[85] Indeed, the doctrine of vocation—of hearing, discerning and responding to God's call in one's daily work—quickly became a rather irrelevant one.

Abstracted, industrialized views of work also corroded the unified, democratic dimensions of vocation. Whereas in the time of the Reformers, one's calling was measured by its respective contribution to the common good, in Rauschenbusch's context it was primarily evaluated upon the grounds of prosperity, be it individual or participatory. The result, Rauschenbusch argues, is a tainted morality, the undermining of the family, a crumbling democracy and a skeptical, wearisome people. What technological and financial achievements were gained through the gradual cooptation of vocation to work as production have been thwarted by human injustice. "Our blessings," Rauschenbusch remarks, "have failed to bless us because they were not based on justice and solidarity."[86] And while the economic loss to the community by this "paralysis of the finer springs of human action" is devastating enough, Rauschenbusch suggests the moral loss is vastly more threatening.[87]

And for Rauschenbusch the social prosperity of a people, the very morality of a people, always depends upon "the wisdom and justice with which the land is distributed and used."[88] Rauschenbusch puts his historical training to work by surveying how land became increasingly privatized rather than socialized. There are those, he writes, who have soil and the bodies to work it and there are those who have no soil, but for subsistence must work it on behalf of others. The latter, farmers who till land they will never own, have become peasants and what Rauschenbusch deems the "disinherited children of our nation."[89] The former, a "few vigorous boys who have secured the cellar key" to America's tenement and waters, have become godlike in their absolute jurisdiction over people's livelihoods and in their re-creation (or de-creation) of our shared natural resources. To this end, Rauschenbusch provides a scathing prophecy of sorts: "No nation can allow its natural sources of wealth to be owned by a limited and diminishing class without suffering political enslavement and poverty."[90]

THE DISRUPTION OF REALIZED HUMAN VOCATION

And it's not just the nation, in Rauschenbusch's case the United States, that risks such an outcome, but also the Christian tradition itself. Indeed, a great deal is lost in the meaning of vocation when the interrelatedness of one's myriad roles is reduced to work, particularly work framed as production or the privileged escape from it. The injustices resulting from such a recasting of vocation make it even more difficult for Christians to discern, imagine, and live out calling. Perhaps this is why Rauschenbusch reverses the Reformers' functional ordering of vocation. Rather than beginning with God's will and expecting obedience or some level of adherence to it, he suggests social order be evaluated, and structures oppressing and inhibiting humankind modified, that all people might have the opportunity to experience true vocation.[91]

Much of the contemporary conversation on the theology of work has sought to do what Rauschenbusch suggested. In the more than one hundred years that have passed since he wrote *Christianity and the Social Crisis in the 21st Century*, liberation, feminist, and post-colonial theologians in particular have begun to re-envision vocation as freedom from such mounting injustices. In Dorothee Sölle's words, "As human beings we are born into the process of liberation. If we fail to take this project seriously, we miss our vocation."[92] In this sense, calling grants a higher place to interrelatedness than to productivity, emphasizing themes of co-creativity with God wherein we participate in unfinished and ongoing creation by finding and choosing solidarity with our fellow workers and creation. However, as we have seen, the entrapping of vocation to work makes such cooperation difficult because it fails to see and reckon with the myriad ways work impacts other relationships, such as family connections, neighborhoods, ecosystems, and global markets. When work is detached from the rest of life, cloistered off as an end unto itself, it is easy, even understandable, to see why so many of us choose careers that fundamentally undermine unity and equity and jeopardize nature. The "golden handcuffs" of prosperity are hard to shake and the principled life most certainly a road less traveled.

It is also easy to see why Christians who *do* value experience in and with the natural world often enjoy it aesthetically, by way of hobby, rather than by immersing their whole selves (work and all) in it. It's enough to find respite in a weekend freshwater canoe adventure, even if the result of one's Monday through Friday, 9 to 5 existence endangers those very waters or one's thoughtless recreational habits do the same. Not only do patterns of injustice related to privileged access to the natural world make it difficult for most to have "wilderness experiences," but they also inhibit the elite's ability to fulfill calling in the everyday. And in both cases, the unfortunate blanching and sanitization of vocation has taken place, and lost is the Reformers' invaluable reminder—that any good theology must take into account the dusty, earthly, and biological realities of life. However, when dirtied up, vocation can be an incredibly fecund and promising ethical resource to us today. As a concept that speaks to matters of both redemption and creation a theology of calling can help bridge the gap between theory and praxis in Christian environmental ethics. To exemplify how, the next chapter highlights three contemporary thinkers, each of whom, as the Reformers did, understands vocation as work, but a work attentive to location, place, and relationship.

NOTES

1. For example, by the end of the sixteenth century, treatises on vocation began to speak about the "good choice" of a calling and as early as 1700 viewed vocation under the guise of spiritual fitness, preference, and inclination. Puritan theology extended this view even further to include profit and individual advantage in the realm of vocation, as evidenced in the works of Richard Baxter.

2. Surprising examples of such students are process theologians Herman Daly and John Cobb, Jr. In their joint work *For the Common Good: Redirecting the Economy Toward Community, the Environment and a Sustainable Future* (Boston: Beacon Press, 1994), they argue that Protestantism "paved the way for the anthropocentrism of the Enlightenment and the relegation of the rest of creation to the status of passive matter to be shaped by human beings to human ends" (391). This was because Protestantism, much more than Catholicism, emphasized the individual's immediacy to God, a reappropriation of the Jewish prophetic tradition. Yet, as we saw in the last chapter, the interrelated nature of creation was fundamental to Luther and Calvin's working doctrines of creation. And as we shall see throughout this chapter, the theological emphasis on soteriology, and justification in particular, was more characteristic of the Reformers' successors than it was of their own work.

3. Notable examples are Karl Barth, Jacques Ellul, Stanley Hauerwas, and Miroslav Volf, whose concerns will be addressed in some detail in chapter 5. These thinkers take note of what the late religious historian Robert S. Michaelsen regarded as a movement beyond original Reformation theology. For the ways Luther and Calvin's successors emphasized the importance of the active life over the contemplative one, they were "true followers of the Reformers, although they went beyond the Reformers in their understanding of the role of the community in covenant relation with God and in their systematic development of the doctrine of vocation" (see "Work and Vocation in American Industrial Society," in *Work and Vocation: A Christian Discussion*, edited by John Oliver Nelson (New York: Harper & Brothers Publishers, 1954), 118–119).

4. The lectures underwent eighteen Latin editions, in addition to numerous translations. Just four years after publication, the University of Cambridge made it required reading, with England's Queen Elizabeth I said to have had it virtually memorized.

5. Robert Kolb, "God Calling 'Take Care of My People:' Luther's Concept of Vocation in the Augsburg Confession and Its Apology," in *Concordia Journal* (January 1982): 4–11.

6. Phillip Melancthon, *The Difference between Worldly and Christian Piety* (1522), in the Post-Reformation Digital Library, https://mail.google.com/mail/u/0/#inbox/15430629330216 63?projector=1 (last accessed April 20, 2016).

7. See, for example, Article XII of the *Augsburg Confession*, which refutes the Anabaptist tradition. Here perfection is rejected because of the real and lasting consequences of sin.

8. Melanchthon, *Apology of the Augsburg Confession* Article XXVII (*Book of Concord* 283.37). This emphasis played out in Melanchthon's writings on Christian education. Alongside Erasmus, Melanchthon is said to be one of the founders of a new educational theory, which focused on the moral lessons found within the writings of antiquity (see Brian McGregor's introduction to Erasmus' "On Good Manners for Boys").

9. Philip Melanchthon, *The Loci Communes*, translated by Charles Leander Hill (Boston: Meador Publishing Company, 1944), 261.

10. Philip Melanchthon, *Paul's Letter to the Colossians*, translated by D. C. Parker (Worcester: Sheffield Academic Press, 1989), 38.

11. Ibid., 41.

12. Ernest Stoeffer, *The Rise of Evangelical Pietism* (Leiden: E.J. Brill, 1965), 183.

13. Einar Billing, *Our Calling*, translated by Conrad Bergendoff (Philadelphia: Fortress Press, 1952), 15.

14. Examples of these include Johann Arndt (1555–1621), Philip Jacob Spener (1635–1705) and August Hermann Francke (1663–1727).

15. William Perkins, *Treatise of Vocations*, ed. John Legatt (1626), in the Digital Puritan Library, http://www.digitalpuritan.net/Digital%20Puritan%20Resources/Perkins,%20William/Treatise%20of%20the%20Vocations%20(OTW%20Version).pdf (last accessed April 16, 2016).

16. Ibid., 22.

17. Perkins, *Treatise of Vocations,* 4. An interesting note is Perkins's brief discussion of extraordinary gifts, which he distinquishes from callings. Perkins cites Luther as an example of one discharged with extraordinary gifts, namely, the "boldness and courage to withstand the whole Church of Rome" (23).

18. Ibid., 13 and 18.

19. Ibid., 4, 16; on how they are not in conflict, 6–7. The theological emphasis on God's providence, or what in other works Perkins referred to as double-predestination, characterized his particular reading of vocation. In true Calvinist form, Perkins sees the chief goal of human life to worship God and praise him forever.

20. Perkins, *The Foundation of the Christian Religion Gathered in Six Principles*, http://www.nesherchristianresources.org/perkins/PerkinsWorks/SixPrin.html (last accessed on April 16, 2016).

21. Perkins, *Treatise of Vocations*, 7.

22. Richard Baxter, "Directions for the Right Choice of our Calling and Ordinary Labour," in *A Christian Directory*, 2nd Edition (London, 1678), 378. Baxter's later contemporary, Richard Steele, wrote one small tract, "The Religious Tradesman: Plain and Serious Hints of Advice" in 1684, which Weber and others use to demonstrate the increasingly intimate relationship between, vocation and trade. In it, Steele argues that Christians should make the most of two inhabited worlds, the sacred and the secular, and earn money not to serve mammon, but God and man.

23. In his article, "Talent and Vocation in Humanist and Protestant Thought," Richard Douglas outlines some of the differences between early humanist and Protestant views on vocation. Erasmus, for example, called upon Petrarch and other late Stoics, describing vocation as a particular way of life (*genus vitae*) and a career related to one's nature, aptitudes, and constitution. One's *genus vitae*, or inclined nature, wasn't chosen. Rather, it was discovered. As was outlined in the previous chapter, the Reformers referred to vocation as a gift from God, very often realized over and against human nature and inclination. So, whereas humanists like Erasmus argued from the irreversibility of his own unique character, Luther and Calvin argued from the irresistibility of a divine command. Hence, the difference in early sixteenth-century terminology, with *eligere* representative of secular views of vocation and *vocari* of more spiritually laden ones (in *Action and Conviction in Early Modern* Europe, edited by Theodore K. Rabb and Jerrold E. Seigel (Princeton, NJ: Princeton University Press, 1969), 261).

24. Michael Northcott, *A Political Theology of Climate Change* (Grand Rapids, MI: Eerdmans, 2013), 62–63. Rather than speaking about phases within one unified Scientific Revolution, MIT Professor Emeritus Thomas Kuhn encouraged students of science to think of this as an era of many revolutions, wherein a priority of paradigms exists (see *The Structure of Scientific Revolutions* (Chicago: The University of Chicago Press, 1996)).

25. Francis Bacon, *Novum Organum* 249, cited in Michael Northcott in *A Political Theology of Climate Change*, 63.

26. As Charles Taylor reflects, secularism's ongoing movement is never merely about subtraction, but always also about growth in a new and different direction (see *A Secular Age* (Cambridge, MA: Harvard University Press, 2007), 22).

27. Paul Marshall, *A Kind of Life Imposed on Man: Vocation and Social Order from Tyndale to Locke* (Toronto: University of Toronto Press, 1996), 84.

28. Jean-Luc Marion, "Cartesian Metaphysics," cited by Michael Northcott in *A Poltical Theology of Climate Change*, 66. Marion is no doubt referring to Newton's explicit attempt to separate special revelation from general revelation. In *Principia*, Newton argued that a true understanding of the phenomena of nature is based upon "rational mechanics," or "reasoning from mechanical principles" of all the phenomena of nature that are formulated according to

"mathematical principles." Contrary to revelation, in the realm of nature the whole plan of the universe lies before us in its undivided and inviolable unity, evidently, waiting for the human mind to recognize and express it (see "Newton's Preface to the First Edition of the *Principia*"in *Newton's Philosophy of Nature: Selections from His Writings*, edited by H. S. Thayer (New York: Hafner, 1974), xvii-iii).

29. John Locke, "Of Study," in *The Educational Writings of John Locke*, edited by J.L. Axtell, 408–411.

30. John Locke, *Conduct of the Understanding* (New York: Burt Franklin, 1971), 43.

31. Locke, "Of Study," 411.

32. Adam Smith, *The Theory of Moral Sentiments* (New York: A.M. Kelley, 1966), 153–154.

33. Adam Smith, *An Inquiry into the Nature and Causes of the Wealth of Nations* (New York: Random House, 1937), 315.

34. For example, in *An Inquiry into the Nature and Causes of the Wealth of the Nations*, Smith outlines four modes of production, or what he calls the four "stages of society:" hunting, pasturing, farming, and commerce. For Smith, commerce is highly valued because it affords individuals the option to decline work.

35. E. G. West, *Adam Smith* (New Rochelle: Arlington House, 1969), 169. Smith differs from his egoist friend, David Hume, in his commentary on the perfection of human nature. In *A Theory of Moral Sentiments* Smith suggests that the truly perfected individual is the benevolent, charitable, and affectionate one. So while individuals make choices primarily based upon an interest in self, in true liberal fashion, Smith believed that what was best for the individual really was best for the community.

36. Miroslav Volf, *Work in the Spirit: Toward a Theology of Work* (New York: Oxford University Press, 1991), 51.

37. We see this transition reflected in patronymics, for example. Whereas one was once a miller because one's father and grandfather were, names began to be applied to immigrants who migrated to cities in search of work.

38. Michael Northcott, *A Political Theology of Climate Change,* 55. The emergence of the guild wasn't about protecting the weak, but about protecting the skill, about trade secrets. This was the artisanal model, wherein one was let into the "secrets of the trade," and this power then inferred responsibility.

39. Ibid., 56.

40. Lewis Mumford, *Technics and Civilization* (New York: Harcourt, Brace & Company, 1934), 14.

41. Mumford, *Technics and Civilization*, 15.

42. Richard Baxter, *A Christian Directory*, chapter X, part I, question 5, answers 3–4. http://www.ccel.org/ccel/baxter (last accessed on February 10, 2016).

43. For example, in *Vocation and the Politics of Work: Popular Theology in a Consumer Culture* (New York: Lexington Books, 2013), Jeffrey Scholes equivocates Troeltsch's views with Weber's, arguing that the Calvinist conception of vocation raised the ordinary work of one's profession to an exercise of faith.

44. Paul Marshall helpfully warns his reader to avoid lifting Weber's famous work on Protestantism from his larger study of capitalism. *The Protestant Ethic and the Spirit of Capitalism* is not Weber's only work addressing the sociological force of religion upon society. The work garnered a great deal of attention, Marshall argues, for its attempt to counter two prevalent theses: 1) the Protestant argument that secularism arose from the rationalism of the French Enlightenment and was henceforth fostered in particularly Catholic environments and 2) the Catholic argument that secularism began with Protestantism itself, a splintering of the one and unified Church (see *A Kind of Life Imposed on Man: Vocation and Social Order from Tyndale to Locke*, 5).

45. Troeltsch, *Social Teachings*, 916.

46. Marshall's late-twentieth-century reading of Weber is similar to Troeltsch's. Weber, while never equivocating Calvinist Protestantism and capitalism, rendered the "Protestant ethic" as a lever or sort of midwife to the momentum of capitalism. It was *one* factor in the rise and growth of capitalism, and perhaps only a contingent factor at that. Marshall contends that

Weber never intended "painting such a foolish and doctrinaire thesis as that the spirit of capitalism could have only arisen as a result of certain effects of the Reformation, or even that capitalism was an economic system is a creation of the Reformation," for the connection wasn't primarily a logical one, but rather psychological (7). This is why Weber's work consistently focuses more on counseling manuals and theological works like Richard Baxter's *A Christian Directory* more than Luther or Calvin's larger works.

47. Troeltsch, *Social Teachings*, 915.
48. Ibid., 643.
49. Ibid., 643.
50. Ibid., 648.
51. Mumford, *Technics and Civilization*, 24–25.
52. Ibid., 27.
53. Charles Dickens, *Dombey and Son* (New York: Mead & Company, 1950), 2.
54. Jean Jacques Rousseau, *Discourse on the Origin of Inequality*, part 1 as cited by James Livingston in *Modern Christian Thought: The Enlightenment and the Nineteenth Century* (Minneapolis: Fortress Press, 2006), 44.
55. James C. Livingston, *Modern Christian Thought: The Enlightenment and the Nineteenth Century*, vol. 1 (Minneapolis: Fortress Press, 2006), 84.
56. Edwards's diaries reveal a particular affection for the work of Cambridge Platonist John Smith. In his essay, "The Existence and Nature of God," Smith describes God as "that Omnipresent Life that penetrates and runs through all things, containing and holding all fast together within himself; and therefore, the ancient philosophy was wont rather to say that the world was in God, than that God was in the world" (Smith, *Select Discourses*, London, 1660, 145). Yet, it should be noted that both Smith and Edwards differentiate the idea of divine self-movement from the Neoplatonic theory of "emanation." Neither was a panentheist in the modern sense of the term. Rather than seeing things *in* God and God in all things, both men saw God *as* all things, the "shadows" or "images" of God in creation being evidence of God's Spirit. Notwithstanding the fact that Edwards uses the latter term, the outward flowing of God doesn't imply the dissolution of all distinctions as it does in Neoplatonic thought. As Augustine said, "God is not diffused through all things as a quality of the world, but as the creative substance of the world, He governs and maintains." The Creator-creature distinction remains essential to Edwards's theology, as it did within Augustine's. As Edwards scholar Douglas Elwood states, "The world of sense objects, in Edwards's system, is at most a world of 'shadows.' Its only real significance lies in God's prior intention that it should image forth spiritual realities and beauties and thus serve as a medium of divine communication to created minds. In this way all creation shares, directly or indirectly, in the divine life. But only persons, endowed with perceptive and reflective powers, are capable of participating in the wisdom and love of God wherein His true glory and beauty consist" (Douglas Elwood, *The Philosophical Theology of Jonathan Edwards* (New York: Columbia University Press, 1960), 99).
57. Edwards, "Sermon on James," in *The Works of Jonathan Edwards*, edited by Patrick H. Alexander (Carlisle, PA: The Banner of Truth Trust, 1995), 1.17. It appears that Edwards was familiar with the Hebraic concept *cabhodh*, which designates the shining forth or flowing outward of God's inexhaustible fullness in communicative streams of light and love.
58. Elwood, *The Philosophical Theology of Jonathan Edwards*, 97.
59. Edwards, "The Mind," as cited by Avibu Zakai in *Jonathan Edwards's Philosophy of History* (Princeton, NJ: Princeton University Press, 2003), 91.
60. The first of the Great Awakenings (roughly 1730–1743) can be characterized as a movement to redefine the relationship between God and the world. The movement sought to reform religious convictions and persuasions expressing God's immediate involvement in the order of creation, resulting in new modes of religious faith and experience. Since the "search for the essence of true religion, as an objective 'presence of things outside myself' appeared to have bankrupted itself," Protestants like Edwards developed a new theology of the heart that emphasized the illumination of the Holy Spirit within the individual. (See Jaroslav Pelikan, *The Christian Tradition: A History of the Development of Doctrine*, vol. V, *Christian Doctrine and Modern Culture (since 1700)* (Chicago: University of Chicago Press, 1989), 119–121).

61. Ralph Waldo Emerson, "Nature," in *Emerson: Essays and Lectures*, edited by Richard Garnett and John Parker Anderson (New York: Library of America, 1983), vol. 1, 38–39.

62. Ibid., vol. 1, 38–39, 44.

63. For example, over 90 percent of contemporary black Americans descended from southern slaves, who up until the mid-twentieth century were intimately familiar with the natural world, which was "at once home, workplace, space for recreation, food source, medical resource, place of magic, stories and legends, and avenue for or barrier to travel or escape" (Carolyn Finney, *Black Faces, White Spaces: Reimagining the Relationship of African Americans to the Great Outdoors* (Chapel Hill, NC: University of North Carolina, 2014), 237–238). Yet, despite this close relationship to the natural world, black citizens were not able to procure land in the same manner as "Caucasian" persons. The Homestead Act of 1862 was denied to ethnic minorities. Instead, legislation was enacted to limit the movement of such persons (i.e., California Land Claims Act of 1851, The Black Codes of 1861–1865, the Dawes Act of 1887 and the Curtis Act of 1989).

64. By the "genius" of reformed Protestantism, I am referring to the Reformation's emphasis on freedom of thought and the role of religion in the formation of morality.

65. Mark S. Stoll, *Inherit the Holy Mountain: Religion and the Rise of American Environmentalism* (New York: Oxford University Press, 2015), 119.

66. Emerson, "Nature," 7.

67. For example, in *Christianity and the Social Crisis in the 21st Century* (New York: Harper One, 2007), Rauschenbusch states, "If Christian men are really interested in the salvation of human lives and in the health, the decency, the education, and the morality of the people, they must wish well to the working people in their effort to secure such conditions for themselves and their dear ones that they will not have to die of tuberculosis in their prime, nor feel their strength ground down by long hours of work, nor see their women and children drawn into the merciless hopper of factory labor, nor be shut out from the enjoyment of the culture about them which they have watered with their sweat" (325).

68. Frederic Henry Hedge, *Sermons* (Boston, 1891), 263, cited by Ronald Vale Wells in *Three Christian Transcendentalists: James Marsh, Caleb Sprague Henry, Frederic Henry Hedge* (New York: Octagon Books, 1972), 131.

69. Hedge, *Sermons*, 263.

70. Hedge, "The Religion of the Present," *Christian Examiner*, LCVII (1859): 50–70, 54.

71. Hedge, "The Doctrine of Endless Punishment," *Christian Examiner*, LXVII (1859): 98–128, 128.

72. Hedge, "The Doctrine of Endless Punishment," 118.

73. Hedge, *Sermons*, 112.

74. Wells, *Three Christian Transcendentalists*, 139.

75. Hedge, "University Reform," *Atlantic Monthly*, XVIII (1866): 301. He was a big advocate for intellectual liberty, self-determined activity, and voluntary study.

76. Cornel West offers a helpful definition of the Social Gospel movement, "a historic movement that wedded the Christian faith to social justice during the Gilded Age of imperial extension, corporate greed and massive immigration." (See Rauschenbusch, *Christianity and the Social Crisis in the 21st Century*, 231).

77. In his afterword in the most recent edition of *Christianity and the Social Crisis in the 21st Century*, Richard Rorty highlights Rauschenbusch's "ascetic ideal," which Rauschenbusch himself credits to non-Christian influences, including Romanticism and transcendentalism. Rorty, a secular humanist, argues that what makes Rauschenbusch's work so compelling to a scholar of his ilk is its dismissal of the Pauline claims of human depravity. While many critiqued Rauschenbusch's optimism, not least of all Reinhold Neibuhr and Karl Barth, Rorty appreciates his push to think of matters like sin and salvation structurally and socially (See "Buds That Never Opened" in *Christianity and the Social Crisis in the 21st Century*).

78. Rauschenbusch, *Christianity and the Social Crisis in the 21st Century*, 30.

79. Ibid., 290.

80. To this end, Rauschenbusch quotes former U.S. President Teddy Roosevelt, who as Commissioner of the New York Police force said, "I would teach the young men that he who has not wealth owes his first duty to his family, but he who has means owest his to the State. It

is ignorant to go on heaping up money. I would preach the doctrine of work to all, and to men of wealth the doctrine of unremunerative work" (*Christianity and the Social Crisis in the 21st Century*, 337).

81. Ibid., 193.

82. Ibid., 193.

83. Ibid., 180. Interestingly, matters of security are of particular interest to many contemporary critics of capitalism. For example, Nobel Laureate and founder of the Green Belt Movement in East Africa Wangari Maathai cites security among ordinary persons as a top priority. When they are able to sustainably support themelves, they will not "feel so marginalized and terrorized by the state" (see Rob Nixon, *Slow Violence and the Environmentalism of the Poor* (Cambridge, MA: Harvard University Press, 2011), 149).

84. Ibid., 180.

85. Rasuchenbusch speaks at length about the wealth disparities of the nineteenth and early twentieth centuries. "When wealth was multiplying beyond all human precedent, an immense body of pauperism with all its allied misery was growing up and becoming chronic. England was foremost in the introduction of machine industry, and the first half of the nineteenth century was one of the darkest times in the economic history of England. While the nation was attaining unparalleled wealth and power, many of its people were horribly destitute and degraded. . . . Men learned to make wealth much faster than they learned to distribute it justly. Their eye for profit was keener than their ear for the voice of God and humanity" (182).

86. Ibid., 193.

87. Ibid., 194.

88. Ibid., 184.

89. Ibid., 186–187. Here Rauschenbusch's forecast for the impending doom of corporate agriculture is startlingly accurate.

90. Ibid., 190.

91. For example, on 300–301 of *Christianity and the Social Crisis in the 21st Century*, Rauschenbusch quotes Pastor Stöcker of Reichstag, who said, "We have put the question the wrong way. We have asked: How much child and female labor does industry need in order to flourish, to pay dividends, and to sell goods abroad? Whereas we ought to have asked: How ought industry to be organized in order to protect and foster the family, the human individual, and the Christian life?" The simple reversal of that question, Rauschenbusch argues, marks the difference between the Christian conception of life and property and the mammonistic.

92. Dorothee Sölle, *To Work and to Love* (Philadelphia: Fortress Press, 1984), 29.

Chapter Five

Voices From the Wilderness

Critical Principles for Contemporary Christian Vocation From the Perspective of a Pastor, Scholar, and Poet

The complexity and urgency of our global environmental challenges require myriad theological resources and a plethora of voices coming from diverse contexts. To further flesh out the ethical nature of vocation, three contemporary Protestant thinkers, H. Paul Santmire, Sallie McFague, and Wendell Berry, represent this needed diversity of thought.[1] Each writer calls upon a different theological tradition: Santmire—Lutheranism, McFague—a reconstructive Reformed theology, and Berry—the Baptist tradition, loosely speaking.[2] Furthermore, each of these thinkers employs a unique style of writing, with Santmire's work being characteristically pastoral and homiletical in nature, McFague's accessibly academic, and Berry's prophetically creative and poetic. In their sermons, articles, books, poems, and stories all three contemporary figures express a mediated ecological ethic, wherein tereology and practice are held in tension. All three address the Protestant concept of vocation and, in ways both explicit and implicit, unpack the doctrine in ecologically meaningful ways, setting forth embodied principles for responsibly enacting Christian vocation.

Each writer has been reflecting on the nexus of Christianity and ecology for over forty years and, in ways big and small, influenced one another along the way. Hence, the order of their appearance here isn't chronological as much as it is dialogical. It is, nonetheless, intentional. First, the pastoral voice of Santmire, because his work most directly addresses the alleged ecological bankruptcy of the Christian tradition. Santmire's working concept of ecological vocation honestly addresses some of the problems within Christianity and sets forth an engaging and hopeful apologetic. Then McFague, as her constructive work in many ways builds upon Santmire's critical readings. McFague's emphasis on metaphorical theology and her retrieval of the theological virtue-ethics tradition brings shape and form to a mediated ethic of vocation. And finally, a sampling of the prolific work of Wendell Berry to envision examples of fulfilled ecological vocation. In an effort to read each thinker on their own terms, I first outline methodology and then move to critical commentary on each thinker's working concept of vocation. In each case we see how an ethic grounded in Christian vocation proves ecologically adequate. I also demonstrate how the larger field of ecological ethics might benefit from added and sustained attention to religious concepts of calling.

THE VOICE OF A PASTOR: PAUL SANTMIRE AND VOCATION AS PARADOX

Having been described as one of the "best searchers for a new, or renewed, Christian ecological vision," one whom, having taken nature seriously, "offers a sorely-needed corrective to much recent Protestant theology," H. Paul Santmire is a well-known name in the field of Christian ecological ethics.[3] Since the early 1970s, with the popular publication of his Harvard dissertation, *Brother Earth: Nature, God and Ecology in a Time of Crisis*, Santmire has been working to retrieve and reclaim what he deems "the ambiguous ecological promise of Christian theology."[4] Generally characterized by its firm location in the liberal Protestant tradition and by its commitment to the construction of an ecological biblical rendering of classical Western theology, Santmire's work exemplifies a terreological approach to Christian ecological ethics. His robustly Trinitarian concept of God coupled with a decidedly Lutheran conception of vocation lends itself to a radically theocentric approach. Yet it is not this emphasis that makes his work unique among other eco-theologians, or what warrants a closer study of his voice here. What qualifies Santmire's work as exceptional is its authentic pastoral quality and keen attention to the balance between theory and practice. Describing his own sense of calling as bivocational, responsible to the academy and the church alike, Santmire's work consistently contextualizes larger terreological questions in light of pastoral care and leadership, and as such serves as model for other pastors and those seeking to serve the church and world in an ecologically just and responsible manner.[5]

Methodology

Santmire's early works take up the question of Christianity's alleged ecological bankruptcy and engage in the debate with an eye for pastoral realism. Critical of those who forfeit what ecological resources Christianity has to offer and dubious that other religious traditions prove more promising, Santmire argues that the enmeshment of Protestant thought in Western cultural ideology requires the engagement of the tradition rather than an escape from it. Reflecting on his own suburban pastoral experience, he claims that highly consumptive North Americans are more likely to change in attitude and behavior if shown an ecologically-sound reading of the Bible or Reformation tradition than if taught more culturally alien ways of Shaminism or Buddhism.[6] There is sense in simply working from where one is, and this is exactly what Santmire as a pastoral scholar does, working from within the theological tradition he knows best, Lutheranism.

Modestly describing himself as "one little Protestant boy over in the corner trying to do his thing . . . to see what can be done with the Reformation tradition," Santmire's concept of vocation is fundamentally ethical, just as it was for Luther.[7] Indeed, the very ecology of vocation or interrelatedness of the myriad roles a person inhabits is far less a doctrinal concern for Santmire than an ethical one. As shown in chapter 3, Luther's democratization of vocation extended the concept of calling to all realms of life. A milkmaid glorifies God in her work every bit as much as a priest in his; a loving parent takes up calling as much as a dedicated monk. Through the gift of faith, everyone receives both a spiritual calling (*vocatio spiritualis*) and a temporal calling (*vocatio extern*), the former a result of Christ's life and death and the latter an opportunity for human response. Yet, as Santmire observes, Protestantism's historical obsession with the doctrine of justification has undermined and distorted the union of Christ's work with His person. The result has led to what he calls ecclesial docetism, where initially the objective nature of vocation *vis-à-vis* the proclamation of the Word (*kerygma*) eclipsed the subjectivity of vocation, prompting in response the rise of pietism and quietist individualism. Both accounts, which Santmire highlights in the theologies of Bultmann and Barth respectively, mistakenly limit the church's identity to that of instrument of salvation rather than reality of salvation.[8] Kerygmatic approaches emphasize the communal and passive nature of calling, but fail to articulate how Christ's patient agency produces personal human action and ethical fruit. Conversely, pietist approaches rightly attend to behavior, but in a privatized moralistic manner that dangerously resembles what Luther regarded as filthy rags.

For Luther, with Santmire in tow, Christ's life and work modeled something different. When Christ's justifying work and real presence in the Word and Spirit are held in tension, questions of vocation are recast. The church's guiding inquiry moves from "called to what?" to "called to whom?" and "called for what purpose?" Being called to particular actions, such as evangelism or holiness, matters insofar as such actions respond to and meet the needs of an actual neighbor. It is the neighbor who is both the means as well as the end of vocation. And for Santmire, much more explicitly than for the medievalist Martin Luther, the neighbor includes the other-than-human because of human beings' undeniable connection to the natural world. Calling and innovating upon Martin Buber's relational schema much the way H. Richard Niebuhr did, Santmire suggests that Christians consider their relationship to the earth and all it hosts as an I-Ens relation (*Ens* from the Latin participle for "being"). This third way of relating and being neither subjugates nature to the place of mere utilitarian object (I-It), as is common among industrial-mechanized societies, nor does it exalt nature to a state of divinity (I-Thou) as is common in biocentric terreologies. Rather, when viewed as innately valuable in theocentric perspective, nature takes on the shape of neighbor through its immediate presence (Buber's *Gegenwart* over *Gegenstand*) and intimate, organic relationship with the human subject.[9] For example a tree, although an object in the strict sense of the term, ought not to be juxtaposed with human subjectivity given humans' biological intimacy and dependency upon the tree. Far from abstract, ethereal, or static, Santmire's working concept of vocation is embodied, localized, and dynamic.

The Church's Calling to Nature

In several essays and in the final chapter of *Nature Reborn,* Santmire explicitly outlines four aspects of the church's calling to nature, qualifying vocation as a way of "reliving the classical Christian story ethically."[10] All four build upon the biblical argument he outlined fifteen years earlier, where he suggested that the androcentric creation account of Genesis 2 be interpreted in light of the more cosmic Priestly narrative and themes of wisdom Christology in the Pauline and Johannine corpuses. An ecologically promising reading of the Christian tradition will uphold the aegis of Hebraic metaphors of migration to a good land and mystical metaphors of fecundity rather than pervasive Greco-Roman metaphors of ascent.[11] Keeping this earthy, incarnational reading of Scripture in mind, Santmire first suggests that Christian calling requires righteous cooperation with nature, meaning that while humans can intervene in the systems of the natural world, acting at times as creators in the fabrication of goods, they are to do so respectfully, attentive to nature's own processes and to related divinely-mandated requirements of social justice.[12] Such conscientiousness employs an I-Ens rubric rather than the I-It paradigm of traditional dominion or stewardship approaches, resembling the mutuality model of Aldo Leopold's proposed land ethic. For Santmire, language like "creation care" doesn't go far enough; it's too anthropocentric in scope and, in the consideration of present and future human welfare, fails to keep justice at the center of the conversation. Practically speaking, calling as cooperation with nature demands a lifestyle of voluntary simplicity, where a working virtue of restraint or temperance is always at play.[13] Pastorally it requires prophetic teaching and radicalized liturgy on both local and global ecclesial levels.[14]

Yet still, in true dialectical form, Santmire also points out that abandoning all language or constructs of care is unhelpful. The second major aspect of ecological vocation *is* to care for nature in the manner of Genesis 2:15—serving and protecting. On this point, Santmire delineates between wild, cultivated, and fabricated nature, noting how different degrees of nature call for various types of involvement. Reticent to promote any one model of care, he notes how in some cases service and protection looks like conservation and in others responsible intervention. So, while concern for eco-justice is of foremost importance to Santmire, particularly in his later works, his overall schema is far from anthropocentric in scope, as some recent critics have suggested.[15] Here one can appreciate Santmire's pastoral sensibilities, which seek to keep in mind both the livelihood of parishioners working the coal mines outside of Akron, Ohio (where he was pastoring at the time) and the flourishing of bioregional ecosystems. What is critical to any Christian ecological vocation, he argues, is the interdependence of all three types of nature. He writes,

> Since we are created by God to live in the midst of all these dimensions of nature, we should make every reasonable effort to see that they overlap and interpenetrate, wherever possible. In particular, the city should have signs of cultivated nature and hints of wild nature. The farmlands should have signs of nearby or distant urban centers and hints of the wilderness. The wilderness may have hints of urban life and signs of agricultural life at its edges.[16]

There is no rural, agrarian ideal in Santmire's paradigm, just as there is no cosmopolitanism. Rather, just as vocation can be found in any station of life, so too a vocation of care must emerge from wherever one is, with due regard for more foreign habitats.

The third aspect of a Christian's calling to nature is awe-filled wonder. More than mere sentiment, wonder requires sustained attention and self-sacrificing appreciation for the *Ens*. If one's attention to the natural world is divided, *Ens* quickly becomes a commodity (It), lacking value of its own accord. Quite fond of Luther's phrase, "If you really examined a kernel of grain thoroughly you would die of wonder," Santmire underscores the mindfulness of vocation.[17] When one chooses to be present in wonder, the created value of nature shines forth leaving human beings more capable of gratitude and delight.[18] In this sense vocation is more of a posture or an attitude toward the neighbor, which in turn informs one's actions and behavioral patterns.

Santmire's final aspect of calling is eschatological in scope. Christians, he argues, are uniquely called to anticipate the reign of God joyfully. Deeply influenced by the late twentieth century's theologians of hope, who emphasized the in-breaking of Christ's consummative power in the here and now, he maintains that despite current ecological trajectories, Christians are to trust in God's promises to renew and heal the earth. Such trust is to be enacted in the actual sacramental life of the church, which he refers to as a "martyr church" for its perennial existence under the sign of the cross. "This martyr church can rise to this historic occasion today, by the grace of God, to respond to what is perhaps an unprecedented calling, to love God and all God's creatures, as one great and glorious extended family, and in so doing to be a light to the nations and a city set upon a hill, whose exemplary witness cannot be hidden."[19]

Vocation as Paradox

To paint Santmire's working concept of vocation in positive terms alone—cooperation, care, wonder, and joy—would be to misinterpret the critical ways he re-envisions Western Protestant theology. Such a reading would also ignore Santmire's pastoral realism, a key attribute of his work. Cumulatively, his work outlines an apology for the ecological promise of Western Protestant thought, but does so in light of terrifying and disheartening scientific and cultural realities. To provide pastoral insight for how to act toward the neighbor or how to be in right relationship with nature, one must also seek to see things for what they really are. As explored in chapter two, normative ethics cannot take place without descriptive ethics.[20] To enact care, wonder, and hope, Christians must also contemplate what Santmire calls "the dark side" of God's majestic vision. Here again, he calls upon Luther, noting how when we contemplate God in, with, and under nature, we humans see through a glass darkly. "The world we see, good as it is and as overflowing with the presence of a good God as it is, is also a world of sin and death, of suffering and destruction. Luther was not, nor do I want to be, some kind of romantic who refuses to see the darkness for what it is."[21]

Thus, for Santmire, vocation occupies the space of paradox. Calling requires affirmation and negation, both a building up and a tearing down. Ethically speaking, vocation uplifts the positive potential of human moral agency while simultaneously acknowledging the liabilities of human ignorance, complacency, and selfishness. To Santmire's eye, the paradox of vocation is illustrated and magnified in the Gospels, where Jesus outlines principles of the Kingdom of God. The Kingdom is, on the one hand, wholly present in the incarnation of Christ, and on the other hand, not yet fully realized. The theological image speaks to the hope for heaven and eternal spiritual restoration *and* the renewal of the city of man. It refers to both a Divine rule and a Divine realm, wherein the reign of God extends beyond Divine-to-human or human-to-human relationships, to include an actual geography. For this reason, Santmire seeks to recast the Social Gospel Movement's reclamation of the image, viewing it as an equally ecologically imaginative and germative theological framework. The paradox of Kingdom of God theology "allows us to conceive of a personal God who relates himself directly both to a personal creature ([hu]man) and to an a-personal creature (the whole of nature) with the same degree of intensity, if not the same kind of intimacy."[22]

For Santmire, this present God who is in, with and under all things is also the hidden and unknowable God. Therefore, what the Christian ultimately has are traces of the Triune God, *vestigial Trinitatis*. Mention of God's mystical presence in nature wasn't explicit in Luther's work, Santmire rightly argues, because creation and redemption weren't binaries for Luther. God's presence and work in all of creation was assumed; the Medieval natural law tradition was taken for granted. Yet, Santmire suggests contemporary Christians extend some of Luther's thinking to include a more decidedly Trinitarian theology.[23] While critical of his emphasis on Divine immanence at the expense of Divine autonomy and transcendence, Santmire admits to being heavily influenced by Jürgen Moltmann's working pneumatology and eschatology. As Moltmann attempts to investigate the *perichoresis* of the Trinity, likewise Christians would do well to pay more attention to the interrelatedness of the Triune persons and the related ongoing creative acts of God (*creatio continua*).[24] In radically theocentric terms, they can think about the Trinity as "a festive communal process" that fills all things like "a powerful, torrential flow."[25]

And this radical, mystical reconception of God, both God's nature and God's work in the world, serves to recast our understanding of calling. With its origin in God's Word, vocation in paradox avoids Western theology's pervasive anthropocentrism, which limits human responsibility to the neighbor to the realm of human relationships. It also steers clear of hyper-personalism, which loses the truly personal aspects of calling, and panentheism, which Santmire understands to be nothing more than a form of metaphorical reductionism.[26] In economic terms, Santmire regards the Triune God as Giver, Gift, and Giving. Immanently the Trinity is mutuality, a realm where perfect giving and receiving takes place. And in less-than-perfect ways, this is what human vocation is, the simultaneous and ongoing process of receiving from God while also sacrificially giving to neighbors in and through Christ.

THE VOICE OF A PROPHETIC SCHOLAR: SALLIE MCFAGUE AND VOCATION AS RESISTANCE

Situating vocation as sacrifice has given many feminists reason to pause and protest, for prescribed roles of woman as helpmate to man and nurturer for children have perennially limited women's work to the domestic realm and have often undermined the important work of truly valuing oneself.[27] Sallie McFague, one of contemporary Christianity's most celebrated feminists, is aware of the liabilities accompanying a kenotic theology. Were it not for her commitment to the liberation of nature alongside women, her work could be easily characterized like much of the neo-liberal feminist tradition.[28] Yet, a distinctive and frequently surprising feature of McFague's voice is her retrieval of the apophatic tradition and her embrace of a radical self-denying practical theology. Demonstrated through attention to her use of metaphor and her retrieval of a quasi-virtue ethics tradition, McFague's conception of kenotic love of God and neighbor proves anything but tritely subservient. Subversive at its core, Sallie McFague evokes a picture of vocation inclusive of radical cultural critique and resistance.

Methodology

Like Santmire and many aforementioned Christian theologians and ethicists, McFague works within the realm of moral terreology, reinterpreting theological concepts, beliefs, and symbols in light of socio-political realities. Generally speaking, her work could be characterized as theocentric in nature, most congruent with historical forms of sacramentalism. However, McFague's feminist and postcolonial sensibilities tailor the type of theocentricism she employs, one that to her mind reimagines theology while taking science seriously. She argues that there have been two major theocentric approaches. The first, an agential theocentric perspective, emphasizes God's agency as realized in history, thus painting the picture of a deeply personal God. Despite her appreciation for the theological emphasis on divine will, McFague is critical of such approaches for the way they've been co-opted by sexist language. God, the creating Father, is little more than a controlling mind or self, or (at very best), the neutered breath that animates life. Not only does such a perspective too quickly disregard the particularities of science, but it also applies an immature anthropology upon the doctrine of God. In true feminist form, McFague argues that all theology is anthropology.[29] We cannot help but bring ourselves to theological reflection; when we think of God, we innately think of ourselves. Feminist theory reminds us that the mature self appreciates difference or particularity for what it is while also crafting identity in terms of interdependence. The relational self, McFague argues, avoids the fusion of the self to other on the one hand and the disjoining of self from the community on the other.[30] As a relational being, therefore, God "is not exhausted by finite being, not even all finite beings, yet God is in all finite creatures and apart from God there is nothing; nor is God apart from anything."[31]

The second theocentric perspective, which McFague refers to as the organic view, closely aligns with process theology differing only in its assumption that a supreme agent guides the evolutionary processes. Organic theocentrism highlights the transformation of all things through their processes of natural growth toward the divine source and goal of their existence.[32] For McFague the problem with this perspective is the lack of personal language. Surely God is much more than a force or energizing principle, as the cosmic Christ took on flesh and dwelled among us![33] Unlike many of her feminist counterparts, and particularly her white peers, she is unwilling to part with personalized language altogether, as it more accurately denotes the ecology of our relationships and honors the intention with which such relationships were established.

This is where the power of metaphor plays a critical role for McFague. Metaphors, she asserts, lead us to the mystical place between nonsense and truth, proving to be principal epistemological tools more than descriptions of reality. When we engage metaphors, we test language against experience, trying them on as if to peel back another layer of waylaid or dormant knowledge. This is why no single metaphor is adequate; all are in need of supplementation from other metaphors. What ultimately makes a metaphor a good one is the relevant shock of recognition that it supplies after a subject's initial stage of disbelief.[34] And so, to imagine the world as God's body is not to limit God to the particularities of any one place or time, as in agential perspectives, nor is it to obtusely conceive of God as entirely impersonal. Rather, McFague's reigning metaphor, and indeed her overall commitment to metaphorical theology, attempts to hold these two approaches in tension. The result is an apophatic bodily theology that focuses upon what McFague deems the very heart of Christian theology: the self-sacrificial emptying of God's body.[35]

Kenosis and Radical Incarnationalism

Like Santmire, McFague regrettably observes how the West has been obsessed with soteriology, particularly justification. By way of contrast, she highlights three parts of the Eastern Christian tradition: *kenosis*, *enosis,* and *theosis*, all of which emphasize a Christology "from below."[36] When we begin discussions of creation (including the discernment of our roles and responsibilities within creation) with the incarnation and the cross as the environment for the doctrine of creation, a different outlook emerges. We become free to embark on what she calls "radical incarnationalism," where suffering has a supernatural purpose rather than a supernatural remedy, and where we move toward God by subtraction rather than by accumulation.[37] To this end, McFague explores the relationship between price and cost, suggesting that price rarely gets at the actual cost of things. Authentic discipleship, for example, has a cost but no price. The work of our hands may have a price, but is not often appropriately and commensurately linked to the actual cost of time, energy, and resources. Christianity, in its embrace of beauty and pain, death and life, can unveil the relationship between these two realities and speak to what vocation actually requires—restraint, sharing, limits, and boundaries.

From this vantage, love of the neighbor is unpossessive, having more to do with empowerment of others or the power to let them be than any emotion or feeling. In the words of one of her intellectual mentors, Iris Murdoch, "love is the extremely difficult realization that something other than oneself is real." In this sense vocation or calling is not first and foremost an individual receiving, heeding and acting upon God's command to love the world, although for McFague it is also that. Rather, vocation is the act of kenotic love itself, a hardheaded, sober analysis of the way things are and the willingness to honor the space another deserves and requires. "This is who we are—world lovers—," McFague writes in the introductory chapter of *Blessed are the Consumers*, "which always means world bearers, for both nature and the neighbor are the 'new poor' in our time."[38]

Vocation as Obligation and Desire

In her most recent work, McFague observes that what surprises us human beings is not that we've lived and are living beyond our means, for deep within ourselves we know this and have known it for some time. Rather, what takes us by surprise is the discovery that our duties toward the neighbor, human and otherwise, also align with our truest desires.[39] Together, obligation and yearning are two critical components of vocation. True to her Reformed roots, McFague understands vocation deontologically, where authentic work is qualified by the requirements of God's mandates. As in Santmire's Lutheran context, vocation remains in the realm of the law. However, for McFague it isn't that vocation leads one to the cross, but rather that the kenotic act of love metaphorically accessible in the cross leads one to vocation. In Barthian terms, the commands become permissions, the obligation a freedom of obedience.

But to leave it at this would be to miss some crucial elements of McFague's second aspect of vocation–desire. Having freedom to grow in Christ's likeness, indeed to be sanctified, remains important to McFague, but not necessarily sufficiently motivating. Akin to Santmire, McFague seeks to be unabashedly realistic in her proposal by asking the difficult question: What will actually prompt us to care for creation as we care for ourselves? Looking to the prophetic tradition, she suggests that responsibility has teeth and staying power when it is coupled with personal fulfillment: "We desire what desires us, and it is in the concrete living out of our response–our yes to God's Yes–that we become who we want to be and were meant to be."[40] Here McFague's working concept of vocation takes on a more teleological tenor, with the focus being a certain kind of intended perfected self.

To this end her detailed commentaries on those she calls "ecological saints" are warranted, for persons like John Woolman, Simone Weil, and Dorothy Day (to name a few of her favorites) exemplify radical obedience as an attractive way of life. In their enlightenment, or kenotic awakening to the other, calling was unavoidable. So while the vocations of the saints may seem unreasonable if not crazy to most, when the lenses of self-centeredness are removed from one's eyes, their lifestyles seem "not only possible but in fact eminently reasonable."[41] Like the Gospel itself, McFague suggests such saints testify to and reveal a truth that makes it impossible for us to idly live in our self-serving mythical worlds.[42] When we read their stories and pass into their lives in order to pass back into our own we see that what God requires of us is that which ultimately satiates us.

The more teleological aspect of McFague's concept of vocation is also apparent in her attention to purposeful appetites. Particularly in her later works, McFague opens the door to the virtue ethics tradition, territory not frequently trodden by Reformed theologians and arguably even less so by those of the feminist persuasion.[43] Seeing the social role of religion as the systematic refusal of autocratic consumption, and self-emptying especially central to the Christian tradition, McFague focuses upon simplicity, community, and resistance.

Vocation as Resistance

In order for kenotic action to take place at the personal and public level, which McFague argues it must, three very counter-cultural realities are to be at play. First, akin to Santmire, she asserts that human beings must see themselves as planetary beings, who are part of a larger *oikos*. Secondly, necessary distinctions must be made between human beings based on matters of class, gender, and race so to avoid unjustly lumping all persons into an essential universal self that evades the responsibilities of privilege and power. And finally, a vocation that insists upon the needs of others over the needs of self requires embodied acts of resistance.[44]

The last of these criteria proves the most incarnational by McFague's standards and is thus particularly applicable to a Christian concept of vocation. As a cruciform life of sacrifice and sharing burdens, calling requires that we rethink and undertake "alternative ways of working, eating, cultivating land, transporting ourselves, educating our children, entertaining ourselves, [and] even of worshipping God."[45] In all of these acts, attention to the embodied needs of the neighbor is primary. Is my preference for meat at every meal or a solo commute indicative of the common good? Does our work and do our visions of success consider the world's most vulnerable and the generations yet to come? These are the types of questions the church can and must ask, and in doing so, the church makes what McFagues considers to be its most important contribution to a global alternative economic paradigm. As a vehicle to re-envision its members in their respective vocations, the church ought not be "as cogs in the wheels of the establishment, but as counter-cultural voices for an alternative kind of abundance life for all members of the global family."[46]

When Christian vocation entails the reframing of a scarcity mentality to one of plentitude, the fundamental question becomes "What must I keep?" over "What should I give?" The latter of these questions operates under the assumption of consumption, with giving being an afterthought, whereas the former assumes that *all* bodies need space and thus functions from a perspective of enough. Resisting the norms of our increasingly esurient culture, McFague's working concept of vocation centers on the space the kenotic God opened up for creation, whose power "lies in giving space for others, dying to self that others might live. This strange reversal—losing one's life to save it—is also the sensibility that is needed if our planet is to survive and prosper."[47]

THE VOICE OF A POET:
WENDELL BERRY AND VOCATION AS AFFECTION

In 2014, the American Academy of Religion recognized Wendell Berry's influence in religious studies, awarding the prolific American writer the Martin E. Marty Award for the Public Understanding of Religion. A decade ago, such an acknowledgement would have fared unlikely, for, as many of Berry's commentators and critics have noted, his agrarian ideal is often realized in contrast to baptized economic forces that undermine and destroy nature's resiliency. "The certified Christian," Berry remarked in a 1992 essay, "seems just as likely as anyone else to join the military-industrial conspiracy to murder creation."[48]

However, for all of his scathing critiques of Christianity, Berry's prophetic voice ultimately rejects cliché indictments of religion. Rather than forsaking the traditions and theological resources of Christianity, as with good cause many an ecologically-minded writer has, Berry innovates. As Lawrence Buell and others have suggested, to read Berry and to read him well is to engage and understand something about the creedal traditions of Western Protestantism.[49] One of the theological resources of Berry's Baptist upbringing most readily retrieved in his work is the doctrine of vocation. As we shall see below, calling, cast as affection for land, animals, and people, is foundational to Berry's envisaged authentic culture.[50]

Methodology

Initially, one might argue that Berry doesn't propose a cohesive ecological ethic in the same way Santmire and McFague do. His literature makes different attempts, uses different tools, and while arguably capable of reaching similar moral outcomes to that of philosophical and theological works, remains distinct. Even more convincing is Berry's resistance to given titles like "American moral prophet" and "literary Christian ethicist." "I'm no moralist," Berry said to a small group of Christian graduate students gathered in his hometown of Port Royal, Kentucky, "and even less so a theologian or Christian writer. What I *am* is a storyteller who has a mind to pay attention to the world around him."[51] Yet, as with a good amount of writing with staying power, Berry's narrative appeals to the classical ontological categories of goodness, beauty, and truth.[52] What marks Berry's voice as unique among other transcendentalists, particularly in contrast to those hailing from the Platonic tradition, is his insistent location of such properties in the fleshy and authentic experience of everyday life.

Berry's reader bears the fortune of taking on his working ethic when entering the Port William story. As its characters and circumstances unravel, the reader is engaged in a sort of literary paideutic, not unlike the Christian Gospels that Berry testifies to having always appreciated.[53] As in the synoptic parables or Johannine anecdotes, where the story serves to both describe and implore, the reader is an externalized observer and a moral agent simultaneously. For example, while reading Jayber Crow's descriptive differences between wise, old farmer James Athey and his foolishly proud son-in-law, Troy Chatham, Berry not only paints a picture of sustainable farming over industrialized land abuse, a contrast of personal character over vain ambition, but also invites the reader to examine such polarities and possibilities within one's self. The story teaches as much as it entertains, exhorts as much as it chronicles. And just as agrarianism focuses on the particularity and locale of ethical questions, ultimately concerned with the life one actually lives above the one conceived of, likewise Berry's ethic is revealed in the palpable realities of Port William relationships rather than through theoretical or universal musings.[54] If anything, Berry's storyline demonstrates how experiences shape and inform beliefs.

Explicit Definitions of Vocation in Berry's Nonfiction

In his 2012 National Endowment for the Humanities Jefferson Lecture, Berry defined vocation as the responsibility each person has to participate in a neighborly and conserving economy. Understanding economy in simple and classical terms, Berry qualifies authentic economy by "terms of thrift and affection, our connections to nature and to one another."[55] However, as much of Berry's writing demonstrates, a second rendering of economy exists, an industrial one. It also makes connections between land and neighbor, albeit by way of what Berry sees as pillage and indifference. The result is a fracturing of the *oikos*. Lamenting this conceptualization of economy, Berry observes how economists "rarely if ever mention the land-communities and the land-use economies. They never ask, in their professional oblivion, why we are willing to do permanent ecological and cultural damage to 'strengthen the economy?'" Yet, to Berry's eye this is the critical contemporary question, for one's vocation or calling is never merely a question of what a person produces, the work accomplished, or even the philanthropic gifts she or he gives.[56] Vocation is defined; rather, by what a person receives freely from God through the needs of the neighbor and in the act of work itself. Earn and strive as we humans will, what we ultimately depend upon—land and relationship—is given. The competing economies of our present day, one oriented toward production and the other rest, depend equally upon the endowed "Great Economy," of biological life, although only the latter recognizes and adheres to the inherent limitations therein. For Berry, when vocation is properly understood as an obligation to receive gifts and honor creation's limitations, work

> moves virtue toward virtuosity–that is, toward skill or technical competency. There is no use in helping our neighbors with their work if we do not know how to work. When virtues are rightly practiced within the Great Economy, we do not call them virtues; we call them good farming, good forestry, good carpentry, good husbandry, good weaving and sewing, good homemaking, good parenthood, good neighborhood, and so on.[57]

In contrast to tenets of American exceptionalism, in which a person or people is thought destined to greatness by virtue of association, and the longstanding ideology of the "self-made-man," Berry construes the outcomes of good work as gifts. Rather than work becoming a vehicle for pride, wherein the mind is easily incapable of wonder and subject to loneliness, work ought to grace us with health and heal us with grace. In Berry's words, work as vocation "preserves the given so that it remains a gift."[58] Unlike unfettered capitalism, which arrogantly measures and values natural goods and relationships as commodities according to a fabricated monetary bottom line, Berry's agrarianism suggests that if more communities viewed productivity as a gesture of return, "the economy would have to accommodate the need to be worthy of the gifts we receive and use."[59] The obvious result would be a lifestyle more readily characterized by constraint rather than consumption, gratitude over greed. Thus, practically speaking, Berry's working concept of vocation is thoroughly Protestant in the way it engenders thankfulness to God on the one hand and responsibility to the neighbor on the other, as made manifest in one's affection for place and people, land and culture.

The place in which a person finds oneself, their particular locale, is central to one's vocation. It is in Berry's mind not where thoughts settle, cease or rest, but rather, where they begin. And not only is calling to a particular place an important theme throughout Berry's writing, but it's also proved an important element in his biography. As anyone even vaguely familiar with his story knows, Berry and his wife, Tanya, have repeatedly declined prestigious invitations to work and teach outside of their native Kentucky. Even Berry's brief tenure at the University of Kentucky proved challenging, as he grew to despise the commute and what he perceived even then to be a growing chasm between academic life and farm life. In prose and lifestyle alike, Berry's working definition of vocation underscores the importance of being rooted in a place, of being in relationship to the land of the place and of entering into community with the people of the place.[60] In one of his more autobiographical essays, "A Native Hill," Berry shares how such groundedness has shaped his vocation as a writer: "I knew that because I was a writer the literary world would always have an importance for me and would always attract my interest," he writes, "[but] I never doubted that the world was more important to me than the literary world; and the world would always be most fully and clearly present to me in the place I was fated by birth to know better than any other."[61] He would be, in the words of his beloved teacher, Wallace Steger, a "sticker" rather than a "boomer."[62]

Implicit Definitions of Vocation in Berry's Fiction

The importance of commitment to and affection for place and people is most evident in the fiction of Berry's Port William Membership. In these novels and short stories, we meet an array of persons. There are some who, by contributing to the local economy while preserving the greater one, enliven the ecology of their respective vocations. There are others who fail to do so, and often at the expense of the community at large. In their recent book, *Wendell Berry and the Restoration of Life*, Matthew Bonzo and Michael Stevens helpfully highlight six categories of interaction in Berry's hospitable world, ranging from those who while born into the Membership leave in search for better options, to those who invest from outside the community and are welcomed as full members, to full members who always dwell along the margins.[63] As Bonzo and Stevens suggest, no one person or particular above category of interaction is dominant in the narrative; there is no signature hero in Port William. For example, Jayber Crow and Hannah Coulter, aliens by birth to the community, are as critical to its well-being as its lifelong residents, Andy Catlett or Mattie Chatman. What Berry depicts in the membership is a dynamic, yet stable, community with bounded space for mutuality and accountability.[64] In a real sense, Berry's protagonist is the community itself, with individuals' respective callings always understood relative to the myriad relationships they inhabit within the community.

To better understand how Berry recasts the Christian concept of vocation in a manner true to the doctrine's original emphasis and in contrast to contemporary conceptions of work three aspects of vocation in the Port William narrative warrant consolidation. First, Berry tethers vocation to place by emphasizing the importance of a common and shared goal. Secondly, vocation is depicted as something given rather than discovered or earned. And finally, Berry employs an intergenerational sense of calling, noting how lives "dead, living and yet to be" influence one's present work.[65]

Vocation and A Common Goal

We begin with the story of the Catlett men, Wheeler and his two sons, Henry and Andy. Two trained as lawyers and the latter a journalist, the Catletts are unique in Port William for their advanced, formal education and professional careers. As Berry implies time and again, these men could have easily led more fiscally comfortable lives elsewhere, embodying a more modern definition of success. But what makes the Catletts truly unique in the narrative is how they utilize their skills and abilities in service to the shared and common life of the Port William Membership. Take, for example, Henry Catlett's aiding and abetting role in the abduction of old Burley Coulter from a Louisville hospital in the short story "Fidelity." Knowing that Coulter's son Danny wished his bachelor father to die in surroundings that he loved, Henry uses his legal prowess and status to deter a legalistic detective and preserve the broader ecology of a communal vocation.

Andy Catlett's prodigal story of return, captured primarily in *Remembering*, also defines vocation in relationship to the needs of community. While presenting the difficulties of small farmers like those in Port William in a paper at a national conference attended by many who had been "off the farm" for decades, Andy has a conversion-like experience. Unlike his literary colleagues, he is burdened by the mounting injustices related to corporate agricultural practices and doesn't wish to be, or think himself able to be, a writer who records the course of farming outside of an actual farming community.[66] Andy, often thought to be Berry's autobiographical character, returns from San Francisco to Port William seeking reconciliation with those he left and begins to write on behalf of his beloved community.

Interestingly, we see a counter example of this story in the life of Caleb Coulter. Using the language of calling, Hannah Coulter describes how "farming was what [Caleb] played before he could work at it."[67] From her vantage, Caleb's call to farm seemed evident. However, as sure as Caleb may have been of such a vocation he is depicted as being equally certain of the expectations laid upon him. His young adult life, heavy with the yoke of potential, was not only Caleb's to live and so began what Hannah refers to as "the distancing." While in school, Caleb was urged to make more of himself than a farmer. Hannah imagines the voices saying, "There's no future for you in farming" and "Why should you be a farmer yourself when you can do so much for farmers?"[68] Ultimately these voices did shape Caleb's perceived calling. He earned a PhD in agriculture, finding some semblance of solace in teaching others about the art of keeping land. To be sure, Berry's fairly neutral depiction of Caleb makes clear that, unlike his colleagues, who championed the ways of booming agribusiness, Caleb remained tethered to the Port William community in his own removed way, promoting responsible participation in small economies. To this end, Caleb's academic vocation is authentic by Berry's standards and undoubtedly serves as a deliberate alternative to the way of the ivory tower that Berry himself entertained and left behind.

And yet, in Berry's latest novel we learn of Caleb's deep dissatisfaction. Seemingly stuck in a laboratory while invariably yearning to break soil of his own, his mother describes his existence as "always trying to make up the difference between the life he has and the life he imagines he might have had."[69] Here, Berry illustrates the dangers of universality over particularity. Caleb's hidden anguish uncovers a tension in Berry's working concept of vocation, the significance of a community's perceived needs and guidance on the one hand and a person's own still, small voice on the other.

Vocation as Given

This location of the individual in the context of community gives way to a free sense of vocation, as briefly mentioned above. In numerous cases, Port William members come into their calling by way of gift. Berry evokes images of apprenticeship and priesthood repeatedly in his unfolding tale, juxtaposing the wisdom of less-than-credentialed characters with those who are teachers and pastors in name only. A clear example of this can be found in the story of Elton and Mary Penn. Initially poor tenant farmers on the outskirts of town, the Penns exhibit genuine interest in the life of the community and are welcomed with open arms, learning the skills of housewifery and husbandry from their neighbors.[70] These relational gifts lead not only to increased knowledge and skill, but also to a recognized identity, indeed a vocation, as good and faithful farmers. In "A Jonquil for Mary Penn," Mary is shown to have gratitude for the friendships she's been given, a "wonderful provisioning" and a "warmth that answered her parents' rejection," given their aspirations of much higher social aims.[71] Elton, fatherless at a young age and estranged from his mother after her second marriage, also lived under the shadow of abandonment and in the same story is said to be enamored by neighbor Walter Cotman's knowledge of the land: "Elton loved his growing understanding of Walter's character and his ways. Though he was a quiet man and gave neither instruction nor advice, Walter was Elton's teacher, and Elton was consciously his student."[72]

After Old Jack Beechum resigns himself to the reality that his only daughter, Clara, and her banker husband, Gladston Pettit, have no intention of caring for his beloved farm, Jack bequeaths a portion of it to the Penns and, with the additional aid of senior lawyer Wheeler Catlett, the Penns become farmers of their own right. When pressed about his generosity, Wheeler democratizes the situation, establishing his position as similar to that of his beneficiary. "I mean you're a man indebted to a dead man. So am I. So was [Jack]. That's the story of it."[73] Here the given precedes the giving. Elton and Mary Penn's calling came by what was given—the knowledge of the trade and possession of property. Likewise, Wheeler Catlett's vocation as social advocate and community philanthropist comes to be through what was first given him. "It's not accountable," Wheeler remarks at the end of the story,

> we're dealing in goods and services that we didn't make, that can't exist at all except as gifts. Everything about a place that's different from its price is a gift. Everything about a man or woman that's different from their price is a gift. The life of a neighborhood is a gift . . . So there is to be no repayment. Because there is to be no bill.[74]

We also see vocation as given in the storyline between Old Jack Beechum and his nephew, Mat Feltner. In "Pray without Ceasing," the young Mat ponders just revenge in response to the murder of his father, Ben. While often regarded as a bitter curmudgeon in the Port William community, it is old Jack Beechum who saves young Mat from such a fate. Unlike the disembodied pastoral figure of Brother Preston, who Berry describes as having "washed his hands of the whole world," Jack sees and understands the vulnerability of Mat's flesh.[75] Like a true priest, he recognizes the beauty and significance of Mat's pain and embodies a kenotic compassion for his nephew. Jack never consciously takes on such a role, nor does he feign importance amidst the tragic circumstances. Rather, he faithfully and silently accompanies Mat, never wholly detached and yet unobtrusive and in so doing is given the vocation of ministry to the entire Feltner family. The role is the fruit of Jack's keen attention to a particular person in a particular place at a particular time and because it's given, Jack's calling extends to multiple generations, as evidenced in the relationship forged with Hannah Feltner (Coulter) some thirty years later. The vocation of priesthood in the Port William Membership, like any worthwhile vocation, is apprenticed to those who are observant and willing to adapt their own lives to the demands of others.[76]

The Intergenerational Nature of Vocation

This brings us to the third component of Berry's working concept of vocation, the intergenerational. As Brent Laytham has shown, Berry's Port William fiction exhibits a reverence for example by highlighting stories of past righteousness and neighborly concern.[77] The Port William Membership most assuredly includes the dead as much as it does the living. Rather than one being replaced after they die, "cast out of place and out of mind . . . to be alone at the last maybe and soon forgotten," as is the case in most modern work environments, in a communal membership one's vocation extends beyond their lifetime. In Andy Catlett's words to Hannah Coulter, membership "keeps the memories even of horses and mules and milk cows and dogs."[78] There is, as Laytham has observed, an almost ecclesial quality to the Membership, wherein those gone before constitute part of the *Communio Sanctorum*.

In *Jayber Crow* we read of Jimmy Chatham's intimate apprenticeship with his maternal grandfather, Athey Craig. From a young age, Jimmy was taken with the simple and holistic techniques fundamental to Athey's farm, in contrast to the mechanized methods of his own father, Troy, and given responsibilities related thereto. Here the transmission of vocation doesn't pass directly from one generation to another, or follow direct bloodlines. In Athey Craig's case, the beauty and dignity found in farming was known and understood by his heir twice removed, and an heir that would be given little power to honor Athey's ways. In the sad conclusion to this tale, we see how the influence of the dead can lead to the undoing of the living, for when Athey Craig passed away, Jimmy Chatham's life began to slip away, leading eventually to drunken oblivion and a life extinguished prematurely under the guise of a necessary war. Jimmy's vocation was, in Berry's words, "lost in what was and what could never be."[79]

As linked to those gone before, calling is equally associated with those yet to come. In the short story "The Wild Birds," for example, we learn of Burley Coulter's desire to bequeath his farm to Danny Branch, not only out of obligation, but also because Danny has proven able to care for the land just as Burley responsibly tended what was given him. Here the validity of vocation has everything to do with what it yields in generations to come, a particularly important aspect of Berry's working concept of vocation in today's environmentally perilous times.

SYNTHESIZING VOICES

While Santmire, McFague, and Berry diverge in methodology and literary style in the crafting and articulation of their respective concepts of vocation, they also coalesce on important matters. Paul Santmire views current ecological projections in light of God's promises as tenuous and ambiguous, the Christian calling ultimately being that of paradox. Sallie McFague regards vocation as both an obligation and a desire, decidedly moved in kenotic action and resulting in a prophetic life of resistance. And finally, Wendell Berry defines vocation in concert with a fostered love of and affection for place. Whether paradox, resistance, or affection, the work of these three contemporaries can be fused in three areas of practical application of vocation: interrelatedness, restraint, and wisdom, all topics taken up in the next and final chapter.

NOTES

1. While I will show how these three thinkers differ in theological emphases and writing style, it remains important to note that all three of these thinkers are Caucasian U.S. citizens, and so while diverse in part, certainly do not adequately represent the whole of Christian thought on ecological ethics.

2. As will be articulated below, Wendell Berry by no means identifies himself as a Christian writer. Nor does he ever support one denomination or train of Christian thought over another. He does, however, identify his own familiar heritage with the Baptist tradition and, as we shall see, does depict that particular sect of Christianity in his fictional work.

3. Robert Booth Fowler, *The Greening of Protestant Thought* (Chapel Hill, NC: University of North Carolina, 1995), 100. Fowler reviews Santmire's work through the mid-1990s in a section on contemporary theology and argues that he is among the most influential eco-theologians of our day. Claude Stewart dedicates an entire chapter to Santmire's work in *Nature in Grace* (Macon, GA: Mercer University Press, 1983).

4. This is the subtitle of his second book, *The Travail of Nature* (Minneapolis: Fortress Press, 1985).

5. In fact, Santmire's latest book *Before Nature: A Christian Spirituality* (Minneapolis: Fortress Press, 2014) is intentionally written to the teachers and pastors of today's seekers and "nones." While organized religion is undoubtedly waning in North America, Santmire argues that the "cathedral of the great outdoors is alive and well, even flourishing" (xiv). He asks his pastor/teacher reader, "What if we were to image the cathedral of the great outdoors engulfing, surrounding, embracing the cathedral of Christian practices, and image ourselves standing at the entrance of that Christian cathedral, contemplating the vastness and the mystery and the beauty of the world of nature before and all around us in the cathedral of the great outdoors?" (xv).

6. Santmire, "Reflections on the Alleged Ecological Bankruptcy of Western Theology," *Anglican Review* 57:2 (April 1975): 147.

7. H. Paul Santmire, "Reflections," 146.

8. H. Paul Santmire, "On the Mission of the Church: Reflections along the Way," *Lutheran Quarterly* 23, no. 4 (Nov 1971): 366–387.

9. H. Paul Santmire, *Nature Reborn: The Ecological and Cosmic Promise of Christian Theology* (Minneapolis: Fortress Press, 2000), 68–70.

10. Santmire, *Nature Reborn*, 115. See also, "The Future of the Cosmos and the Renewal of the Church's Life with Nature" in *Word & World* IV:4 (1984). The word "nature" is in the title of each book Santmire has written. In *Ritualizing Nature: Renewing Christian Liturgy in a Time of Crisis* (Minneapolis: Fortress, 2008), he speaks to the ambiguity of the term. Nature "resists definition," he remarks, much like time and other such mythic words in our Western vocabularies (32). The word has been fraught with misunderstood social meanings, leading many like leading French sociologist Bruno Latour to abandon the term altogether. Santmire decidedly uses the word "nature" for pastoral cause; it bears a commonplace understanding that has some teeth in actual liturgical communities. The closest he comes to defining it himself is,

"the material-vital aspect of God's creation," which is visible in wilderness, cultivated and fabricated nature alike (32–33).

11. Santmire, *The Travail of Nature*, 183. Santmire unpacks each of these theological motifs in great detail in chapter 2 and then links each of them to respective historical thinkers: Ireneaus with the good land metaphor and Bonaventure with the metaphor of fecundity.

12. Santmire, *Nature Reborn*, 120.

13. Celia Deane-Drummond notes how Santmire's concept of vocation closely aligns with virtue ethics approaches to nature. Like most Lutherans, Santmire's ethical methodology is decidedly deontological in scope, but as Deane-Drummond demonstrates in *Ethics of Nature*, his expansion of "the neighbor" leads one to also consider classical virtues such as prudence and temperance (*Ethics of Nature*, (Malden, MA: Blackwell Publishing, 2004), 215).

14. Santmire describes the latter with great detail in *Ritualizing Nature*. His long-time involvement with the LCA and ELCA's task forces on environmental justice and his current leadership with Lutherans Restoring Creation and Eco-Reformation also testifies to this aspect of his work.

15. Ecotheologian Gretel Van Wieren recently critiqued Santmire's work, arguing that his attention to justice in the fabrication or modification of nature and the role of humans as co-creators is too anthropocentric in scope (*Restored to Earth: Christianity, Environmental Ethics and Ecological Restoration* (Washington, DC: Georgetown University Press, 2013), 105). What Van Weiren fails to appreciate, however, is Santmire's earnest pastoral realism and holistic picture of justice. True restoration of the natural world, or even the wilderness as Santmire categorizes it, isn't possible if humans don't live into the responsibility set before them within more fabricated environments. The latter is impacting the former to such an extent that to ignore the unique role humans play in maintaining and fabricating nature is to misunderstand restoration entirely.

16. Santmire, *Nature Reborn*, 126.

17. Martin Luther, *WA*, 14:496. For more on this, see Heinrich Bornkamm. *Luther's World of Thought*, trans. Hart H. Bertram (St. Louis, MO: Concordia, 1959), 182.

18. Santmire, *Nature Reborn*, 70–71.

19. Ibid., 128.

20. Here I am referring to the work of Santmire's Lutheran colleague, Cynthia Moe-Lobeda. In "Climate Change as Climate Debt: Forging a Just Future" in *Journal of the Society of Christian Ethics* 36:1 (Spring/Summer 2016): 27–49. She distinguishes between the work of normative ethics and descriptive ethics, arguing that for a transformative ethics to take place, our communities must attend first to reality and then attend to questions of moral behavior and action.

21. Santmire, *Before Nature*, 143.

22. Santmire, *Brother Earth: Nature, God and Ecology in a Time of Crisis* (New York: T. Nelson, 1970), 102.

23. Santmire, *Before Nature*, 143.

24. Santmire, *Before Nature*, 140, 189.

25. Ibid., 144–145.

26. Ibid., 138. He specifically mentions Brunner and Barth with regards to personalism. The hyper-personalism he has in mind refers to Paul Tillich's work. While he doesn't go into great detail, he is outspoken against the panentheistic Trinitarian theologies of Sallie McFague and Jürgen Moltmann.

27. For example, in *To Work and to Love* (Philadelphia: Fortress Press, 1984), Dorothee Sölle speaks at length about the worth and dignity of the individual in the context of community.

28. Here I am thinking of the examples listed in chapter one of Cristina L. H. Traina's work *Feminist Ethics and Natural Law: The End of the Anathemas* (Washington, DC: Georgetown University Press, 1999). She uses Beverly Wildung Harrison's work as a case in point, which regularly uses slogans of reason, rights, and common humanity to argue for reforms in gender relations. Wilding Harrison adopts the liberal tradition's peculiar understandings of fact and nature and their disconjunction from both culture and value, and in Traina's opinion this bifurcation undermines the feminist project by promoting thin rather than thick theories of the

good, providing uncritical confidence in human reason, overemphasizing the self over community and ignoring embodiment (26–28).

29. McFague, *A New Climate for Theology: God, the World and Global Warming* (Minneapolis: Fortress Press, 2008), 129.

30. McFague, *Super Natural Christians: How We Should Love Nature* (Minneapolis: Fortress Press, 1997), 104.

31. McFague, *The Body of God* (Minneapolis: Fortress Press, 1993), 149. It is noteworthy to mention here McFague's criticism of panentheism, even though many classify her work as panentheistic in nature, if not pantheistic in some respects. She argues that saying all things are somehow held in God, making God indefinitely immanent, does not minimize God's otherness and transcendence. Twentieth-century Trinitarian theologians (not coincidentally, predominately male and European-Caucasian in ethnicity) emphasizing the immanent Trinity over and above the economic Trinity would do well to heed the feminist tension–that one can be interdependent and yet wholly particular.

32. McFague, *The Body of God*, 141.

33. In speaking about energizing principles, we call to mind the brilliant work of Teilhard deChardin. Sallie McFague's work is often linked with the late Catholic paleontologist for the ways she reinterprets Christian concepts of creation in light of evolution and unfolding scientific discoveries. However, deChardin saw nature as marked by the double drive toward increased complexity and deeper interiority and thus culminated in the phenomenon of human life. While his schema isn't thoroughly anthropocentric (humans are never the center of creation), human beings are the cosmic anthropic principle from which we can work backward to understand the material world. In short, humans are the keys to the cosmos. McFague is very reticent to make such claims. In fact, in her recent works on climate change, she depicts humanity as the force undermining and forever modifying the cosmos.

34. McFague, *A New Climate for Theology*, 130–131.

35. McFague, *Blessed are the Consumers: Climate Change and the Practice of Restraint* (Minneapolis: Fortress Press, 2013), 174. McFague makes the argument that because theology is necessarily metaphorical, it is also fundamentally kenotic. The limits of language, she writes, make us "more aware of the 'is not' shadowing its statements, rather than the 'is.' Hence, both in content and in style, theology for the twenty-first century should, I believe, be kenotic—vulnerable, lowly, limited, self-emptying" (174). For McFague, kenotic love and humility ought to shape *how* we do theology. She continues, "I am less concerned here to be total, covering all issues, or systematic, doing so in an orderly fashion, than I am in being suggestive, invitational, and probing" (174).

36. To flesh out these themes, McFague is largely working from two recent works: Norman Russell's *The Doctrine of Deification in the Christian Tradition* (Oxford, UK: Oxford University Press, 2004) and Stephen Finlan and Vladimir Kharlamov, eds., *Theosis: Deification in Christian Theology* (Eugene, OR: Pickwick, 2006), as cited in *Blessed are the Consumers*, 188.

37. McFague, *Blessed Are the Consumers*, 33, 58.

38. McFague, *Blessed are the Consumers*, 19.

39. Throughout her works, McFague uses the term "neighbor" to include extra-human life. Rarely does she take the time to explain her reasoning for this extension; rather, it is often assumed. The best place to trace her human-world connection is in *The Body of God*, where she outlines the relational anthropology described above and links it to a hopeful ethic.

40. McFague, *Blessed are the Consumers*, 11.

41. Ibid., 56.

42. Ibid., 71.

43. There are exceptions to this, however. Catholic feminists Celia Deane-Drummond and Jean Porter, for example, read the Aristotelian virtue perspective through a feminist lens.

44. McFague, *Blessed Are the Consumers*, 129–135.

45. McFague, *Life Abundant: Rethinking Theology and Economy for a Planet in Peril* (Minneapolis: Fortress Press, 2001), 198.

46. McFague, *Life Abundant*, 198. It is noteworthy to highlight McFague's early use of the phrase "ecological reformation," a term now widely used in the wake of the 500th Anniversary of the Protestant Reformation. She uses it intentionally, calling to mind the role of active

resistance in the larger movement. So while from this stage in world history one can see how the Protestant Reformation focused too heavily upon the human person in salvation history, counter-cultural characteristics of the movement still appeal and apply to our contemporary context.

47. McFague, *A New Climate for Theology*, 138.

48. Wendell Berry, "Christianity and the Survival of Creation," in *Sex, Economy, Freedom & Community* (New York: Pantheon, 1992), 94.

49. Lawrence Buell goes so far as to suggest that Berry's writing is more emphatically creedal and denominational in manner than many other American environmental writers, such as Willa Cather, Henry Thoreau, John Muir, Robinson Jeffers, Ralph Waldo Emerson, and James Fenimore Cooper. See "Religion and the Environmental Imagination in American Literature," in *There before Us: Religion, Literature, and Culture from Emerson to Wendell Berry*, edited by Roger Lundin (Grand Rapids, MI: Eerdmans, 2007), 219.

50. Berry's critique of the historical application of the doctrine of vocation largely relates to the nature and purpose of work. In "The Gift of the Good Land," for example, Berry laments how Christianity has always emphasized the spiritual at the expense of the physical, thereby devaluing what he calls "earthy work" (See *The Gift of Good Land: Further Essays Cultural and Agricultural* (San Francisco, CA: North Point, 1981), 267. Over a decade later, Berry remarks, "If you are going to destroy creatures without respect, you will want to reduce them to 'materiality;' you will want to deny that there is spirit or truth in them, just as you will want to believe that the only holy creatures, the only creatures with souls, are humans—or even only Christian humans." (See "Christianity and the Survival of Creation" in *Sex, Economy, Freedom & Community*, 104). Criticisms of disembodied theology surface throughout the Port William fiction, particularly through the musings of young seminarian turned town barber, Jayber Crow, who often wondered why "Everything bad was laid on the body, and everything good was credited to the soul" (see *Jayber Crow* (Berkeley, CA: Counterpoint, 2000), 49). The essay "God and Country" also criticizes Christianity for its tacit approval of (and enmeshment with) capitalism. In Berry's opinion, the malformed ecology of capitalism misconstrues anthropology and cheapens the dignity of work (the essay is found in *What Are People For?* (San Francisco, CA: North Point, 1990)).

51. Taken from unpublished notes from a personal interview at the annual Au Sable Graduate Fellows retreat in Port Royal, KY, on January 20, 2014.

52. In his 2012 National Endowment for the Humanities Jefferson Lecture, Berry explicitly mentions these categories, suggesting that we give our affection to things that embody such principles rather than to things that are destructive, toxic and corrosive. "It All Turns on Affection," accessible at: http://www.neh.gov/about/awards/jefferson-lecture/wendell-e-berry-lecture (last accessed on June 3, 2015).

53. One of Berry's most theologically astute characters, Jayber Crow, makes similar remarks: "I saw the Bible as pretty much slanting upward until it got to Jesus, who forgave even the ones who were killing Him while they were killing Him, and then slanting down again when it got to St. Paul. I was truly moved by the stories of Jesus in the Gospels. I could imagine them. The Nativity in the Gospel of Luke and the Resurrection in the Gospel of John I could just shut my eyes and *see*. I could imagine everything until I got to the letters of Paul" (in *Jayber Crow*, 50).

54. This is in contrast to other American environmental writers, such as Barry Lopez, whose migratory stories paint a picture of elsewhere and aggressively address anthropocentrism more than the practiced ethics of place. See, for example, "Renegotiating the Contracts," in *This Incomperable Lande: A Book of American Nature Writing* (Boston: Houghton, 1989), 381–388.

55. Berry, "It All Turns on Affection."

56. Berry is critical of philanthropy or charity that has little to no relational connection to the receiving subject. Furthermore, he demonstrates the frequency with which charitable gifts are given from the proceeds of monies earned in harmful and unjust ways. To this end, he highlights James L. Duke, the philanthropic founder of Duke University, in "It All Turns on Affection." Berry argues that Duke, while undeniably financially generous, made his money on the backs of small tobacco farmers by monopolizing the markets and pigeonholing families into tenant farming contracts.

57. Wendell Berry, "Two Economies," in *Home Economics* (San Francisco, CA: North Point, 1987), 73–74.

58. Wendell Berry, "Healing," in *What Are People For* ? (San Francisco, CA: North Point, 1990), 9–10.

59. Wendell Berry, "The Agrarian Standard," in *The Essential Agrarian Reader, edited by Norman Wirzba,* (Louisville, KY: The University Press of Kentucky, 2003), 27. Here we see how Berry, like other agrarian thinkers, fundamentally rejects the reigning capitalist logic of "trade offs," wherein ecological integrity and the well-being of the poor are sacrificed for maximized economic growth. As Willis Jenkins explains in a recent chapter on economies of desire in *The Future of Ethics* (New York: Oxford University Press, 2014), on a whole, agrarianism is distinguished from the impoverishment wrought by globalizing capitalism. It denies the claim that human development must inevitably encroach upon ecology and exploit the poor. "Economic reasoning is not about making choices among rivalrous goods to maximize benefit," Jenkins summarizes, "but about cultivating forms of wealth that satisfy an entire membership. An economy could develop differently, producing habitat for others while producing food for humans. Economy should be the skillful art of blessing, not the dismal math of scarcity" (270).

60. Todd Edmondson, *Priest, Prophet and Pilgrim: Types and Distortions of Spiritual Vocation: The Fiction of Wendell Berry and Cormac McCarthy* (Eugene, OR: Pickwick Publications, 2014), 70.

61. Wendell Berry, "A Native Hill," in *Long-Legged Horse* (New York: Shoemaker & Hoard, 2004), 173–75.

62. In his "It All Turns on Affection" lecture, Berry is referencing Wallace Steger's *Where the Bluebird Sings to the Lemonade Springs* (New York: Random House, 1992), xxii, 4.

63. See the introduction of J. Matthew Bonzo and Michael R. Stevens's *Wendell Berry and the Cultivation of Life* (Grand Rapids, MI: Brazos Press, 2008).

64. Bonzo and Stevens, *Wendell Berry and the Cultivation of Life*, 143.

65. Wendell Berry, "The Wild Birds," in *That Distant Land: The Collected Stories* (Berkeley, CA: Counterpoint, 2007), 363.

66. Wendell Berry, *Remembering in Three Short Novels* (Berkeley, CA: Counterpoint, 2008), 137–140.

67. Wendell Berry, *Hannah Coulter* (Berkeley, CA: Counterpoint, 2004), 126.

68. Ibid., 128.

69. Ibid., 131.

70. Ibid., 201.

71. Wendell Berry, "A Jonquil for Mary Penn," in *That Distant Land*, 201.

72. Ibid., 201.

73. Berry, "It Wasn't Me," in *That Distant Land*, 284.

74. Ibid., 288.

75. Berry, *A Place on Earth* (Berkeley, CA: Counterpoint, 2001), 32.

76. Edmondson, *Priest, Prophet and Pilgrim*, 132.

77. Brent Laytham, "The Membership Includes the Dead: Wendell Berry's Port William Membership as Communio Sanctorum," in *Wendell Berry & Religion: Heaven's Earthly Life*, ed. Joel James Shuman and L. Roger Owens (Louisville: University Press of Kentucky, 2009), 174.

78. Berry, *Hannah Coulter*, 133–134.

79. Berry, *Jayber Crow*, 293.

Chapter Six

Ecology of Vocation

The Reclamation and Reformation of a Vital Protestant Doctrine

As evidenced in the work of Santmire, McFague, and Berry, interest in the Protestant doctrine of vocation has resurged in recent decades, correlating with renewed general interest in early Reformation thought. Yet, as I've argued throughout, very little scholarship pragmatically addresses *how* the doctrine of vocation proves promising in the formation and sustained practice of an eco-ethic and the ways the doctrine may need to be reformed.[1]

Due to the focus vocation brings to appropriate response to the action of God and neighbor on the self, the doctrine is an ecologically promising theological resource. And in so doing vocation speaks to the most pressing questions of our day: What is going on and how should we respond? The doctrine addresses the first because of its clear and fundamental connection to creation, which focuses on questions of origin, sin, providence, preservation, and future. But contrary to some historical readings of the Protestant doctrine of vocation, the doctrine doesn't speak to the realm of creation alone. Vocation addresses the second critical question by being tethered to concepts of redemption, which center upon themes of kenotic relationship, reparation, and restoration. As a lynchpin doctrine, vocation, holding space between creation and redemption respectively, speaks less about *doing* the right thing or *being* the right thing and more about *relating* in a right or appropriate fashion. For this reason, vocation must be recast as something far greater than work, as even "ethical" forms of work speak primarily to the realm of rule and underestimate the complex interrelationality of one's inhabited roles. This is also why vocation mustn't be understood as a romantic retreat from work, for many of the relationships we find ourselves inhabiting are forged as a direct result of our embodied day-to-day responsibilities.

Learning to respond "rightly" is the work of vocation, and this work is corporate and personal at once. It is corporate because as evident in ecosystems themselves, no individual exists without context or community. We depend upon communities of all kinds, human and natural, just as we likewise shape them. In the same manner, vocation is personal because communities exist and change as a result of individual identities and practices. We act upon one another as we are also acted upon and through our responses to all such action craft the porous, dynamic identities of one another. Ethical choices, then, speak to *how* we act upon one another, responsively, actively, and reflexively.[2] Therefore, if our personal and corporate vocation is to relate to God and neighbor "rightly" or "responsibly" we must ask, "How is this done?" Some past conceptions and applications of Christin vocation have answered this in part, and these aspects of vocation warrant retrieval. Others have failed to do so and continue to fall short in light of contemporary environmental challenges; here the Protestant doctrine of vocation requires reform.

RETRIEVAL: WHAT THE REFORMERS GAVE US

As discussed in chapter three, the early Reformers' revolutionary views on soteriology and ecclesiology radically changed the face of the pre-modern church. Luther and Calvin's grave perspectives on human anthropology coupled with their hope and trust in the ongoing generative presence of the Holy Spirit limited the role of human agency, particularly in the case of the priest, while yet extending the reach of all persons. To be sure, one of the most fruitful legacies of early Protestant thought is the "priesthood of all believers," which directly resulted in the democratization of calling, or the flatlining of vocational distinctions.

Vocation as Conscientiousness and Responsibility

A direct benefit of democratization was (and is) the valuation of all callings. In today's environmental context it is perhaps more apparent that the work of a responsible farmer is equally important to that of the environmental lawyer, the cumulative influence of a conscientious stay-at-home-parent as critical as a climate scientist's academic contributions. After all, we must *all* play our part. However, what remains underappreciated about the Reformers' revolutionary doctrine of vocation is its challenge to our very understanding of calling. Each and every one of us occupies multiple callings simultaneously. That parent isn't just a mom or dad; that lawyer isn't just a lawyer. There is, as it were, an actual ecology to our respective vocations. I, for example, am a mother, wife, daughter, teacher, writer, pastor, friend, citizen, and more. Opportunities arise to responsibly love God by seeing, acknowledging, and meeting the needs of the neighbor manifest in all of these roles, and often in interrelated ways. If by the power of the Spirit I am living conscientiously, I cannot help but recognize how the content of my study and what I explore within the walls of my classroom inform my domestic life and vice versa. The same could be said for how my civic engagement relates to personal and professional life. In both cases attention to the Reformers' democratization of vocation can lead me, and all of us, to consider how life might become too easily categorized, with aspects like work being separated from discipleship, citizenship from home life. When our various vocational capacities are removed one from another, calling is typically reduced to one role, most frequently monetized forms of work. And when roles are siloed the potential promulgation of structural injustice looms large. For example, many of the financial institutions Christians utilize individually and corporately (banks, hedge fund organizations, investment services, etc.) profit from the abuse of vulnerable communities and lands, and yet most of us entrust them with the hard-won earnings of our labor and the wellbeing of our domestic and professional lives. Little regard is paid to the ecology of our vocation, wherein one's role in the workplace and one's role as neighbor and ecological citizen are interrelated. Envisioning vocation in this light—as the relatedness between our respective vocational roles—promotes greater authenticity in our multifaceted lives and affords us more opportunity to live with an integrity that befits the Gospel.

Just as a retrieved doctrine of vocation can lead us to greater awareness, it can also lead us to greater responsibility, for if all callings are valuable and each person actively lives into many at one time, then all persons play a part in the establishment and preservation of the common good. Here the Apostle Paul's metaphor of the body is particularly applicable. The foot, the hand, ear, and eye are equally indispensable and therefore responsible in the functioning of the whole body. When one part proves weaker than another it is to receive more honor, not less, for the sake of the community. In Paul's words, "God has so composed the body, giving greater honor to the part that lacked it, that there may be no division in the body, but that the members may have the same care for one another. If one member suffers, all suffer together; if one member is honored, all rejoice together. Now you are the body of Christ and individually members of it" (1 Corinthians 12:25–27). This is not to say that all have been granted equal access to freely and fully live out vocation. Nor is it to say that culpability for inequities and injustice falls to all in the same manner. As shown in greater detail below, retribution and restitution remain real and important factors in contemporary quests for justice, particularly when considering matters of race, class, and gender, as in cases of environmental racism and climate debt for example. But it *is* to say that as a theological resource the democratization of vocation evokes us to take on responsibility individually and corporately and to recognize calling as a way of life which makes possible the thriving of the neighbor.

Vocation's Connection to Creation

A second invaluable implication of the early Protestant doctrine of vocation is its clear connection to creation. Linking calling to creation and redemption extenuates vocation's relationship to our ever-changing world and climate. As earth rapidly fluctuates, the needs of our other-than-human and human neighbors are drastically changing, calling for reciprocally flexible and responsive callings. These "new decalogues" reveal God's law afresh and lead us to more thoroughly consider the Holy Spirit's role than any rote appeal to divine command.

The connection to creation also underscores the interrelated nature of callings, both in the intrapersonal sense as discussed above, as well as in the interpersonal, for not only is our changing environment recasting our working sense of neighbor and therefore promoting novel concepts of vocation, but so too our respective vocations with the lifestyles they endorse and promote are changing the environment. In fact, we are changing more than our immediate environment, but also the scope and potential of other human vocations, including those of generations to come. Avoiding hyper-spiritualized notions of vocation and tethering vocation to creation as a form of *creatio continua* is critical, lest our ambitions of today eclipse the promises of those who shall come tomorrow.

Vocation as Embodiment

Such realities, while daunting, lead us to consider yet another positive of the Reformers' emphasis on creation-embedded vocation; namely, that all calling must take on an embodied form. As we've seen in the case of vocation as work, Enlightenment detachment of essence from substance leads to injustice in one way or another, be it vocation rendered as production with little regard for wholeness and sustainability, or vocation cast as privileged retreat without due appreciation for the necessary and mundane. However, when vocation is retrieved in fundamentally embodied ways it is linked to an actual place at an actual time, complete with all of the real-life consequences of relationship.

To say that vocation is the interrelatedness between myriad roles rather than any one said role doesn't consign vocation to the incorporeal or abstract. On the contrary, our bodies carry untold memory and expertise, often making physiological connections between experiences in one realm of life with another. Growing literature in affect theory, which speaks to how emotional states take on bodily responses, supports this.³ Recent study on trauma does the same, demonstrating how a devastating experience in one event or relationship can indirectly or directly shape the formation of future experiences and/or relationships, including one's relationship with the Divine.⁴ In tragic ways environmental racism as a form of environmental injustice also speaks to the embodied realities of interrelatedness. As Dorceta Taylor has documented, the "call" for people of color to labor in environmentally toxic work environments insidiously impacts nearly every facet of life. This is particularly so for women of color, whose callings to motherhood can be significantly altered due to exposure of toxins in the pre-natal weeks.⁵ Vocation is never solely about spiritual discernment and gift, as if the realm of the Spirit was so removed from the elements of the Sacred. For better or worse, vocation is received, executed, and confirmed in the fragility and viscerality of the human body.

CONTEMPORARY CRITIQUES OF LINKING VOCATION TO CREATION

For all of the aspects of the Protestant democratization of vocation worthy of retrieval, I would be remiss to overlook contemporary critiques of the Reformers' doctrine of vocation. As interest in the doctrine has mounted, many Protestants have voiced concern over the doctrine's historical connection to creation, a critical aspect if the doctrine of vocation is to remain a helpful theological resource in today's Anthropocene. Due to the perils of ascriptivism and dangers of inflated self-importance, thinkers like Karl Barth and more recently Miroslav Volf and Stanley Hauerwas, have sought to distance vocation from the doctrine of creation, theologically linking it instead to a revelatory Christology and unfolding pneumatology. Viewing calling as more a matter of being transformed despite worldly systems than participating in them, they have critiqued the notion of vocation as a means of co-creation, wherein human beings participate in God's *creatio continua*.

Karl Barth, for example, saw the Reformers as taking the division of labor in society for granted, hence subjecting any divine imperative of calling to such divisions.

> What about the superiority of the divine calling over all other prescribed stipulations of the human sphere of operation? Is not its freedom forfeited again if it must coincide ipso facto with the well-known limitation of a human station and vocation? . . . Ought not the divine calling and man's obedience necessarily entail the transformation and new definition and form of the sphere or operation?⁶

For Barth calling should be transformative because God's identity as Creator is inseparably related to God as Reconciler and Redeemer. The essence and act of God are one in the same for Barth, making any human ethic measurable in light of the Incarnation and the Holy Spirit's presence, not creation per se. As evidenced in his famous debate with friend and colleague Emil Brunner, Barth didn't think anything meaningful could be said about creation without the inclusion of Christology.[7] When cited as having subjected Christian ethics to a baptized variety of monism, limiting ethics to abstract concepts, Barth argued that a response to Christ always takes place at a particular time and in a particular place and as such proves to be a definite, concrete ethical event.[8] This is why for Barth a response to God's call has less to do with what one *ought* to do and more to do with what one *does*.

Miroslav Volf also focuses on such "freedom of obedience," as Barth put it, but goes a step further in firmly locating vocation within the pneumatological. It isn't that God calls us to fulfill roles within the orders of creation, but more so that God gives gifts (*charisms*) for the sake of the Christian community. By focusing on creation, Volf argues, Luther and his counterparts threatened to collapse internal vocation to the external, over-spiritualizing the alienation of much modern work and thereby rendering it meaningless for most.[9] Volf suggests a better translation of "call" in 1 Corinthians 7 attends to the moment *when* one is given a gift rather than focusing on *what* station one is called to. He asserts this is especially important in contemporary context, where persons are likely to have myriad careers throughout a lifespan, and possibly multiple jobs at any given time.

Stanley Hauerwas shares many of Volf's concerns and proposals. He too critiques vocation's connection to creation for the ways calling can then be valued as an end unto itself, or a means for glorifying God. It is the community aspect of vocation, he argues, that gives calling value, not its close connection with creation. In response to Pope John Paul's encyclical on work Hauerwas wrote, "We do not need to attribute ultimate significance to our work because we see how our work helps sustain the lives of other people. Moreover, we know that work can estrange as easily as it can unify—we therefore require a community whose unity can see us through the conflicts that our interaction in work can so easily entail."[10]

These concerns, while valid and helpful for the way they tease out essential differences between distinctively Christian and secularized conceptions of calling, do not nullify the overt benefits to linking calling to the natural world. Neither Luther nor Calvin placed vocation solely within the realm of creation, although such contemporary readings of their working doctrines suggest this was the case. As noted earlier, early Protestant renderings of vocation spanned the chasm between creation and redemption. This is why for Luther, all persons, no matter their spiritual identity, have a calling. It is also why some are said to have fused their external vocation with their spiritual one. While the early Reformers' bifurcation of Christian vocation brings with it risks of vocational hierarchy (recall Calvin's distinction between the pastor and the cobbler, for example), considering the explicitly external manifestations of vocation makes calling accessible to all. For the ways vocation has garnered secular value and purpose in recent decades, it seems that this more inclusive view of vocation is warranted and indeed helpful toward the aim of humans living out our shared planetary calling.

Critics of a creation-embedded doctrine of vocation also underestimate the manner in which the natural world has and is changing our very perceptions of calling. In chapter four I argued that modernity's emphases on individualism and industrialism altered Protestant understandings of vocation rather than any said "Protestant work ethic" leading to the rise of industrial capitalism. The same line of logic applies here. Biblical concepts of vocation have always been articulated within the realm of a particular, localized context. The most overt reference to calling in the New Testament is found in 1 Corinthians 7:20–24, where Paul reminds Christians to faithfully proclaim God from within whatever station they find themselves. The overarching concern of the passage is equality despite differences, a theological theme threaded throughout the epistle. In this instance, it isn't that Paul sought to apply some universal template of calling upon the Christians of Corinth, but rather that his commentary on calling arose amidst the realities within that first-century community. Here station is not a role reinforcing status quo, but neither is it simply a spiritual gift, as Volf would have us think. The myriad vocations to which Christians and others are called, which together comprise an ecology of vocation, do not exist *in spite* of environmental realities, or *alongside* such realities, but rather *because* of environmental realities. In their agrarian context of nobility and emergent nationalism, the Reformers understood this. And in our times, oddly characterized by both plutocracy and emergent populism, the Reformers' instinct to connect calling to the embodied realities of life on earth remains all the more critical.

HISTORICAL EMPHASES WORTH REVISITING

To revivify the Christian doctrine of vocation for ecological purposes, today's Church need not return solely to the voices of the Reformers, for as I began to demonstrate in chapter four some Protestants living during and after the Industrial Revolution were critical of the co-optation of vocation to the particular aim of work, and particularly inciting when it came to industrial capitalism's influence on Christian conceptions of work. Much of what Henry Hedge and Walter Rauschenbusch decried and renounced at the turn of the twentieth century applies yet today. These subversive voices of resistance emphasized the dignity of work, underscoring its importance for all, and related to this, linked social prosperity to ecological justice. Both of these emphases warrant greater attention in our contemporary Christian communities.

The Dignity of Work

Because today's common parlance equivocates vocation as work, we yet again pause to remember that earlier Christian conceptions were never restricted to the realm of work. Both the biblical texts and the work of the early Reformers articulate a much more expansive, integrated view of vocation. This understood, in the U.S. context, use of vocation as an ecologically promising theological resource requires extra attention to the workplace due to the gradual secularization of vocation and because of the central role work plays in contemporary family systems. In a general sense, Americans are obsessed with work, and some subcultures are more than others. As my international friends have helped me see, work is often core to our stated identities (i.e., someone asks, "Tell me about yourself" and the response is, "I work at such-and-such and am a . . ."), requires vast amounts of our time, and continues to be a political focal point in our larger civic debates.[11] This isn't to say that we've got it all wrong and work should simply matter less. In fact, as Rauschenbusch and others lead us to see in fresh view, work is a necessary and empowering aspect of life. The Christian need look no further than Christ's parables or Paul's warnings against idleness to glean such insight.[12] But in light of our changing workplaces and planet what hasn't been articulated well enough is *how* work ought to appropriately relate to the other aspects of one's vocation. In a very real sense work is useful insofar as it relates to some thing, a person, or a place; namely a relationship. In working one works on, for, or toward something and conducts such work in a particular location. From a distinctively Christian point of view the purpose of such work is not simply the product of such labor, but also the rest and revelry that follows the work. And this is why as an aspect of vocation work must always be linked to creation, for in a real sense we Christians work to rest in a manner resembling the God of the Priestly accounts, who creatively worked to ultimately enjoy the Sabbath fruits of labor. Work as we understand it today must not dwarf or occlude our other callings, such as being a restful presence to our families and children, listening to and responding to the land, and engaging and serving within our civic communities.

Nor must work eliminate the value of the individual from within the community. Just as the Social Gospel Movement positioned work within a larger framework so too it emphasized the self-possessed nature of work, how at its best work it is a necessary expression of self. This is to say, first of all, that work affirms some semblance of autonomy, or the ability to define and complete work according to one's own satisfaction. Here again, the creative work of the Divine serves as example. The world in all its mystery and splendor is created through the power of lyrical world, an expression *of* the Divine.

To express one's self in work is also to set personal parameters around time. The work of varied seasons and thresholds of life make for different needs around time, some more intensive and some less. Yet, much of modern industrialized work deprives us of naming and honoring this fluctuation by making a commodity of our time. Work as defined by the corporate clock rather than by an internal measure or the changing needs of a community easily becomes the all-too-familiar grind, drain, or mindless and purposeless treadmill. Writing now as a mother of young children, this element of dignified work seems particularly crucial. As an academic and clergyperson, I personally know of no one more effective with their time and faithful to their work than working moms. And yet, most women in my professional and personal circles fear judgement and/or demotion for the keeping of an alternative calendar. This anxiety is the residue of a narrow and antiquated view of vocation, one that reduced the complexity of vocation to the monetized work of today by overlooking and undervaluing the uncompensated long-game of parenthood. In my view, the Church will practically reform the doctrine of vocation and lift high the dignity of work if and when it listens well to the experience and expertise of women, and in suit freely follow our leadership.

In addition, self-expression as work values the process of production as much if not more than the product itself. Rather than being alienated from the final product as a mere cog in the larger wheel of production, subject to what Marx called "the abstraction of work," the self-expressive worker actively participates in the crafting or care of a product, thereby serving as an agent of creativity and change.[13] In light of contemporary environmental challenges, which illustrate well the devastating fallout from perennially detaching ecological realities from the process of production, this aspect of work proves particularly imperative.

Joy in work is yet another retrievable element of the Social Gospel Movement and twentieth-century resistance movements that followed. While finding joy in work is far from a modern ideal (Thomas Aquinas, who as we've discussed above, limited vocation in a way the Reformers would not, responded to the cloistered problem of *acedia* by suggesting that no joy in life could be found without joy in work), the need to recover it in our daily work remains a present and pressing issue.[14] It's urgent for two reasons. First, some measure of joy and fulfillment in work is a basic human need, without which the slow perishing of self is bound to take root. Secondly, as we shall discuss in greater detail below, fulfillment or contentedness in our work (a notable difference from defining joy as happiness) dialectically leads us to see and appreciate what has been given in the material world and otherwise, and can motivate us to preserve rather than exploit, keep rather than use, cherish rather than scorn. As Dorothee Sölle argued in her seminal book on work, "The task of theology is to uncover, to unmask, to critique the repressive tradition and to reveal the true meaning of human work and the identity of its agent, the worker. . . . We need to understand ourselves as co-creators who require constructive and joyful work in which we are challenged to develop our creative potential."[15]

Linking Social Justice with Ecological Justice

A second promising element of progressive twentieth-century views of vocation is the obvious link between social justice and ecological justice, a critical connection rarely recognized even in our current century. Prophetic leaders, like Rauschenbusch, related the natural world and its fecund resources to the ecology of vocation. He understood how the renewal of society necessarily required a renewed moral ecology of everyday life, wherein both the values and the output of work serve to reconcile human communities to a larger, shared biological one.

Faith leaders from communities of color have long led this raised consciousness, but particularly so since the terror of Jim Crow officially began to lift in 1964.[16] Some like the Rev. Dr. Martin Luther King explicitly called upon Rauschenbusch's thought. For example, the careful and astute reader will find elements of Rauschenbusch's thought emerge in King's final speech, "I've Been to the Mountaintop," delivered to the Memphis sanitation workers, who in April of 1968 invited King to join their strike in protest of the dangerous, toxic, and inequitable working conditions of black employees.

Since that time a great many faith communities in predominately communities of color began to blow the whistle on environmental racism, calling the church to respond to the needs of the neighbor in more holistic ways.[17] One such effort took place in Warren County, North Carolina, in the late 1970s-early 1980s. This watershed tale of environmental injustice illustrates themes and challenges similar to many other documented incidents of environmental racism, including the critical role of faith communities as resistors.

In the summer of 1978, Robert Burns and family of the Ward PCB Transformer Company of Raleigh, North Carolina, illegally, deliberately, and discretely dripped 31,000 gallons of PCB oil along 240 miles of state highway. Prior to 1979 polychlorinated biphenyls (PCBs) were widely used in the construction of electrical products, and when disposed improperly among organic materials, the PCBs were known to bioaccumulate in the food chain, resulting in highly toxic carcinogens that lead to the disruption of human hormones and low birth weights in pregnant women. Under the Toxic Substances Control Act of 1976 such contaminated soils were to be buried in dry-tomb toxic waste sites, like the one built in Warren County shortly thereafter. However, due to its proximity to the water table the tomb failed within months. In 1982, after numerous ineffective quick-fixes were made to the tomb, the EPA reinstated the dumping of contaminated soil in Warren County and for over six weeks those driving the roughly 10,000 trucks of PCB soil were met by black bodies strewn in protest across the road. Hundreds were arrested, mostly black women from churches in Afton, a nearby poor and predominately African American town. Unfortunately, the dumping continued until 1993 with little to no publically-disseminated information regarding PCBs long-term effect on public health, when the Governor finally guaranteed landfill clean-up, a promise that took another decade to fulfill. To this day no reparations have been made to the residents of Warren County or to their kin.

Stories like this led other faith-based groups to begin connecting the dots between social and ecological justice. In 1986 the United Church of Christ responded to its shared, corporate calling by financing the Commission for Racial Justice's investigation into other examples of environmental injustice. The report was published a year later; "Toxic Wastes and Race in the United States" was the first national study to correlate waste facility sites and demographics. Among other disturbing findings, the study found race to be the most likely variable in predicting where waste facilities would be placed, particularly those facilities housing toxic materials.

In large measure, this document and the vocational faithfulness of a few to heed the need of the neighbor in real, embodied ways led to the First National People of Color Environmental Leadership Summit in 1991. For four days faith leaders partnered with community activists from all fifty states and Puerto Rico to discuss how environmental realities relate to matters such as public health, worker safety, land use, transportation, housing, resource allocation, and community empowerment. The Summit resulted in the crafting of the *17 Principles of Environmental Justice*, a resource now considered to be the founding document of the contemporary environmental justice (EJ) movement in the United States. While not a theological document per se, the *Principles* lift up religious underpinnings of the EJ movement.[18] For example, the preamble articulates a desire to re-establish a "spiritual interdependence to the sacredness of our Mother Earth" while promoting "economic alternatives which would contribute to the development of environmentally safe livelihoods;" and, to secure "political, economic and cultural liberation that has been denied for over five hundred years of colonization and oppression, resulting in the poisoning of our communities and land and the genocide of our peoples." At numerous points, the *Principles* reference vocation, as defined in the integrated fashion articulated here. To this end, the document speaks to the environmental rights of all workers, who have a right to a "safe and healthy work environment, without being forced to choose between an unsafe livelihood and unemployment." It also affirms the rights of those whose primary vocation is enacted in the home, to "be free from environmental hazards." The document identifies the vocation of citizenship as central, noting the importance of education and the need for all persons to "participate as equal partners at every level of decision-making including needs assessment, planning, implementation, enforcement and evaluation."

Interestingly, much of this language is mirrored in President Bill Clinton's later 1994 Executive Order on Federal Actions to Address Environmental Justice in Minority Populations and Low Income Populations (E.O 12898).[19] And when the executive order was honored and celebrated by President Barack Obama on its twentieth anniversary in 2014, the act was said to have emerged from the leadership of activists who "took on environmental challenges long before the Federal Government acknowledged their needs." In his remarks on our contemporary challenges, President Obama himself evokes the language of calling, "We remember how Americans—young and old, on college campuses and in courtrooms, in our neighborhoods and through our places of worship—called on a Nation to pursue clean air, water, and land for all people. On this anniversary, let us move forward with the same unity, energy, and passion to live up to the promise that here in America, no matter who you are or where you come from, you can pursue your dreams in a safe and just environment."[20] As Rauschenbusch reflected roughly one hundred years prior, we all have individual and social callings and both are as inextricably bound up with the biological world that we inhabit as they are with one another. The biological is personal and the personal necessarily political.

REFORMING THE PROTESTANT DOCTRINE OF VOCATION

The intuition and foresight of thinkers like Rauschenbusch, King, the women of Warren County, and the delegates of the 1991 National People of Color Environmental Leadership Summit leads to a second major question of consideration: How ought the Protestant doctrine of vocation be reformed? Put otherwise, what new questions must Christians ask when discerning and acting upon calling?

In order for the doctrine of vocation to be an effective eco-ethical resource, the remediation of increasingly secularized renderings of callings is needed. It must be clear how the distinctively Christian concept of vocation differs from secular ideas of calling and why the Christian is particularly called to care for the earth in and through the interconnectedness of vocational roles. A quest for such answers requires the utilization of the Scriptures, tradition, and a variety of other disciplines toward the aim of what H. Richard Niebuhr called "objective relationalism." Related to this, contemporary conceptions of vocation must practically address the necessary steps to enact and measure vocation.

Reclaiming Distinctively Christian Concepts of Calling

In chapter 4, I outlined the historical factors leading to the cooptation of calling and the eventual whittling down of vocation to the particular aim of work. I described the philosophical, theological, and industrial factors leading to such theological anemia and demonstrated why it remains so pervasive today. We need only recall the very recent use of the term "Voc-Tech schools" or consider how university and college centers for vocation measure success by the percentage of graduates finding employment to testify to this effect. Even the term's common use in our newspapers, podcasts, and newsreels calls upon this limited and misinformed view of vocation.

This dyed-in-the-wool understanding must be eradicated for many reasons, not least of all for the ways it has artificially disconnected work from the living world upon which we all depend. To the Christian, this disunion should be particularly concerning, given the Gospel's dictum to be "salt and light in the world." Given Christian understandings of the Spirit's diffuse presence in the world through the church, work can never be "just work," but rather another place to respond to God and neighbor. Likewise, vocation can never be about the tasks of work alone, for the Christian brings their whole self—which, to call upon the binaries of the New Testament, like Christ is simultaneously body and spirit in the undertaking of any specific task.

Although Millennials and Generation Z are increasingly characterized by a decided lack of connection to any formal religious entity (i.e., the None generation, as in no religious affiliation), few would likely qualify vocation in such a disembodied way. New data on young adults suggests twenty-somethings and those in their young thirties are envisaging and recrafting work. As corporate coach Jerry Colonna indicates, such young adults see what a bifurcated life has cost their baby-boomer parents and want little to do with it.[21] When the young workforce clocks in, they're not content to simply check at the door their lives as activists, parents, and spiritual-seeking people, to "let work be work." Instead, they're requiring that such aspects of their lives, or what I would call vocational roles, influence the work itself as an interconnected aspect of it. From this vantage, a reformation of vocation ought to exhibit a concerted effort to rid ourselves and our communities of stymied definitions of calling while also opening ourselves to new ways of knowing and being. In the context of faith communities, be they churches, academic institutions, or non-profits, leaders will do well to listen to and learn from the young, even as we return afresh to the voices of old. Vocation is the connectedness of our lived realities, which take place in bodies marked by race, gender, a spectrum of ability, and age.

But lest I present too optimistic a view of contemporary secular conceptions of vocation, another competing view bears mentioning—that of vocation as self-discovery. One need only visit the self-help section of the library or local bookstore to witness the lure of a rife contemporary mantra, "be your best self." Titles on finding one's purpose and calling in life package the doctrine of vocation as product, something to find in punctiliar time and assume for one's own ends. We are often encouraged to shop for a vocation, paying particular attention to what makes us "sing" or brings to us and for us the greatest happiness. And when we think we've found it, fleeting though it may be, we're encouraged to consume it by narrowly focusing our attention upon that one path and pursuing it without abandon. Some call this "finding one's passion." But because this self-absorbed conception of vocation focuses little on responding to the action of God or the realities of the neighbor, it typically proves isolating and unfulfilling. When one conceives of vocation in this way, the end result is very often another trip to the same Barnes & Noble aisle with the aim of trying on another idea, and ultimately a hyper-individualized life built on little more than shifting sand of whim and the next-best-thing.[22]

Even more nuanced conceptions of vocation as the intersection of one's passions with the needs of world smack of prevalent cultural narcissism in the way that they frequently prioritize the consideration of self and grossly miscalculate the actual and dynamic needs of the neighbor. Extreme versions of this rendering include the all-too-familiar white savior complex notable in the history of Christian missiology; for example, wherein one (usually the white man backed by colonial power) shares the entanglement of both his expertise and his Gospel with the "savage" who asked neither for the help nor the enculturation. However, more subtle and insidious versions of this passion-meets-need reading of vocation also exist in liberal, Protestant circles, which often proudly characterize service in contrast to such problematic evangelical approaches. Take, for example, the accompaniment model of missions within my denominational home, the Evangelical Lutheran Church of America (ELCA). Until recently, this missiological approach emphasized the need for a missionary to come alongside rather than to lead, to share one's passions with others as needed and when appropriate. What it didn't highlight was the mutuality between church leaders and their global companions, or how the very passions of the missionary might be formed by the community they've come to serve. Indeed, any time vocation is conceptualized as the individual becoming some kind of benefactor, even if the most humble of sort, the radical divine gift of vocation is lost.

The Reformers insisted that in matters of faith it is Christ who comes to us rather than we who come to Christ. Christian vocation is ultimately a response to the promises of God, made through the action of God, and the action of the neighbor upon the self.[23] Vocation is received and lived out in and through relationship, not individually discovered and then executed by way of relationship. Cast in this light, calling is fundamentally connected to the Gospel. In Einar Billing's words, "My call is the form my life takes according to how God himself organizes it for me though his forgiving grace."[24] Christian vocation doesn't solely emerge from the demands of every new age or even the desires of one's heart, but instead in one's pursuit of God through them and sometimes in spite of them.

Therefore, the clear connection between vocation and redemption is grounds for resisting and reforming authority, particularly within the realm of work. Through the salvific act of Christ and the power of the Spirit, we can be conformed to Christ. This is not by imitating Christ or more perfectly emulating him, but rather by receiving his gift and his power. Faith is gifted; vocation is endowed. These gifts, together a promise, mark Christian identity. Living into such an identify affords Christians the opportunity to rebrand vocational authority. The power one occupies in a vocation has less to do with domination or even leadership than it does responsive service, and likewise vocational recognition less to do with public accolade than spiritual fulfillment. The result is a more expansive view of vocation which necessarily includes the unsexy roles many—and particularly women—occupy (caregiver, parent, volunteer, housemaker, tenant of the land, etc.).

Not only does the link between vocation and redemption lift up the legitimacy of a great many "hidden" vocations, but it also helps Christians distinguish calling from coaxing. The Reformers also insisted on this. Not all jobs or tasks are callings; not all work is counted as such on Christian grounds. Indeed, many jobs undermine the radical message of the Gospel, as evidenced by the first-century Jewish community's discourse in the book of James and the Reformers' later diatribes on usury, human trafficking, the mistreatment of animals, and more. Yet, so much of contemporary jargon surrounding vocation pushes us to "make our lives count for something," to pursue the exceptional, the original, the "important," even if it entails unjust means toward some perceived righteous end. Here the words of a missionary whose multivalent vocation was formed by his community ring true. William Schweitzer notes,

> Only a person who can find a value in every sort of activity and devote himself to each one with full consciousness of duty, has the inward right to take as his object some extraordinary activity instead of that which falls naturally to his lot. Only someone who feels his preference to be a matter of course, not something out of the ordinary, and who has no thought of heroism, but just recognizes a duty undertaken with sober enthusiasm, is capable of becoming a spiritual adventurer such as the world needs. There are no heroes of action: only heroes of renunciation and suffering, and of such there are plenty. But few of them are known, and even these not to the crowd, but to the few.[25]

Because Christian calling is discerned and acted upon within the mundane, it is itself a spiritual act of renunciation, of resistance.[26] This implies the resistance of notoriety on the one hand, but also the resistance of certain forms of work. To have full consciousness of duty, as Schweitzer puts it, necessarily requires the Christian to decline work affiliated with decided environmental harm and related structural systems of social injustice. Christian communities and individuals seeking to remain faithful to the Scriptures and Christian witness must re-envision work, keeping eco-social concerns near the fore of deliberation.

Inspirational to People and Communities

But is this realistic and pragmatic? I return again to the question posed by Rev. Dr. Leah Schade in the introduction: is it reasonable to expect Christians to choose an ecologically-mindful calling over economic gain when cultural tides emphasize the latter and when, for many, a job is necessary for survival? Does the concept of biblical vocation still wield enough influence among Protestants to enact resistance against cultural norms and the provision for newly envisioned work opportunities? For, while conceptual clarity is necessary, it alone does not suffice. As Larry Rasmussen's work remind us, what matters are not good ideas, critical though they be, but good communities.[27]

Like Rev. Dr. Shade's parishioner, who despite earning long-awaited financial comfort left his job with a fracking company, some within our Christian communities demonstrate the depth of character to deny themselves security and forgo the pleasures of affluence (or in this instance, just plain sustenance!) in faithful response to God's call upon their lives. And indeed all of us ought to, for this is the heart of discipleship. Yet, if we're honest, most of us lead a bargaining life akin to the Gospel writer's rich young ruler, hoping to honor God while yet pleasing our families and ourselves with the comforts and security of monetary goods. We straddle sustainability but consume at the same rate and in the same manner we always have. Some justify working where the money is by giving more. We promise ourselves we'll compromise for a season, only to find ourselves replaying the same complacent narratives decades down the road, often incarcerated by the golden cuffs and bars of affluence. These failures are the result of vocation cast as disembodied, modern individualism rather than a deeply interconnected response to God and neighbor.

Interestingly, a good deal of contemporary anthropological and sociological research indicates that beyond financial security, authentic community is what most of us actually desire and value. Brené Brown's research and bestselling works on shame and vulnerability showcase this by demonstrating the adult need to live "with courage, purpose, and connection," which necessarily requires "taking off the armor we use to protect ourselves, putting down the weapons that we use to keep people at a distance, showing up, and letting ourselves be seen."[28] In theological terms, Miroslav Volf's recent work with the Yale's Happiness Project and research on thriving articulates similar findings, noting the role relationship plays in the cultivated art of living, as opposed to what some contemporary philosophers call instrumental rationality, or the ability to accomplish tasks with no attention to ends.[29] We are motivated by our need to be seen and loved, and we're particularly satisfied when we're granted opportunities to recognize how our strengths and abilities benefit others. And even if subconsciously, such data suggests we're also strengthened in knowing how our weaknesses and liabilities might be supplemented or met by the neighbor. To traffic as a useful concept in today's context, individualistic renderings of vocation must be thrown off and replaced with the generative messiness of interrelatedness.

The good news is that we're already familiar with the mess; even the most solitary among us. We encounter the messiness of relationship in our families and workplaces, through the impact of markets and big weather, and in the vanishing species or face of the climate refugee. And at their best, our communities have the qualities of a safe haven, sacred places open to creative risk. *This* is what Protestant communities must continually strive to be, adaptive networks where it is possible to imagine the world as it might be and reorder possibilities for new and renewed practices. Ecological vocation as realized in such communities then becomes less of a response to what is and more a posture or way of life. Through the many roles one inhabits, the ecology of vocation is an anticipation of need, emerging through the accumulation of numerous small-scale efforts and changes.[30] Collectively such efforts, such fulfillment of calling, can amount to a cultural tipping point where bioregional values and practices make possible the transnational impact sorely needed in this anthropocenic era.[31] How one responds to the needs of the *actual* neighbor, human or otherwise, in *actual* time and space *actually* affects our global realities. Why? Because we belong to each other. Our very identities are comprised by the relationship of our responses to the action of God and neighbor upon us.

The remainder of this book will address such small-scale efforts to get at our pressing question—how might Protestant communities practically understand vocation, and how might the impact of Christian calling be measured?

VOCATION AS RESPONSIBILITY AND PRACTICAL VIRTUE

Because the many realms of one's life comprise the ecology of vocation, the doctrine has the potential to address complex environmental realities on the household, organizational, and political level. That is, with practice. Linking vocation with the development and practice of the virtues is one of the most practical ways to enact vocation. This is not because good human habits guarantee the earth will flourish, nor is it for the ways virtues can help communities and individuals cope with anthropogenic despair, although some certainly can. Rather, reified traditions of virtue reinvent possibilities of moral agency and provoke our Christian communities to reconsider what a called life might look like on a planet in peril.[32] As discussed in chapter 2, realities like climate change present tremendous challenges to our inherited moral systems because they organize around discrete acts of harm, when in reality moral agency is increasingly ambiguous. This is why limiting ethical foci to right behavior or compliance with a certain set of rules falls short. By contrast, rendering Christian responsibility as the cultivation of virtues speaks to the individual insofar as virtue redefines the goods that enable a person to flourish and fulfill calling. And, as Michael Doan has helpfully noted, appeals to virtue also make clear why individuals remain complacent or fail to do what they should. Understood within the framework of motivational vices, moral inertia is more easily exposed and addressed.[33]

Practically reading vocation as the development and practice of virtue also speaks to structural and corporate matters by clarifying the habits necessary for global humanity to act more responsibly. For even when vice leads to the corrosion and failure of entire institutions, responsibility yet falls to communities of individuals, either to "solve the problems themselves, or if this is not possible, to create new institutions to do the job."[34] In this way, virtue underscores responsibility and provides an account for how individual practices and habits contribute to collective action.

To categorize some practical ways vocation is lived out on these levels I return to the insights of Santmire, McFague, and Berry. Their contemporary reflections on vocation point to three major virtues capable of tempering calling: humility, restraint, and wisdom. And to these I add justice and the theological virtue of hope, as decidedly Christian vocation must always tend to the manner of one's relationship with the neighbor and center itself in the promises of God. When practiced these five virtues carry with them respective fruits such as biodiversity, accountability, sufficiency, gratitude, and equity.

Humility in Interrelatedness

For humans the word calling immediately evokes a related task, listening. Practically speaking, religious vocation is first and foremost the act of listening for and discerning the voice of God. And if ecological vocation is understood within the context of a radical theocentrism listening to the land becomes integral to the fulfillment of calling.[35] As Santmire's work underscores, listening begins with the realization that our role as co-creative beings is not more valuable than the unfolding creative nature of other life forms, but rather is grounded in an embodied realization of our dependent nature. As earthen beings, we belong to each other and to earth; we're called to share *koinonia* with all of life.

Related to a humility rooted and discovered through an awareness of dependency lies a call to be people of a place. Just as we find ourselves living in a particular point in history, so too we all inhabit particular locales and spaces. The vocational nature of a Christian anthropology that seeks to responsibly situate one's love of self in relationship to God and others must attend to these particulars and respond accordingly. In my St. Paul, Minnesota home, for example, salty winter runoff from interstates and highways has reduced the presence of ditch clover, thereby undermining systems of pollination throughout the entire state of Minnesota. In addition to driving less and reducing the use of ice salts, this localized problem can be addressed in my own yard, for when natural clover, often viewed as petulance and sprayed or cut away, is left to grow, regional birds and bees and the ecosystems they support, thrive.[36] For me at this place and at this time, part of what it means to be human is to partner with pollinators. That is, the moral nature of our anthropologies must adopt an adaptive ethic beginning with local experience while not being limited to it. To live out vocation, we must hear what our place has to say and respond in the most considerate and conserving manner.

The practical fruits of realized humility in interrelatedness are many. First, conscious dependence upon other life forms met with a modest view of self promotes the environmental principle of biodiversity, which manifests in virtues of respect and receptivity. These virtues practically address the deficient vices of conceit and self-sufficiency on the one hand and excessive vices of addiction to overuse on the other.[37] Secondly, as Christians draw deeper into a calling of interrelatedness, more intimacy and solidarity among humans and other-than-humans is possible. In this case, our motivation to care for the natural world stems from something deeper than the need to self-sustain and becomes more of a posture of reciprocity. As the earth abundantly gives to us, we as biological consumers give what we can by standing with the earth in its evolving need. It is our affection for the land that makes possible our willingness to suffer along with it. And as McFague clarifies, we don't suffer with creation because such love provides a supernatural remedy; rather, we love in and through suffering for the ways it provides supernatural purpose. Like any healthy relationship, intimacy requires attentiveness and sacrifice. And the more this intimacy is fostered the greater accountability we will have within our communities, making it increasingly difficult to disassociate one's own experience or particular community from the wellbeing of the biotic community at large.

Restraint

A second quality of fulfilled Christian vocation is restraint, as characterized by refrain, resistance, and rebuilding. And here again vocation proves anything but novel, for the concept of living within one's creaturely limits is an ancient one. This is likely due in part to the premodern realities of daily life, which regularly reminded humans of their fragility and dependence upon the earth. Ancient communities ascribed the comings and goings of the natural world to the Divine. As outlined in chapter 4, there were ample problems with such pre-modern, theocentric views, which led to more recent quests for divine-like power over nature, through mechanical, technological, and biological means. This shift reflects a slow and gradual change of attitude, one where humans became God's equal, or rival, able to destroy the natural world just as God had created it. It is an attitude yet familiar to us today, a problem of "becoming creators," as Wendell Berry puts it, where "we have felt ourselves greatly magnified." So why, Berry and others ask, "should one get excited about a mountain when one can see almost as far from the top of a building, much farther from an airplane, farther still from a space capsule?"[38] In other words, why practice the virtue of restraint over and above intervention, enhancement, or change?

As a growing number of ecological exegetes have uncovered and emphasized, the Scriptures are replete with imperatives to let creation be and to enjoy it for what it is. In fact, when it comes to human encounters with the earth and its lifeforms, a great deal more is said about restraint and a letting be than about intervention.[39] Not only is our human liberty curbed by our limitations as creatures, as the ancients understood, but also by our calling to see creation as fundamentally good in and of itself. Lifestyles characterized by restraint are born out of this perspective and put into practice through the habitual practice of repentance. We seek to use only what we need because in humility we are reminded of the effects of greed. We refrain from exploitation of the earth's resources because the practice of the virtues puts us into closer relations with other-than-human life. We protest against the ubiquitous messages of materialism and consumerism because Christ modeled a radical alternative. And we cooperate with the good, finding pleasure in the beauty and honor of simple things. In short, when one seeks to mindfully tend to the ecology of vocation, the fruit of restraint is less an occasional lifestyle option and more so a way of life, characterized by gratitude and contentedness.

In classical virtue theory, restraint is commonly regarded as impulse control, wherein temperance protects the integrity of the soul. And while abstinence of many kinds remains an aspect of Christian vocation, the doctrine's emphasis on the self as fundamentally related to the neighbor also requires a more communal and active practice, resistance.[40] The cultivation of restraint calls for enjoyment just as much as it does detachment, the act of having just as much as abstaining. To this end, Medieval understandings of temperance have merit yet today, as the "habit of being consistently moved and pleased in a beautiful and honorable manner by attractive objects of sense experience."[41] Of course the key word here is "honorable," which speaks to the connection between restraint and resistance. When structures, be they economic, political, or material, dishonor life they are not only to be avoided; they are to be actively resisted.

Out of resistance new forms of life and possibilities emerge. As a form of denial, the practice of restraint exposes our greed and carelessness and prompts us to respond in repentance. As a form of resistance, restraint can redirect our energies toward the sustainable pleasure of creation. When we practice it, we grow in our ability to enjoy what we *do* have and become increasingly attuned to what God has done and is doing in creation. It is in this act that we learn to find tranquility and joy in creation, cooperate with the good and work to preserve the beauty and honor of the other-than-human world.

In recent decades, literature from many disciplines has explored the connection between human flourishing and nature-connectedness, or the working Biophilia Hypothesis, which suggests humans have evolved with an innate tendency to affiliate with other forms of life. In places where the relentless pursuit of wealth, beyond modest income levels, and its close relative consumerism are prevalent, happiness is waning if not altogether diminished.[42] In environments where people are increasingly detached from the land or the outdoors, depression and anxiety are on the rise.[43] Some studies now show children with limited access to nature and the outdoors suffer from Nature Deficit Disorder, an unclassified behavioral or emotional disorder that effects neurological and biological functioning.[44] Keeping such emergent research in mind, a logical positive outcome of vocation lived out as restraint is the gained sense of sufficiency and the immeasurable contentedness one is likely to experience as a result.

But for the Christian, contentedness lies beyond the psychological benefits of caring for creation. In the Scriptures, contentedness has everything to do with hiding oneself in God, relying not on the circumstances of life, but instead upon God's promises despite them. Therefore, when the Christian adopts a mindset of service to creation and enacts this perspective by means of abstinence and resistance, they are recognizing God's creative act in all of its complexity and are participating in nothing short of worship.

Wisdom

To practice interrelatedness and restraint requires a certain level of discernment, or what might more theologically be considered wisdom. Wisdom has long been hailed the most excellent of the acquired virtues for the way it directs all other moral virtues and provides the measure that all virtues are to attain.[45] In more modern times, wisdom has been reduced to the concept of reason, despite much more expansive definitions in ancient thought. Much of Greek thought, for example, saw wisdom as an innate ability of the human soul, a sort of "divine spark," which provided life with purpose and meaning. As a natural propensity it required practical application, hence Aristotle's emphasis on *phronesis*. The more a person put wisdom to practice, the more likely it was to grow. Hence, it wasn't merely that one needed to gain more knowledge to be wise, but rather that one had to gain a richer and greater sense of purpose and meaning to become wise, which was itself cyclically connected to the procurement of wisdom. Certainly Christians seeking to fulfill God's call upon their lives are summoned to both knowledge and a growing sense of purpose. To do so, we must remain well informed about the violent consequences of our consumptive habits and the resulting climate impacts. More than this, we need to allow such information to inform and reshape our individual and corporate desires. Simply having more information about our environmental problems doesn't lead to greater knowledge on how we might respond, just as knowing something about the neighbor doesn't equate to responding to their need. Wisdom is the link between the two, and growth in wisdom requires purpose and practice.

The biblical texts, while in many ways harmonious with Greek thought, depict wisdom as a gift more than an inclination.[46] The Hebrew Bible paints an even bolder picture, with wisdom personified as the bearer of life itself. Wisdom is the midwife working with those in pain to bring about new creation (Psalm 22:9–10). She is the One knitting life together (Psalm 139). Here the connection between wisdom and creation is overt, particularly with regards to God's presence within creation, and is easily connected to the person of Jesus. As Franciscan scholar Denis Edwards makes clear, Christ took on flesh not merely to save, but also to reveal more about creation.[47] Wisdom, therefore, is available through any and every creature, as all are self-expressions of Christ as wisdom. Practically addressing the created world as a manifestation of Christ is yet another specific way to fulfill Christian vocation. This perspective has the force to prophetically change our teaching and preaching and presents the germinal power to radically redefine our liturgies and worship.[48]

The fruits of wisdom need not be as clearly articulated as those of interrelatedness or restraint, for who can deny the clear benefits of increased knowledge or sense of purpose? Yet, perhaps an overlooked fruit of gained wisdom is its essential ingredient of increased self-actualization. Considering vocation to be the pursuit of wisdom prompts the Christian to pay more careful attention to their views of nature as well as their demands of it, and with skill and good judgment discipline their relations with the natural world. For most of us putting wisdom to work and seeking to increase it constitutes a major shift in consciousness. We need to rethink the ways we eat, work, transport, and educate ourselves. In the words of many environmental activists, it demands that we change everything about the way we live on this planet.[49]

Justice

Conceivably the three virtues just mentioned could be practiced individually, although I've argued our very understanding and habitual practice of humility, restraint, and wisdom cannot be reified apart from community. Nevertheless, the practice of justice is different; it necessarily functions socially. Classically understood as the constant and perpetual will to give everyone that which is due them—*justitia est constans et pertetua voluntas just suum unicuique tribuendi*—justice speaks to the appropriate relationship between self and neighbor in the pursuit of calling. But as aforementioned complications of moral agency in the Anthropocene make clear, simple application of the Golden Rule falls short. When seemingly inexorable problems like climate change present as intergenerational challenges, we cannot simply frame our ecological actions in terms of the other who is present here and now. Nor can those of us from places of privilege in the North American context realistically consider what we would desire "done unto us" from our positions of power and affluence. As Jürgen Moltmann has rightly observed, justice in contemporary context must extend beyond distributive justice to more decidedly emphasize the security of law in a restorative way. To fulfill calling as justice, then, requires a keen and honest desire to listen and respond to the voice of victims rather than an effort to expiate ourselves as perpetrators. This kind of justice, "embraces all aspects of saving and having compassion, helping and healing, justifying and putting right. It is not confined to human beings but actually applies first to the earth, with which human beings live and suffer."[50] And Protestantism doesn't present a particularly helpful track record here. Theological emphases on grace and justification have readily lent themselves to a focus on the sinner rather than upon justice for the victim. Yet the Scriptures, and indeed Christ himself, provide critical resources for reorientation, as justice is most powerfully demonstrated in Christ who takes on the weight of the perpetrator, yes, but *while* dwelling among the powerless and the weak.

A favorite passage of mine, the calling of Matthew Levi, illustrates this practice well. What I take to be an individual who is both "up" and "out," Matthew lives excluded from virtually every community in which he finds himself. He is a Jew, but not a ritually clean one given his professional association with imperial Rome and frequent exposure to those outside the Temple sect. He was likely a well-to-do tax collector, but because of his religious heritage and affiliation not entirely at home in this fold either. Indeed, the text gives us good reason to view Matthew as a perpetrator, one who endorsed and promulgated an unjust economic system that afflicted the Jewish majority in concrete and devastating ways. Perhaps this is why the Pharisees so self-righteously inquire of Jesus' disciples, "Why does your teacher eat with such tax collectors and sinners?" (Matthew 9:11). Speaking to the transformative power of relationship with Christ, Jesus himself provides the answer: "It is not the healthy who need a doctor, but the sick. But go and learn what this means: 'I desire mercy, not sacrifice.' For I have not come to call the righteous, but sinners" (9:12–13). Here, justice is enacted through Christ's solidarity with the perpetrator, with Matthew and the bad company he keeps, but in its context the lesson of Matthew's calling doesn't stop there. Later in the narrative we read of Matthew's work with Jesus among the most vulnerable, those "harassed and helpless, like sheep without a shepherd" (9:36). Matthew's calling is not only a narrative of personal repentance and requital, but also a powerful example of *justitia justificans*, or the justifying justice that prioritizes and focuses upon the experience of victims. It is to this ministry that Matthew is called.

For calling to be understood in this manner, contemporary Protestants must first recognize the suffering of victims and the role of personal guilt. And by guilt I don't mean shame, but rather a clear sense of misappropriated moral agency. For some, this has meant a lack of action. For others, it's the wrong action. For most of us, it is both. To enact vocation as justice requires that one see and understand the difference, repent, and work toward restitution by relying upon the long memories of victims (as opposed to the short memories of perpetrators).[51] As we consider our collective calling and the vocation of today's church, key questions emerge. Their answers are indicative of how the enactment of Christian vocation might be measured. First, are our faith communities prioritizing hearing the voices of the global poor, who are most impacted by problems like climate change? And secondly, how are our communities, shared experiences of worship, and curricula encouraging true repentance for the explicit and complicit ways we harm our human and other-than-human neighbors?

Here, I want to say a word about repentance, the second step of enacting vocation as justice. In the socially progressive Protestant contexts I frequent, the concept of turning-from-one's-sin is often shortlisted as legalism, or a harkening back to constrictive ideas of what it means to be a Christian in society. As the trope goes, in light of grace who's to say what sin is anyway? Cheap grace abounds. And when it does, disproportionate damage is done to and within the human and biotic communities already living in harm's way. For the cultivation of justice to be a decided aim of Christian vocation, the work of self-awareness is paramount. As H. Richard Niebuhr helps us see, the self is always impacted by the action of God and neighbor, making the journey of self-awareness an ongoing one. But keen attention to the impact of the self on the neighbor is particularly needful in contexts where privilege is frequently ignored or underplayed, like that of my own faith community, which purportedly attends to injustices of many kinds and yet remains 98 percent white, affluent by any comparative standard, and split many times over by debates on the role of women and LGBTQI in leadership.[52] Seeing injustice is one thing, but reckoning with the ways we ourselves aid it is quite another. Christian vocation, then, necessarily includes a deep, sustained interrogation of the ways one lives at the expense of the earth and the marginalized communities the earth supports. It is a reorientation of consciousness with an eye toward the wellspring of all life.

And finally, when in and through repentance Christian vocation fuels the individual and collective power to eliminate bringing about further damage to our communities, the practice of justice requires restitution. Vocation that is centered upon *satisfactio operum*, compensation through something performed, fixates upon matters of mending, restoring, and creatively re-creating. It is a calling that, like Matthew's, begins with God's grace, but then moves outward toward radical and countercultural compassion (literally "to be broken with"), or solidarity with the victim, be they personal, creaturely, or inanimate.

Hope

But how does this happen? What of our filthy rags and our hearts turned in on themselves? Can there be hope despite ourselves? Part of keeping the doctrine of creation central to vocation as the early Reformers modeled is to acknowledge God's promises for creation and ways the Spirit continues to create anew.

In Romans 8, creation is said to be subjected to futility or frustration by God, to have travailed, that it might be liberated from bondage to decay and obtain the "freedom of the glory of the children of God." *Creatio nova*, then, appears as a mirror image of *creatio originalis*, for whereas other-than-human life was created before the *imago Dei* in the Priestly creation account, the eschatological image highlights human redemption as a precedent to the salvation of creation. Here, the subject living in hope is creation, not humans awaiting salvation, as is often assumed. It is the earth that with eagerness anticipates the day humans will *finally* nourish and care for our shared sacred planet. In this sense, we can learn much from the soils, waters, and animals, who make clear—lament does not stifle hope, but neither does hope suppress lament. As in the Easter story, hope is foregrounded in a recognition of pain, suffering, and loss and includes a reckoning with grief.

But Paul continues, as the Spirit leads human beings to a knowledge of and trust and hope in God, the Spirit as a midwife transforms creation's groaning as in childbirth into a groaning of joy. As the writer of the fourth Gospel observes, the laboring woman has pain because her hour has come, and when her child is born healthy and happy into her arms, she no longer remembers the anguish because of the joy set before her (John 16:21). There is hope in travail. And so, as Paul Santmire rightly notes, it is the ongoing and unfolding work of the Spirit in creation that makes possible a viable spirituality of cosmic hope which stands in stark contrast to those of despair or indifference.[53]

Because hope is cosmic and ultimately a gift of the Spirit, it is more a state of mind than a response to the state of the world. For vocation to be enacted as hope, circumstances need not be good; hope encompasses much more than an easy, fickle response to positive conditions. Vocation is lived out as hope when the response to *any* action upon the self anticipates the goodness of God. Hope is a holding out for something other than what is and vulnerably opening oneself to such a possibility. It's not naiveté or the dismissal of fear, but rather courage. Nor is hope a well-reasoned sense of optimism, but instead a certainty that something—be it the next thought, word, or action—makes sense no matter what the outcome because God promises to meet us there.

Living into the promise of God's abiding presence permits ample space for pain, loss, and grief, affective realities many contrast with hope. This "gift of tears" as the early Desert Fathers called it, is a necessary element of spiritual maturity and a critical factor in discerning and living out vocation. We must remember the Easter story. Before Mary was called to proclaim the Good News, she persisted in grief. Alone, she stayed at the tomb, wailing and weeping. And from the providential future not unlike the road set before the tomb, Christ came to her, calling her by name. Arguably, the entire hermeneutic trajectory of the Scriptures leads us to consider this story and what these promises mean in light of today's sorrows. As eschatological theologies, or what some call theologies of the future, helpfully remind us the hope of what is to come colors our experience of today and makes possible our very vision. Therefore, the Christian's attempt to seek humility and wisdom, and practice restraint and the enactment of justice is not a vain and futile effort. It is, rather, to anticipate God's working all things for good despite and in spite of our failures. It is in prayer and action trusting what is not yet seen. And as our environmental challenges grow increasingly complex with their solutions seemingly arbitrary to even the world's most qualified minds, vocation as a habit of hope can confront without hysteria and seek to repurpose despair to some form of reimagined creativity.

In this sense, hope is something we *do* rather than something we *have*, as Joanna Macy succinctly puts it. It is active, not passive, having less to do with waiting for external agencies—God even—to bring about what we desire and more to do with acting upon what we would like to see redeemed. Hope is a state of mind that does the next best thing. In the language of vocation, it is first paying attention to what God is communicating through the action of the neighbor upon the self and then actively and appropriately responding. In hope, we hear the call and live out the response. As Christians we're free to make mistakes in our responses but are not free to live without response. Vocation enacted as hope doesn't require a right answer to the challenges set before us, especially when it comes to wicked, complex problems like climate change where any one response proves trite and simplistic. Nor does hope mandate a certain orientation of will, as if any of us can simply muscle our way to hope no matter the emotional weight of environmental loss. In reality hope is simpler. It is the actual stepping out in faith, the real and embodied response we choose when experiencing the action of God or neighbor upon ourselves in the midst of the darkness and despair. And when vocation is enacted as hope in this way, we're more free to honestly name, face, and reckon with all that's been lost while also acknowledging the fecund, verdant, and resilient world we all share.

NOTES

1. As early as 1954, Robert Michaelsen suggested that the reification of Christian vocation would be possible only with 1) realistic and pragmatic theological approaches; 2) a recovered sense of community wherein vocation has no basis apart from the relationships one holds; and 3) a realistic critique of the impact of industrialism. "If," Michaelsen argues, "the Church is concerned with the revival of Christian vocation in our time, it will need to consider the worker in his total environment and not only as an individual, the effects of industrialism upon his work, his relationship to the industrial enterprise, and his citizenship in an industrial or other type of work community. It will need also to consider the common motivations to work in our time, and the possibilities of changing or redeeming these motivations. It will need to see these and many other questions in an effort to be as realistic as possible about the worker in his present situation." (See "Work and Vocation in American Industrial Society," in *Work and Vocation: A Christian Discussion*, edited by John Oliver Nelson (New York: Harper & Brothers Publishers, 1954), 154–155.)

2. H. Richard Neibuhr outlines four types of responsible actions toward others: 1) personal action, where we react to another person's action 2) interpretative action, where we interpret someone else's action 3) accountability, where our own deeds impact a community or 4) responsive-responsible action, where one responds to one's own action and owns it.

3. Joanna Macy's work is particularly enlightening on this topic. Her recent co-authored works, *Coming Back to Life* and *Active Hope* speak to the role of the body in dealing with climate despair and other related emotional realities.

4. See Serene Jones's work, *Trauma and Grace: Theology in a Ruptured World* (Louisville, KY: Westminster John Knox Press, 2019) and Karen O'Donnell, *Broken Bodies: The Eucharist, Mary & the Body in Trauma Theology* (London: SCM Press, 2019) and Shelly Rambo, *Spirit and Trauma: A Theology of Remaining* (Louisville, KY: Westminster John Knox Press, 2010).

5. See *Toxic Communities: Environmental Racism, Industrial Pollution and Residential Mobility* (New York, NYU Press, 2014).

6. Barth, CD 3/4: 645.

7. Ibid., 3/4:30.

8. Ibid., 2/2:733.

9. Miroslav Volf, "Human Work, Divine Spirit, and New Creation: Toward a Pneumatological Understanding of Work" in *Pneuma*, 9, no. 2 (Fall 1987): 181.

10. Stanley Hauerwas, "Work as Co-Creation: A Critique of a Remarkably Bad Idea," in *Co-Creation and Capitalism: John Paul II's Laborem Exercens* (Washington, DC: University Press of America, 1983), 42–58.

11. In 1992, Juliet Schor, author of bestselling book *The Overworked American*, demonstrated how "Americans" work an average of one more month per year than in 1970. Recent studies suggest that this number has since increased (see Joanna Ciulla's study on the culture of work in the United States in *The Working Life: The Promise and Betrayal of Modern Work* (New York: Oxford University Press, 2000), Jill Andresky Fraser's *White Collar Sweatshop* (New York: Norton & Norton, 2002), and most recently, *Unfinished Business* by Anne-Marie Slaughter (New York: Random House, 2015).

12. See, for example, the Parable of the Talents in Matthew 24:14–30 or Paul's commentary on idleness in 2 Thessalonians 3:6–13.

13. This is in contrast to the Hegelian view, which understood work within the infrastructure of a master-slave relationship. Such a relationship, Hegel argued in *Phenomenology of the Spirit*, automatically gives rise to human alienation because the servant's productivity is usurped by the master, whose supremacy rests solely on his owning the means of reproduction, not on his own merits or accomplishments. To the master, the wage earner is just another object to be exploited.

14. *Acedia* was often understood as laziness in an existential sense, whereby a person experienced listlessness, malaise and a lack of energy. Aquinas also referred to it as a "sadness of the soul."

15. Dorothee Sölle, *To Work and to Love* (Philadelphia: Fortress Press, 1984), 85.

16. Other notable examples are more thoroughly documented in my article, "White Blight and the Legacy of Protestant Ecotheology" *Word & World* 38:2 (Spring 2018).

17. Many of Robert Bullard's works lift up such examples, including *The Quest for Environmental Justice: Human Rights and the Politics of Pollution* (San Francisco: Sierra Club Books, 2005).

18. The *17 Principles of Environmental Justice* can be accessed many places including: www.ejnet.org (last accessed June 22, 2019).

19. https://www.archives.gov/files/federal-register/executive-orders/pdf/12898.pdf (last accessed July 24, 2019)

20. https://obamawhitehouse.archives.gov/the-press-office/2014/02/10/presidential-proclamation-20th-anniversary-executive-order-12898-environ (last accessed July 24, 2019).

21. See the Reboot website for Jerry's podcast and a list of publications, https://www.reboot.io/ (last accessed June 23, 2019).

22. As Jeffrey Scholes observes, "Either a vocation derives from a God who infuses a vague purpose into work no matter the job, or a vocation is enlisted to legitimize or delegitimize a career choice based on whether the choice matches desire. In both cases, a vocation has become an idea that has little traction in the concrete work world. And such a disengaged, depoliticized and dematerialized, and free-floating vocation is predisposed for use by self-help authors who prefer to push more palatable, less contentious concepts for popular consumption." (See *Vocation and the Politics of Work: Popular Theology in a Consumer Culture* (New York: Lexington Books, 2013), 6.

23. See, for example, John 15:16, Matthew 22:3–4, Proverbs 8:1–4.

24. Einar Billing, *Our Calling*, translated by Conrad Bergendoff (Philadelphia: Fortress Press, 1952), 8.

25. Schweitzer, *Out of my Life and Thought: An Autobiography*, translated by C. T. Campion, postscript by Everett Skillings (New York: Henry Holt and Co., 1949), 91.

26. William Perkins argues this is the case because we are first bound unto God and then unto man (see *The Works of William Perkins*, ed. Ian Breward (Nashville: Abingdon Courtney Press, 1970), 457.

27. I am paraphrasing Larry Rasumussen here, from *Earth-honoring Faith*, 226.

28. Brené Brown, *Rising Strong: The Recknoning. The Rumble. The Revolution* (New York: Spiegel & Brau, 2015), 276. See Brown's recent TED Talks for more on this theme on her website: http://brenebrown.com, last accessed April 21, 2016.

29. Miroslav Volf, *Flourishing: Why We Need Religion in a Globalized World* (New Haven, CT: Yale University Press, 2016).

30. And while Christian communities can and *should* be anticipatory in outlook, such communities are by no means be defined by the religious realm. Scientific communities can also be categorized as reactive or anticipatory. For example, some reactive communities primarily embrace adaptive techniques, which address the negative consequences of climate change. Others go a step further and focus on abatement, measuring practices that lessen emissions. More anticipatory scientific communities deliberate mitigation practices like geoengineering, carbon neutralizing oceanic fertilization, and solar radiation management (See Jamieson, *Reason in a Dark Time*, 204–205).

31. The language of "cultural tipping point" is Larry Rasmussen's, from *Earth-Honoring Faith*. Along the lines of bioregional anticipatory communities, it is important to highlight recent critiques. Rob Nixon, for example, buttresses postcolonial criticism against bioregionalism in the last chapter of *Slow Violence and the Environmentalism of the Poor*. Noting the many positives that come from bioregionalism, he argues that localized perspectives often open into transcendentalism more than transnationalism, making for an environmental vision "that remains inside a spiritualized and naturalized national frame" (238). He suggests that bioregionalism, particularly American agrarian thought, tends toward a style of spiritual geography that is premised on what he calls spatial amnesia. "Within a bioregional center-periphery model, the specificity and moral imperative of the local typically opens out not into the specifics of the transnational but into transcendental abstraction. In this way, a prodigious amount of American environmental writing and criticism makes expansive gestures yet remains amnesiac toward non-American geographies in which America is implicated, geographies that vanish over the intellectual skyline. The spatial amnesia that often attends a bioregional ethic has temporal implications as well: shelter through the legacies of wars or our outsized consumerism, we have a history of forgetting our complicity in slow violence that wreaks attritional havoc beyond the bioregion or the nation" (238–239).

32. For more on the role of virtue in climate ethics, see Willis Jenkins's "The Turn to Virtue in Climate Ethics: Wickedness and Goodness in the Anthropocene," *Environmental Ethics* 38 (1:2016): 77–96.

33. Michael Doan, "Climate Change and Complacency," *Hypatia* 29, no. 3 (2014): 634–650.

34. Stephen Gardiner, "Is No One Responsible for Global Environmental Tragedy?: Climate Change as a Challenge to our Ethical Concepts" in *The Ethics of Global Climate Change*, ed. Denis Arnold (Cambridge, UK: Cambridge University Press), 54.

35. In the aforementioned "The Option for Life," I unpack Luther's working understanding of vocation's ecology, arguing that in as much as environmental matters impact and relate to all four of the classically Lutheran mandates, creation might easily be added as a fifth: "When the function of other callings is directed toward creation and on behalf of creation, love is enlarged to include all of life. For example, the economics of business or home must be directed toward a triple bottom line. From the Christian perspective, when motherhood and fatherhood, church service, politics and personal occupation are viewed in light of creation and as interrelated to the integrity of creation, such callings more holistically respond to God's command and more practically reorient human beings toward the neighbor" (202).

36. See Minnesota Public Radio's reports by Dan Gunderson at http://www.mpr.org/search?site=mpr&client=mpr&ie=UTF-8&oe=UTF-8&output=xml&entqr=3&filter=p&numgm=5&access=p&start=0&num=10&q=Gunderson+Bees, last accessed on April 19, 2016.

37. For more on this see Stephen Bouma-Prediger's, "Response to Louke van Wensveen," in *Christianity and Ecology*, edited by Dieter T. Hessel and Rosemary Radford Ruether (Cambridge, MA: Harvard University Press, 2000), 173–182.

38. Wendell Berry, quoted by Bill McKibben in *The End of Nature* (New York: Random House, 2006), 67.

39. Old Testament scholar Ellen Davis makes this point repeatedly in *Scripture, Culture and Agriculture: An Agrarian Reading of the Bible* (New York: Cambridge University Press, 2009), as does New Testament scholar David Horrell in *The Bible and the Environment: Towards a Critical Ecological Biblical Theology* (London: Equinox, 2010).

40. For example, in most cases, the vocation of marriage requires fidelity and abstaining from fulfilling other sexual desires. Likewise, any parent will likely agree that the vocation of parenthood fundamentally requires a saying "no" to self. Environmental vocation also requires forms of abstention, such as refusing certain products and abstaining from a variety of self-indulgent practices.

41. Diana Fritz Cates, "The Virtue of Temperance," in *The Ethics of Aquinas*, edited by Stephen Pope (Washington, DC: Georgetown University Press, 2002), 322.

42. For example, see R. E. Lane, *The Loss of Happiness in Market Democracies* (New Haven, CT: Yale University Press, 2001).

43. Richard Jackson, MD, the chair of Environmental Health Services in the Department of Public Health at UCLA, has argued this point in numerous articles and in his book *Healthy Communities*, with Stacy Sinclair (San Francisco: John Wiley & Sons, 2011).

44. It is important to note that Richard Louv's findings, articulated in his book *The Last Child in the Woods* (Chapel Hill, NC: Alcoquin Books, 2005), have not yet been endorsed by the wider psychological community. Louv connects his proposed "Nature Deficit Disorder" with other conditions such as: depression attention deficit disorder and obesity.

45. Aquinas is an obvious source to this end. See Thomas Aquinas, *Summa Theologiae*, trans. T. Gilby (London: Blackfriars, 1973), Ia IIae, q. 66, a. 3, ad 3. It is important to note that on occasion Aquinas will delineate between wisdom and prudence, the latter being the highest intellectual virtue in its execution to a fitting and appropriate end behavior and the former containing and ruling understanding. For more on this, see Etienne Gilson's *The Christian Philosophy of St. Thomas Aquinas* (New York: Random House, 1956).

46. See, for example, Job 28 and Proverbs 4, among others. For more on these differences, see Colin Gunton, "Christ, the Wisdom of God: A Study in Divine and Human Action," in *Where Should Wisdom be Found*, ed. Stephen Barton (Edinburgh: T & T Clark, 1999), 249–261.

47. Edwards remarks, "We might once again take up the language of Wisdom to speak of the deepest mystery of Jesus Christ, and that this Christology, by continually making manifest the interrelationship between creation and incarnation, can form the basis for a contemporary ecological theology" (*Jesus the Wisdom of God: An Ecological Theology* (Maryknoll, NY: Orbis Books, 1995), 56).

48. For more on this, see Bruce T. Morrill's *Anamnesis as Dangerous Memory: Political and Liturgical Theology in Dialogue* (Collegeville, PA: Liturgical, 2000).

49. For more popularized environmental treatises, see Bill McKibben's *Eaarth: Making a Life on a Tough New Planet* (New York: Times Books, 2010) and Naomi Klein's *This Changes Everything: Capitalism vs. the Climate* (New York: Simon & Schuster, 2015).

50. Jürgen Moltmann, *Ethics of Hope* (Minneapolis, MN: Fortress Press, 2012), 177.

51. I've explored the topic of vocation as repentance in greater detail in "Repentance and the Virtues toward the Fulfillment of Ecological Vocation," in *Journal of Lutheran Ethics* (March 2013).

52. I hail from the Evangelical Lutheran Church in America. For more on the church's demographics, social statements and history, see: www.elca.org.

53. Paul Santmire, *Before Nature: A Christian Spirituality* (Minneapolis: Fortress Press, 2014), 212.

Epilogue

In my years of researching Protestant ecological ethics and historical renderings of the doctrine of vocation, I've regularly pondered the question of inspiration, not as to whether the biblical texts inspire care for creation, nor whether Protestants themselves can be inspired persons, but rather *how* Protestant communities are (or are not) inspired to rethink and re-feel our shared ecological destiny with theological resources like the doctrine of vocation.

Given Protestantism's recent celebration of the 500th anniversary of Martin Luther's Wittenberg Theses and related emphases on the church's call to continually reform (*Ecclesia sempra reformanda est*), I am particularly interested in how the church might reevaluate its rich theological resources and apply them in new ways. Does this beloved doctrine speak to our contemporary ecological realities? This is of course asking in part a much larger question; namely, whether Christian doctrine is ecologically relevant and if so, how? With regards to the latter question I've assumed Christianity can and must speak to our contemporary environmental challenges. If even at its fringes, among its prophets and its mystics, Christianity always has. This is not to say that the development of all Christian theology, doctrinal concepts included, endorses an integral, earth-centered perspective. As I've noted throughout this book, Protestantism has a particularly disappointing track record to this end given the tradition's sometimes longstanding narrow reading of biblical anthropology and ongoing focus on the justification of humans. However, while many theological doctrines require significant reform *vis-à-vis* a more critical examination of the cultural contexts through which they emerged, others offer surprising ecological promise as well as practical insight. I've argued that the Protestant doctrine of vocation is one of these, albeit but one resource among many in a rich quiver of theological resources.

Overall this work has sought to explicitly relate the Protestant concept of vocation to ecological ethics in a way that other ecotheological literature utilizing the term has not. Throughout, I have overtly drawn out the connection between calling and creation and have sought to clarify not only what is meant by a Christian "ecological vocation," as one among many callings, but also how the interdependent nature of vocation brings an ecological dimension to every calling one inhabits. Calling is the relationship shared between and among these myriad roles. In this way, I have demonstrated how vocation's ecology can mediate between divergent metaethical approaches to ecological ethics, resembling a responsibility ethic, and provide practical measures for the Christian in society.

The critical retrieval of vocation that I've set forth also challenges overly spiritualized conceptions of calling. Theologically speaking, vocation serves as a lynchpin doctrine, bridging the void between the doctrines of creation and redemption respectively. Vocation is always received and in this sense a gift of God, the *karis* of salvation, but always in and through the action of the neighbor upon the self and therefore also fundamentally connected to the realm of creation. In this work I've highlighted the clear connection between vocation, creation, and redemption to speak to historically erroneous understandings and applications of the doctrine. Because vocation is tethered to the universal gift of redemption it cannot be reduced to monetized work in the way it has been predominately cast since the onset of the Industrial Revolution. Not only is vocation much more than compensated labor, but even as work it is first and foremost the expression of self in response to the action of God and neighbor upon the self. Therefore, vocation requires a sense of autonomy and dignity, one seldom provided to the majority of today's working class. On the other hand, it is vocation's connection to creation that calls into question contrasting renderings like those which emerged among nineteenth-century North American transcendentalists. Coupled with a newfound appreciation for the sublimity of nature many of these thinkers understood calling to be the mindful escape from work's banality and an enlightenment experienced through elite retreat from life's daily rigors. This too is a distortion of vocation for the ways it disembodies calling and pays no regard for one's particular location in a place and a time. Calling is neither of these—work or the escape from it—but rather the interrelatedness of spiritual and creaturely realities alike.

This book also showcases how the Protestant doctrine of vocation became increasingly secularized, leading to contemporary emphases on calling as passion and/or "becoming your best self." Such prevalent individualized conceptions of calling may be useful toward aims of self-discovery and self-awareness, but they're not decidedly Christian. I've shown how the centering of the neighbor's needs, including those of our other-than-human neighbor, remains paramount to uniquely Christian conceptions of vocation. Our very identity encompasses that of God and neighbor, and so naturally the interrelatedness of the many roles any person inhabits is discerned within community and for the sake of community.

As is the case with any beginning work, much here remains uncovered and underexplored. For example, in the first chapter I praised responsibilist approaches to ecological ethics for their dual commitment to a radical theocentricism and openness to scientific realism as well as their cathecontic methodology, making the connection between the "other" and the natural world explicit. I did not, however, comprehensively grapple with critiques perennially directed at H. Richard Niebuhr's working schema. More can and should be done to this end, with particular attention paid to H. Richard Niebuhr's fusion of moral agency with value and the role of character formation.

I've also begun to practically extend vocation to the realm of personal and corporate virtue, although my primary goal has been to explore how theory (terreology) and practice relate to one another within the context of vocation. Given some of the historic entrapments of vocation, my project has more heavily addressed the theoretical, or how vocation can and does function as a form in Protestant communities. However, much more needs to be said about what vocation looks like practically and how it might be helpfully distilled to the realm of virtue. As I've attempted to make clear, vocation must manifest in this way, not solely in the structural systems we do or do not participate in. Deeper work on these "virtues" will also be helpful moving forward.

Finally, a major element of my overall argument warrants further study, that is the cooptation of work. As ecotheological literature continues to address the implications of corporate capitalism, the Christian community will necessarily need to reevaluate the nature of work, especially as *an* element of vocation rather than *the* manifestation of it. In this way attention to theologies of work in the 1980s may very well resurface, but now with more holistic attention to the work/rest continuum. More analysis is needed on how the contemporary nature of work impacts our overall vocations, or what I've called the ecology of vocation, as well as our ability to perceive them. In addition to this, we need to ask how the changing landscape of work, one forecasted to further distance us from the processes of production, will inform working conceptions of vocation. With hundreds of new jobs emerging throughout the past decade it is possible, indeed even likely, that my young children will pursue professional fields not yet conceived of. And so, as work diversifies Protestant communities will need to ask how a robust understanding of vocation's ecology might simplify our choices and serve to ground our professional decisions.

This unfinished business aside, it is my hope that the ethical retrieval and reformation of calling offered here can practically serve Protestant communities at the fore of what promises to be a very challenging quincentennial.

As a recast theological resource, may vocation speak to the "new decalogues" being written by our new and changing earth and provide form and language toward a decidedly Protestant ecological ethic. And as characteristic of the Reformers gone before us, may God give us the brazen courage and renewed hope to live out the ecology of our calling in the face of environmental adversity, that all life may flourish and God might be glorified.

Bibliography

Alexander, Patrick H., ed. *The Works of Jonathan Edwards*. Carlisle, PA: The Banner of Truth Trust, 1995.
Althaus, Paul. *The Ethics of Martin Luther*. Minneapolis: Fortress, 2007.
Aquinas, Thomas. *Summa Theologica*. Translated by Fathers of the English Dominican London: Burnes Gates and Washbourne, Ltd., n.d.
———. *Contra Gentiles*. Translated by Vernon Bouke. Notre Dame, IN: University of Notre Dame, 1975.
Badcock, Gary D. *The Way of Life*. Grand Rapids, MI: Eerdmans, 1998.
Baker-Fletcher, Karen. *Sisters of Dust, Sisters of Spirit: Womanist Wordings on God and Creation*. Minneapolis: Fortress Press, 1998.
Barbour, Ian. *Religion in an Age of Science*. San Francisco: Harper & Row, 1990.
———. *Ethics in an Age of Technology*. San Francisco: Harper & Row, 1993.
Barth, Karl. *Church Dogmatics*. Four Volumes. Edinburgh: T & T Clark, 1958–1961.
Bartholomew, Patriarch. *On Earth as in Heaven: Ecological Vision and Initiatives of Ecumenical Patriarch Bartholomew*. New York: Fordham University Press, 2011.
Barton, Stephen, ed. *Where Should Wisdom Be Found*. Edinburgh: T & T Clark, 1999.
Bauckham, Richard. *The Bible and Ecology*. Waco, TX: Baylor University Press, 2010.
Bauman, Whitney A., Richard R. Bohannon II and Kevin J. O'Brien, Eds. *Inherited Land: The Changing Grounds of Religion and Ecology*. Eugene, OR: Pickwick, 2011.
Baxter, Richard. *A Christian Directory*, Chapter X, Part I, Question 5, Answers 3–4. http://www.ccel.org/ccel/baxter.
———. "Directions for the Right Choice of our Calling and Ordinary Labour." In *A Christian Directory*, 2nd Edition (London, 1678).
Beisner, E. Calvin. *Where Garden Meets Wilderness: Evangelical Entry into the Environmental Debate*. Grand Rapids, MI: Eerdmans, 1997.
Berry, R. J., Ed. *Environmental Stewardship: Critical Perspectives Past and Present*. New York: T & T Clark International, 2006.
Berry, Thomas. *The Dream of the Earth*. San Francisco: Sierra Club Books, 1988.
Berry, Wendell. *A Place on Earth*. Berkeley, CA: Counterpoint, 2001.
———. *Hannah Coulter*. Berkeley, CA: Counterpoint, 2004.
———. *Home Economics*. San Francisco, CA: North Point, 1987.
———. "It All Turns on Affection," accessible at: http://www.neh.gov/about/awards/jefferson-lecture/wendell-e-berry-lecture, last accessed on June 3, 2015.
———. *Jayber Crow*. Berkeley, CA: Counterpoint, 2000.
———. *Living the Sabbath: Discovering the Rhythms of Rest and Delight*. Grand Rapids, MI: Brazos Press, 2006.

———. *Long-Legged Horse*. New York: Shoemaker & Hoard, 2004.
———. *Sex, Economy, Freedom & Community*. New York: Pantheon, 1992.
———. *That Distant Land: The Collected Stories*. Berkeley, CA: Counterpoint, 2007.
———. *The Gift of Good Land: Further Essays Cultural and Agricultural*. San Francisco, CA: North Point, 1981.
———. *Three Short Novels*. Berkeley, CA: Counterpoint, 2008.
———. *What Are People For?* New York: North Point Press, 1990.
Berry, Wendell, and Norman Wirzba. *The Art of the Commonplace: The Agrarian Essays of Wendell Berry*. Washington, DC: Shoemaker & Hoard, 2002.
Billing, Einar. *Our Calling*. Translated by Conrad Bergendoff. Philadelphia: Fortress Press, 1964.
Billings, Todd. *Calvin, Participation, and the Gift*. Oxford, UK: Oxford University Press, 2008.
Black, John. *The Dominion of Man: The Search for Ecological Responsibility*. Chicago: Aldine Publishing Company, 1970.
Blanchard, Kathryn B., and Kevin J. O'Brien. *An Introduction to Christian Environmentalism*. Waco, TX: Baylor University Press, 2014.
Bonzo, Matthew J., and Michael R. Stevens. *Wendell Berry and the Cultivation of Life: A Reader's Guide*. Grand Rapids, MI: Brazos Press, 2008.
Bornkamm, Heinrich. *Luther's World of Thought*. Translated by Hart H. Bertram. St. Louis, MO: Concordia, 1959.
Brennan, Patrick M., Ed. *The Vocation of the Child*. Grand Rapids, MI: Eerdmans, 2008.
Breward, Ian, ed. *The Works of William Perkins*. Grand Rapids, MI:Abingdon Courtneny Press, 1970.
Brown, Brené. *Rising Strong: The Reckoning. The Rumble. The Revolution*. New York: Spiegel & Brau, 2015.
Bouma-Prediger, Steven. *For the Beauty of the Earth: A Christian Vision for Creation Care*. Grand Rapids, MI: Baker Academic, 2001.
Buell, Lawrence. "Religion and the Environmental Imagination in American Literature." In *There Before Us: Religion, Literature, and Culture from Emerson to Wendell Berry*. Edited by Roger Lundin. Grand Rapids, MI: Eerdmans, 2007.
Bullard, Robert. *The Quest for Environmental Justice: Human Rights and the Politics of Pollution*. San Francisco: Sierra Club Books, 2005.
Calvin, John. *Commentaries on the First Book of Moses Called Genesis*. Grand Rapids, MI: Eerdmans, 1948.
———. *Commentary on II Thessalonians*. Translated by John Pringle. Edinburgh: Calvin Translation Society, 1855.
———. *Institutes of the Christian Religion*. Edited by John T. McNeill and translated by Ford Lewis Battles. Philadelphia: Westminster Press, 1960.
———. *Treatises Against the Anabaptists and Against the Libertines*. Edited and translated by Benjamin Wirt Farley. Grand Rapids, MI: Baker Academic, 2001.
Canlis, Julie. *Calvin's Ladder: A Spiritual Theology of Ascent and Ascension*. Grand Rapids, MI: Eerdmans, 2010.
Chryssavgis, John. "The World of the Icon and Creation: The Orthodox Perspective on Ecology and Pneumatology." In *Christianity and Ecology*. Edited by Dieter T. Hessel and Rosemary Redford Reuther. Boston, MA: Harvard University Press, 2000.
Cicero. *On Old Age, On Friendship, on Divination*. Translated by W. A. Falconer. Boston, MA: Harvard University Press, 1923.
Ciulla, Joanna. *The Working Life: The Promise and Betrayal of Modern Work*. New York: Oxford University Press, 2000.
Cobb, John. *Sustainability: Economics, Ecology and Justice*. New York: Orbis, 1992.
Crutzen, P. J., and E. F. Stoermer. "The Anthropocene." *Global Change Newsletter* 41 (2002): 1–18.
Daly, Herman, and John Cobb Jr. *For the Common Good: Redirecting the Economy toward Community, the Environment and a Sustainable Future*. Boston: Beacon Press, 1994.

Davis, Ellen. *Scripture, Culture and Agriculture: An Agrarian Reading of the Bible.* New York: Cambridge University Press, 2009.
Deane-Drummond, Celia. *A Handbook in Theology and Ecology.* London: SCM Press, 1996.
———. *The Ethics of Nature: New Dimensions to Religious Ethics.* Malden, MA: Blackwell, 2004.
———. "Theology, Ecology and Values." In *Christianity and Ecology: Seeking the Well-Being of Earth and Humans.* Edited by Dieter T. Hessel and Rosemary Radford-Ruther. Cambridge, MA: Harvard University Press, 2000.
DeWitt, Calvin. *Earthwise: A Guide to Hopeful Creation Care.* Grand Rapids, MI: Faith Alive Christian Resources, 2011.
———. *Missionary Earthkeeping.* Atlanta, GA: Mercer University Press, 1993.
———. *The Environment and the Christian.* Grand Rapids, MI: Baker Publishing, 1991.
———. *The Just Stewardship of Land and Creation.* Grand Rapids, MI: Reformed Ecumenical Council, 1996.
Dickens, Charles. *Dombey and Son.* New York: Mead & Company, 1950.
Dillenberger, John, Ed. *Martin Luther: Selections from His Writings.* New York: Anchor Books, 1962.
Doan, Michael. "Climate Change and Complacency." *Hypathia* 29, no. 3 (2014): 634–650.
Douglas, Richard. M. "Talent and Vocation in Humanist and Protestant Thought." In *Action and Conviction in Early Modern Europe.* Edited by Theodore K. Rabb and Jerrold E. Seigel. Princeton, NJ: Princeton University Press, 1969.
Edenhofer, O. et al (eds). "2014: Summary for Policymakers." In *Climate Change 2014: Mitigation of Climate Change. Contribution of Working Group III to the Fifth Assessment Report of the Intergovernmental Panel on Climate Change.* New York: Cambridge University Press, 2014.
Edmondson, Todd. *Priest, Prophet, Pilgrim: Types and Distortions of Spiritual Vocation in the Fiction of Wendell Berry and Cormac McCarthy.* Eugene, OR: Pickwick, 2014.
Edwards, Denis. *Jesus the Wisdom of God: An Ecological Theology.* Maryknoll, NY: Orbis Books, 1995.
Ellul, Jacques. *The Technological System.* New York: Continuum, 1980.
Elwood, Douglas. *The Philosophical Theology of Jonathan Edwards.* New York: Columbia University Press, 1960.
Finlan, Stephen, and Vladimir Kharlamov, eds. *Theosis: Deification in Christian Theology.* Eugene, OR: Pickwick, 2006.
Finney, Carolyn. *Black Faces, White Spaces: Reimagining the Relationship of African Americans to the Great Outdoors.* Chapel Hill, NC: University of North Carolina, 2014.
Foucault, Michel. *The Order of Things: An Archeology of the Human Sciences.* New York: Random House, 1994.
Fowler, Robert Booth. *The Greening of Protestant Thought.* Chapel Hill, NC: University of North Carolina, 1995.
Foxe, Matthew. *The Coming of the Cosmic Christ: The Healing of Mother Earth and the Birth of a Global Renaissance.* San Francisco: Harper Collins, 1988.
Fraser, Jill Andresky. *White Collar Sweatshop.* New York: Norton & Norton, 2002.
Fröhlich, Karlfried. "Luther on Vocation." In *Harvesting Martin Luther's Reflections on Theology, Ethics and the Church.* Edited by Timothy Wengert. Grand Rapids, MI: Eerdmans, 2004.
Gardiner, Stephen Mark. *A Perfect Moral Storm: The Ethical Tragedy of Climate Change.* New York: Oxford University Press, 2011.
———. "Is No One Responsible for Global Environmental Tragedy? Climate Change as a Challenge to Our Ethical Concepts." In *The Ethics of Global Climate Change.* Edited by Denis Arnold. Cambridge, UK: Cambridge University Press, 2011.
Garnett, Richard and John Parker Anderson, Eds. *Emerson: Essays and Lectures.* New York: Library of America, 1983.
Gebara, Ivone. *Longing for Running Water: Ecofeminism and Liberation.* Minneapolis: Fortress Press, 1999.

Gilson, Etienne. *The Christian Philosophy of St. Thomas Aquinas*. New York: Random House, 1956.

Giordan, Giuseppe, Ed. *Vocation and Social Context*. Boston: Brill, 2007.

Gnanadason, Aruna. *Listen to the Women!: Listen to the Earth!* Geneva: WCC Publications, 2005.

Gottlieb, Roger S. *A Greener Faith: Religious Environmentalism and Our Planet's Future*. New York: Oxford University Press, 2006.

———. "Transcendence of Justice and the Justice of Transcendence: Mysticism, Deep Ecology and Political Life." *Journal of the American Academy of Religion* 67, no. 1 (1999): 149–166.

Grabill, Stephen J. *Rediscovering the Natural Law in Reformed Theological Ethics*. Grand Rapids, MI: Eerdmans, 2006.

Gregorious, Paulos. *The Human Presence: An Orthodox View of Nature*. Geneva: World Council of Churches, 1978.

Gustafson, James. *Ethics from a Theocentric Perspective*. Chicago: University of Chicago Press, 1981.

———. *A Sense of the Divine*. Cleveland, OH: Pilgrim Press, 1996.

Habel, Norman C., David Rhoads & H. Paul Santmire, eds. *The Season of Creation: A Preaching Commentary*. Minneapolis: Fortress Press, 2011.

Hackett, Jeremiah. *A Companion to Meister Eckhart*. London: Brill, 2012.

Hauerwas, Stanley. "Work as Co-Creation: A Critique of a Remarkably Bad Idea." In *Co-Creation and Capitalism: John Paul II's Laborem Exercens*. Edited by John W. Houck and Oliver F. Williams. Washington DC: University Press of America, 1983.

———. *The Peaceable Kingdom: A Primer in Christian Ethics*. Notre Dame, IN: University of Notre Dame Press, 1983.

Hedge, Frederic Henry. *Sermons* (Boston, 1891).

———. "The Doctrine of Endless Punishment," *Christian Examiner*, LXVII (1859): 98–128.

———. "The Religion of the Present," *Christian Examiner*, LCVII (1859): 50–70.

———. "University Reform." *Atlantic Monthly*, XVIII (1866).

Hessel, Dieter T. and Larry Rasmussen, Eds. *Earth Habitat: Eco-Injustice and the Church's Response*. Minneapolis: Fortress Press, 2007.

Hessel, Dieter T. and Rosemary Radford-Ruther. *Christianity and Ecology: Seeking the Well-Being of Earth and Human*. Cambridge, MA: Harvard University Press, 2000.

Hogue, Michael S. *The Tangled Bank: Toward an Ecotheological Ethics of Responsible Participation*. Eugene, OR: Pickwick Publications, 2008.

Horrell, David. *The Bible and the Environment: Towards a Critical Ecological Biblical Theology*. New York: Equinox, 2010.

Jackson, Richard. *Healthy Communities*. San Francisco: John Wiley & Sons, 2011.

Jamieson, Dale. *Reason in a Dark Time: Why the Struggle against Climate Change Failed and What It Means for Our Future*. New York: Oxford University Press, 2014.

Jenkins, Willis. "After Lynn White: Religious Ethics and Environmental Problems" *Journal of Religious Ethics* 37, no. 2 (June 2009): 283–309.

———. *Ecologies of Grace: Environmental Ethics and Christian Theology*. New York: Oxford University Press, 2008.

———. *The Future of Ethics: Sustainability, Social Justice, and Religious Creativity*. Washington DC: Georgetown University Press, 2013.

———. "The Turn to Virtue in Climate Ethics: Wickedness and Goodness in the Anthropocene." *Environmental Ethics*, no. 1 (2016): 77–96.

Jennings, Willie. *The Christian Imagination: Theology and the Origins of Race*. New Haven, CT: Yale University Press, 2010.

Johnston, Lucas F., and Samuel Snyder. "Practically Natural: Religious Resources for Environmental Pragmatism." In *Inherited Land: The Changing Grounds of Religion and Ecology*. Eugene, OR: Pickwick, 2011.

Jones, Serene. *Trauma and Grace: Theology in a Ruptured World*. Louisville, KY: Westminster John Knox Press, 2019.

Jordan, William. *The Sunflower Forest: Ecological Restoration and the New Communion with Nature*. Berkeley, CA: University of California Press, 2003.
Jorgenson, Kiara. "The Option for Life." *Dialog: A Journal of Theology* Vol 54, no. 2 (Summer 2015): 197–204.
———. "Repentance and the Virtues toward the Fulfillment of Ecological Vocation." *Journal of Lutheran Ethics* 13:2 (March 2013).
———. "White Blight and the Legacy of Protestant Ecotheology." *Word & World* 38:2 (Spring 2018): 180–189.
———. "Wild Rumpus Revisited: The Benefits of Outdoor Play in the Vocation of the Child." *Word and World* 35, no. 4 (Fall 2015): 358–367.
Katz, Eric. *Nature as Subject*. Lanham, MD: Rowman & Littlefield Publishers, 1996.
Kellert, Stephen R. *Birthright: People and Nature in the Modern World*. New Haven, CT: Yale University Press, 2012.
———. *Building for Life: Designing and Understanding the Human-Nature Connection*. Washington, DC: Island Press, 2005.
———. *Kinship to Mastery: Biophilia in Human Evolution and Development*. Washington, DC: Island Press, 1997.
Klein, Naomi. *This Changes Everything: Capitalism vs. The Climate*. New York: Simon & Schuster, 2014.
Kolb, Robert. "Called to Milk Cows and Govern Kingdoms." *Concordia Journal* (Spring 2013): 133–141.
———. "God Calling 'Take Care of My People:' Luther's Concept of Vocation in the Augsburg Confession and Its Apology." *Concordia Journal* (January 1982): 4–11.
Kolden, Marc. "Christian Vocation in Light of Feminist Critiques." *Lutheran Quarterly* Vol. X (1996).
Kuhn, Thomas. *The Structure of Scientific Revolutions*. Chicago: University of Chicago Press, 1996.
Lane, R. E. *The Loss of Happiness in Market Democracies*. New Haven, CT: Yale University Press, 2001.
Latour Bruno. "Agency at the Time of the Anthropocene." *New Literary History* 45 (2014): 1–18.
———. *An Inquiry into Modes of Existence: An Anthropology of the Moderns*. Cambridge, MA: Harvard University Press, 2013.
Lear, Linda, Ed. *Lost Woods: The Discovered Writing of Rachel Carson*. Boston: Beacon Press, 1998.
———. *Rachel Carson: Witness for Nature*. New York: Henry Holt, 1997.
Leopold, Aldo. *A Sand County Almanac with Other Essays on Conservation from Round River*. New York: Oxford University Press, 1966.
Light, Andrew. "The Case for Practical Pluralism." In *Environmental Ethics: An Anthology*. Edited by Andrew Light and Holmes Rolston. Malden, MA: Blackwell, 2003.
Light, Andrew and Eric Katz. *Environmental Pragmatism*. New York: Routledge, 1995.
Livingston, James. *Modern Christian Thought: The Enlightenment and the Nineteenth Century*. Minneapolis: Fortress Press, 2006.
Locke, John. *Conduct of the Understanding*. New York: Burt Franklin, 1971.
———. "Of Study." In *The Educational Writings of John Locke*. Edited by J. L. Axtell. Cambridge, MA: Cambridge University Press, 1968.
Lopez, Barry. *This Incomperable Lande: A Book of American Nature Writing*. Boston: Houghton, 1989.
Louv, Richard. *Last Child in the Woods: Saving Our Children from Nature-Deficit Disorder*. Chapel Hill, NC: Algonquin Books of Chapel Hill, 2005.
———. *The Nature Principle: Reconnecting with Life in a Virtual Age*. Chapel Hill, NC: Algonquin Books of Chapel Hill, 2012.
Lubchenco Jane., "Entering the Century of the Environment: A New Social Contract for Science." *Science* 279, no. 5350 (1998): 491–497.
———. J. Lubchenco, et al. "The Sustainable Biosphere Initiative: An Ecological Research Agenda." *Ecology* 72, no. 2 (1991): 371–412.

Luther, Martin. *Luther's Works*. 78 Volumes. Edited by Jaroslav Pelikan, et al. St. Louis, MO: Concordia Publishing House, 1955–2015.

MacIntyre, Alasdair. *After Virtue: A Study in Moral Theory*. Notre Dame, IN: University of Notre Dame Press, 2007.

Macy, Joanna, and Chris Johnstone. *Active Hope: How to Face the Mess We're in Without Going Crazy*. Novato, CA: New World Library, 2012.

Macy, Joanna, and Molly Brown. *Coming Back to Life: The Updated Guide to Work That Connects*. Gabriola Island, British Columbia: New Society Publishers, 2014.

Manoussakis, John Panteleimon. "*Physis* and *Ktisis*: Two Different Ways of Thinking of the World." In *Toward an Ecology of Transfiguration*. Edited by John Chryssavgis and Bruce C. Foltz. New York: Fordham University Press, 2013.

Markowitz, E.M. and A.F. Shariff. "Climate Change and Moral Judgement." *Nature Climate Change* 2, no. 4 (2012): 243–247.

Marshall, Paul A. *A Kind of Life Imposed on Man: Vocation and Social Order from Tyndale to Locke*. Toronto: University of Toronto Press, 1996.

Martin-Schramm, James B. *Climate Justice: Ethics, Energy, and Public Policy*. Minneapolis: Fortress Press, 2010.

Martin-Schramm, James B. and Robert L. Stivers. *Christian Environmental Ethics: A Case Method Approach*. Maryknoll, NY: Orbis Books, 2003.

McDonagh, Sean. *Passion for the Earth: The Christian Vocation to Promote Justice, Peace and the Integrity of Creation*. London: Geoffrey Chatman, 1994.

McDuff, Mallory. *Natural Saints*. New York: Oxford University Press, 2010.

McFague, Sallie. *A New Climate for Theology: God, the World, and Global Warming*. Minneapolis: Fortress Press, 2008.

———. *Blessed Are the Consumers: Climate Change and the Practice of Restraint*. Minneapolis: Fortress Press, 2013.

———. *Life Abundant: Rethinking Theology and Economy for a Planet in Peril*. Minneapolis: Fortress Press, 2001.

———. *Super Natural Christians: How We Should Love Nature*. Minneapolis: Fortress Press, 1997.

———. *The Body of God*. Minneapolis: Augsburg Fortress, 1993.

McGinn, Bernard. "Do Christian Platonists Really Believe in Creation?" In *God and Creation*. Edited by David Burrell and Bernard McGinn. Notre Dame, IN: University of Notre Dame Press, 1991.

———. *The Presence of God: A History of Christian Mysticism*. New York: Crossroad Publishing, 1992.

———, ed. *Meister Eckhart and the Beguine Mystics: Hadewijch of Brabant, Mechthild of Magdeburg, and Marguerite Porete*. New York: The Continuum Publishing Company, 1994.

McKibben, Bill. *Earth: Making a Life on a Tough New Planet*. New York: Times Books, 2010.

———. *The End of Nature*. New York: Random House Trade Paperbacks, 2006.

Meilander, Gilbert. *The Freedom of a Christian: Grace, Vocation and the Meaning of Our Humanity*. Grand Rapids: Brazos Press, 2006.

Melanchthon, Philip. "Apology of the Augsburg Confession" in *The Book of Concord*. Macomb, MI: Lutheran Heritage, 2011.

———. *Paul's Letter to the Colossians*. Translated by D. C. Parker. Worcester, UK: Sheffield Academic Press, 1989.

———. *The Difference between Worldly and Christian Piety* (1522). In the Post-Reformation Digital Library, https://mail.google.com/mail/u/0/#inbox/1543062933021663?projector=1, last accessed April 20, 2016.

———. *The Loci Communes*. Translated by Charles Leander Hill. Boston: Meador Publishing Company, 1944.

Moe-Lobeda, Cynthia. "Climate Change as Climate Debt: Forging a Just Future." *Journal of Society of Christian Ethics* 36:1 (Spring/Summer 2016): 27–49.

———. *Resisting Structural Evil: Love as Ecological and Economic Vocation*. Minneapolis: Fortress Press, 2013.

Moltmann, Jürgen. *Trinity and the Kingdom*. Minneapolis: Fortress Press, 1991.
———. *God in Creation*. Minneapolis: Fortress Press, 1993.
———. *Sun of Righteousness, ARISE!* Minneapolis: Fortress Press, 2010.
———. *Ethics of Hope*. Minneapolis: Fortress Press, 2012.
Moore, Kathleen Dean, and Michael P. Nelson. *Moral Ground: Ethical Action for a Planet in Peril*. San Antonio, TX: Trinity University Press, 2010.
Morrill, Bruce T. *Anamnesis as Dangerous Memory: Political and Liturgical Theology in Dialogue*. Collegeville: Liturgical, 2000.
Mumford, Lewis. *Technics and Civilization*. New York: Harcourt, Brace & Company, 1934.
Nash, James. *Loving Nature: Ecological Integrity and Christian Responsibility*. Nashville: Abingdon Press, 1991.
Nelson, John Oliver, ed. *Work and Vocation*. New York: Harper & Brothers Publishers, 1954.
Niebuhr, Reinhold. *Interpretation of Christian Ethics*. New York: Harper & Brothers, 1935.
Niebuhr, H. Richard. *Radical Monotheism and Western Culture*. Louisville, KY: Westminster/John Knox Press, 1970.
———. *The Meaning of Revelation*. New York: Macmillan, 1962.
———. *The Responsible Self*. New York: Harper Row, 1963.
Nixon, Rob. *Slow Violence and the Environmentalism of the Poor*. Cambridge, MA: Harvard University Press, 2011.
Northcott, Michael S. *A Political Theology of Climate Change*. Grand Rapids, MI: Eerdmans, 2013.
———. *The Environment and Christian Ethics*. New York: Cambridge University Press, 1996.
O'Donnell, Karen. *Broken Bodies: The Eucharist, Mary and the Body in Trauma Theology*. London: SCM Press, 2019.
Outka, Paul. *Race and Nature: From Transcendentalism to the Harlem Renaissance*. New York: Palgrave Macmillan, 2008.
Padgett, Alan. *Science and the Study of God: A Mutuality Model for Theology and Science*. Grand Rapids, MI: Eerdmans, 2003.
Peacocke, Arthur. *Creation and the World of Science*. Oxford, UK: Clarendon Press, 1979.
Pelikan, Jaroslav. *The Christian Tradition: A History of the Development of Doctrine*, vol. V, *Christian Doctrine and Modern Culture (since 1700)*. Chicago: University of Chicago Press, 1989.
Perkins, William., *The Foundation of the Christian Religion Gathered in Six Principles*. http://www.nesherchristianresources.org/perkins/PerkinsWorks/SixPrin.html.
———. *Treatise of Vocations*. Edited by John Legatt (1626). In the Digital Puritan Library. http://www.digitalpuritan.net/Digital%20Puritan%20Resources/Perkins,%20William/Treatise%20of%20the%20Vocations%20(OTW%20Version).pdf.
Peters, Jason. *Wendell Berry: Life and Work*. Lexington: University Press of Kentucky, 2007.
Pew Center on Global Climate Change. *Climate Change 101: Understanding and Responding to Global Climate Change*. Arlington, VA: Center for Climate and Energy Solutions, 2011.
Plumwood, Val. *Environmental Culture*. London: Routledge, 2002.
Pope, Stephen, ed. *The Ethics of Aquinas*. Washington, DC: Georgetown University Press, 2002.
Rabb, Theodore K., and Jerrold E. Seigel, eds. *Action and Conviction in Early Modern Europe*. Princeton, NJ: Princeton University Press, 1969.
Radford-Ruether, Rosemary. *Gaia & God: An Ecofeminist Theology of Earth Healing*. San Francisco: Harper Collins, 1992.
Rahner, Karl. *Theology of Death*. New York: Herder & Herder, 1961.
Rambo, Shelly. *Spirit and Trauma: A Theology of Remaining*. Louisville, KY: Westminster John Knox Press, 2010.
Rasmussen, Larry L. *Earth-honoring Faith: Religious Ethics in a New Key*. New York: Oxford University Press, 2013.
———. "Environmental Racism and Environmental Justice: Moral Theory in the Making?" *Journal of the Society of Christian Ethics* 24, no.1 (2004): 4–23.
Rauschenbusch, Walter. *Christianity and the Social Crisis in the 21st Century*. New York: Harper One, 2007.

Rolston, Holmes III. *A New Environmental Ethics: The Next Millennium for Life on Earth.* New York: Routledge, 2012.

———. *Conserving Natural Value.* New York: Columbia University Press, 1994.

———. "Environmental Ethics: Some Challenges for Christians." *The Annual Society of Christian Ethics.* Washington, DC: Georgetown University Press, 1993.

———. "Value in Nature and the Nature of Value." In *Philosophy and the Natural Environment.* Edited by Robin Attfield and Andrew Belsey. New York: Cambridge University Press, 1994.

Russell, Norman. *The Doctrine of Deification in the Christian Tradition.* Oxford, UK: Oxford University Press, 2004.

Santmire, H. Paul. *Before Nature: A Christian Spirituality.* Minneapolis: Fortress Press, 2014.

———. *Brother Earth: Nature, God and Ecology in a Time of Crisis* (New York: T. Nelson, 1970).

———. *Nature Reborn: The Ecological and Cosmic Promise of Christian Theology.* Minneapolis: Fortress Press, 2000.

———. "On the Mission of the Church: Reflections along the Way." *Lutheran Quarterly* 23, no. 4 (Nov 1971): 366–387.

———. "Partnership with Nature According to the Scriptures: Beyond the Theology of Stewardship" *Christian Scholar's Review* 32:4 (Summer 2003): 381–412.

———. "Reflections on the Alleged Ecological Bankruptcy of Western Theology." *Anglican Review* 57, no. 2 (April 1975): 131–152.

———. *Ritualizing Nature: Renewing Christian Liturgy in a Time of Crisis.* Minneapolis: Fortress Press, 2008.

———. *The Travail of Nature: The Ambiguous Ecological Promise of Christian Theology.* Minneapolis: Fortress Press, 1985.

Schaefer, Jame. *Confronting the Climate Crisis: Catholic Theological Perspectives.* Milwaukee, WI: Marquette University Press, 2011.

Schaeffer, Francis. *Pollution and the Death of Man: The Christian View of Ecology.* Wheaton, IL: Tyndale Publishers, 1970.

Scholes, Jeffrey. *Vocation and the Politics of Work: Popular Theology in Consumer Culture.* Lexington, KY: Lanham Books, 2013.

Schor, Juliet. *The Overworked American: The Unexpected Decline of Leisure.* New York: Basic Books, 1992.

Schuurman, Douglas. *Vocation: Discerning Our Callings in Life.* Grand Rapids, MI: Eerdmans, 2004.

Schweitzer, Albert. *Out of My Life and Thoughts.* Translated by C. T. Campion. New York: Henry Holt and Company, 1933.

Scott, Ernest F. *Man and Society in the New Testament.* New York: Charles Scribner's Sons, 1946.

Scoville, Judith. "Fitting Ethics to the Land: H. Richard Niebuhr's Ethic of Responsibility and Ecotheology." *Journal of Religious Ethics* 30, no.2 (2002): 207–229.

See, Ruth Douglas. *The Protestant Doctrine of Vocation in the Presbyterian Thought of Nineteenth-Century America.* New York: New York University Press, 1952.

Shuman, Joel James and L. Roger Owens, Eds. *Wendell Berry and Religion: Heaven's Earthly Life.* Lexington, KY: University Press of Kentucky, 2009.

Simpson, Gary. "Written on Their Hearts: Thinking with Luther on Scripture, Natural Law and the Moral Life," *Word and World* 30, no. 4 (Fall 2010): 419–428.

Sinden, Amy. "Climate Change and Human Rights." *Journal of Land, Resources, and Environmental Law* 27 (2007): 255.

Singer, Peter. *Animal Liberation.* New York: Harper Collins, 2002,

———. *Practical Ethics.* New York: Cambridge University, 2011.

Sittler, Joseph. "A Theology for the Earth." In *Environmental Stewardship: Critical Perspectives Past and Present.* Edited by R. J. Berry. New York: T & T Clark, 2006.

Slaughter, Anne-Marie. *Unfinished Business: Women, Men, Work, Family.* New York: Random House, 2015.

Smith, Adam. *An Inquiry into the Nature and Causes of the Wealth of Nations*. New York: Random House, 1937.
———. *The Theory of Moral Sentiments*. New York: A.M. Kelley, 1966.
Sölle Dorothee. *To Work and to Love*. Minneapolis: Fortress Press, 1984.
Srinivasan, U. Thara et al. "The Debt of Nations and the Distribution of Ecological Impacts from Human Activities." *Proceedings of the National Academy of Science* 105:5 (February 5, 2008): 1763–1773.
Steger, Wallace. *Where the Bluebird Sings to the Lemonade Springs*. New York: Random House, 1992.
Steele, Richard. *The Religious Tradesman: Plain and Serious Hints of Advice*. Trenton, NJ: Francis Wiggins, 1823.
Stewart, Claude. *Nature in Grace: A Study in the Theology of Nature*. Macon, GA: Mercer University Press, 1983.
Stoeffer, Ernest. *The Rise of Evangelical Pietism*. Leiden, UK: E.J. Brill, 1965.
Stoll, Mark S. *Inherit the Holy Mountain: Religion and the Rise of American Environmentalism*. New York: Oxford University Press, 2015.
Stott, John. *Christian Mission in the Modern World*. Downers Grove, IL: InterVarsity Press, 1975.
Swoboda, A.J., ed. *Blood Cries Out: Pentecostals, Ecology, and the Groans of Creation*. Eugene, OR: Wipe & Stock, 2014.
———. *The Dusty Ones: Why Wandering Deepens Your Faith*. Grand Rapids, MI: Baker Books, 2016.
Taylor, Bron. *Deep Green Religion: Nature, Spirituality and the Planetary Future*. Berkeley: University of California Press, 2010.
Taylor, Charles. *A Secular Age*. Cambridge, MA: Harvard University Press, 2007.
Taylor, Dorceta. *Toxic Communities: Environmental Racism, Industrial Pollution and Residential Mobility*. New York, New York University Press, 2014.
Thayer, H. S., ed. *Newton's Philosophy of Nature: Selections from His Writings*. New York: Hafner, 1974.
Torgerson, Mark Allen. *Greening Spaces For Worship and Ministry: Congregations, Their Buildings, and Creation Care*. Herndon, VA: Alban Institute, 2012.
Townes, Emilie. *In a Blaze of Glory: Womanist Spirituality as Social Witness*. Nashville, TN: Abingdon Press, 1995.
Traina, Cristina L.H. *Feminist Ethics and Natural Law: The End of the Anathemas*. Washington DC: Georgetown University Press, 1999.
Troeltsch, Ernst. *The Social Teaching of the Christian Churches*. Translated by Olive Wyon. New York: The Macmillan Company, 1931.
Tucker, Mary Evelyn. "Religion and Ecology: The Interaction of Cosmology and Cultivation." In *The Good in Nature and Humanity: Connecting Science, Religion, and Spirituality with the Natural World*. Edited by S. Kellert and T. Farnham. Washington, DC: Island, 2002.
Van Wensveen, Louke. *Dirty Virtues: The Emergence of Ecological Virtue Ethics*. Amherst, NY: Humanity Books, 2000.
Van Wieren, Gretel. *Restored to Earth: Christianity, Environmental Ethics, and Ecological Restoration*. Washington, DC: Georgetown University Press, 2013.
Volf, Miroslav. "Human Work, Divine Spirit, and New Creation: Toward a Pneumatological Understanding of Work." *Pneuma*, 9, no, 2 (Fall 1987): 173–193.
———. *Flourishing: Why We Need Religion in a Globalized World*. New Haven, CT: Yale University Press, 2016.
———. *Work in the Spirit: Toward a Theology of Work*. New York: Oxford University Press, 1991.
Warren, Karen, ed. *Ecofeminism: Women, Nature and Culture*. Indianapolis: IN. University Press, 1997.
Weber, Max. *The Protestant Work Ethic and the Spirit of Capitalism*. New York: Charles Scribner's Sons, 1958.

———. *The Vocation Lectures: Science as Vocation and Politics as Vocation.* Edited by David Owen and Tracy B. Strong. Translated by Rodney Livingstone. Indianapolis, IN: Hackett Publishing Company, 2004.

Wells, Ronald Vale. *Three Christian Transcendentalists: James Marsh, Caleb Sprague Henry, Frederic Henry Hedge.* New York: Octagon Books, 1972.

Wendel, Francois. *Calvin: The Origins and Development of His Religious Thought.* New York: Harper & Row, 1950.

West, E. G. *Adam Smith.* New Rochelle, CA: Arlington House, 1969.

Westhelle, Vítor. *Transfiguring Luther: The Planetary Promise of Luther's Theology.* Eugene, OR: Cascade, 2016.

White, Lynn. "The Historical Roots of Our Ecologic Crisis." *Science* 155 (March 1967) 1967: 1203–1207.

Wilson E. O. *Biophilia.* Cambridge, MA: Harvard University Press, 1984.

Wilson, Jonathan R. *God's Good World: Reclaiming the Doctrine of Creation.* Grand Rapids, MI: Baker Academic, 2013.

Wingren, Gustaf. *Luther on Vocation.* Philadelphia: Muhlenberg Press, 1957.

———. *Creation and Law.* Philadelphia: Muhlenberg Press, 1961.

———. *The Flight from Creation.* Minneapolis: Augsburg Publishing House, 1971.

Winright, Tobias L. Ed., *Green Discipleship: Catholic Theological Ethics and the Environment.* Winona, MN: Anselm Academic, 2011.

Wirzba, Norman. *The Essential Agrarian Reader.* Berkeley, CA: Counterpoint, 2003.

Zakai, Ayibu. "The Mind." In *Jonathan Edwards's Philosophy of History.* Princeton, NJ: Princeton University Press, 2003.

Zizioulas, John. "Proprietors or Priests of Creation." In *Toward an Ecology of Transfiguration.* Edited by John Chryssavgis and Bruce C. Foltz. New York: Fordham University Press, 2013.

Index

Adam and Eve, 19, 21, 49, 64
Amsdorf, Nicholas, 78
Anabaptist theology, 62, 78, 96n7
Anthropocene era, 16, 25, 48, 57, 131, 149
anthropocentric ethical approach:
  ecological subjectivity, seeking to address, 37; endorsement of, 43, 51; godly dominion approach, 17–20; henotheism, as mimicking, 46; paradigmatic approach, as a framework in, 16; priesthood approach, 23–25; reformation *vs.* rejection of, 34; stewardship approach, 20–23; transnational impact of bioregional practices, 143
Aquinas, Thomas, 25, 59, 73n58, 135, 154n14, 156n45
ascriptivism, 37, 58, 63, 64–65, 69n2, 131
Augsburg Confession, 76, 96n7
Augustine, Saint, 19, 60, 69n7, 73n57, 74n64

Bacon, Francis, 17, 38n21, 81
Barth, Karl, 26, 43, 61, 71n25, 131–132
Bartholomew I of Constantinople, 24
Bauckham, Richard, 19–20, 22–23, 54n12
Baxter, Richard, 79–80, 84, 85
Beisner, Cal, 18–19, 20, 38n24
Berry, Thomas, 30
Berry, Wendell: agrarian perspective, 15, 114; Baptist background, 103, 114; on ecological vocation, 103–104, 115–117; humans as creators, on the problem of, 146; vocation in fiction of, 115–121
Bible and Ecology (Bauckham), 22
Billing, Einar, 64, 72n40, 78, 141
biocentric ethical approach, 16, 30–31, 106
biophilia, moral imperative of, 35–36, 147
Birch, Bruce, 30, 31
Black, John, 17–19, 38n23
Blessed are the Consumers (McFague), 112
Bonzo, Matthew, 117
Bouma-Prediger, Steven, 22
Brother Earth (Santmire), 104
Brown, Brené, 142
Brunner, Emil, 70n20, 123n26, 132
Buber, Martin, 106
Buell, Lawrence, 34, 114
Burns, Robert, 136

Calvin, John and Calvinism: Anabaptist lines of thinking within Calvinism, 78; capitalism, affinity with Calvinism, 85–87, 98n46; on creation as manifesting divine glory, 89; doctrine of vocation, democratizing, 57, 58, 75, 128; the dust, emphasizing fundamental attachment to, 64; natural law tradition, reading Calvin within, 61, 70n20; nature, seeing God's radical presence

in, 89; obedience to God, understanding vocation as, 82; the ordinary, on pursuing vocation in, 62–63, 65, 98n43; Perkins, prioritizing holiness more than Calvin, 79; personalism as an issue in works of Calvin, 58; radical prudence of Calvin, 88; spiritual and intimate understanding of vocation,, 81; on vocational hierarchy, 66, 133
Cambridge Platonism, 88–89
Carson, Rachel, 11, 37n2, 46, 48–49
Christian agrarianism, 35
Christian Directory (Baxter), 80, 85, 98n46
Christian ethics: Barth, accused of veering towards monism, 132; Berry, rejecting title of literary Christian ethicist, 115; on ecological matters, 3, 4, 43; environmental ethics as a burgeoning field, 12–16; H. Richard Niebuhr on the threefold relations of, 45; Santmire, terreological approach to, 104; universal human ethics, convertibility with, 47; vocation as the foundation of, 7, 43, 57, 86. *See also* terreology
Christianity and the Social Crisis in the 21st Century (Rauschenbusch), 92, 95
climate change: charity and imagination as lacking in response to, 14; dominion proponents as climate deniers, 20; flexibility in calling as necessary to address, 130; human behavior, partial origin in, 51; intergeneraltional challenges of, 149; local environmental impact on, 21; as a moral issue, 144; perfect moral storm in current response to, 50, 52, 54n15; stewardship model as inadequate for addressing, 23; vocation-as-hope in relation to, 153
Clinton, Bill, 138
Cobb, John, 30, 31, 41n69, 41n73
Colonna, Jerry, 139
the common good, 73n47, 79, 82, 94, 113, 129
Comte, Auguste, 16
Cone, James, 53
Confessionalism, 78
constructivism, 33–35
Copernicus, Nicolaus, 80

Cornwall Alliance, 18, 55n26
creation care concept, 106–107

Deane-Drummond, Celia, 21–22, 123n13, 124n43
democratization of vocation: Calvin and Luther as emphasizing, 58, 65–66, 75; contemporary critiques, 131–133; in early Protestant thought, 50; ethical privatization, release of the doctrine from, 45; Perkins on the threefold sense of, 79; priesthood of all believers, linked with the concept of, 128; the privileged as undervaluing, 92; responsibility ethic and, 57–58; thriving of the neighbor, making possible, 52, 130; vocational roles, relatedness between, 129. *See also* Protestant doctrine of vocation; vocation
deontological ethics, 19, 22, 25, 27, 45, 48, 112
Descartes, Renes, 81–82
DeWitt, Calvin, 21–22, 39n34
Dickens, Charles, 88
Dirty Virtues (Wensveen), 22
Doan, Michael, 144
dominion theology, 17–20, 21, 22, 25, 43, 68, 106

Earth-honoring Ethics (Rasmussen), 19
ecclesial docetism, 105
Eck, Johann, 76
ecological ethics. *See* Christian ethics; terreology
ecological saints, 113
ecological subjectivity, 35–37
Edwards, Denis, 148, 156n47
Edwards, Jonathan, 79, 84, 89, 99n56–99n57
Emerson, Ralph Waldo, 84, 89–90
environmental justice (EJ), 36, 52–53, 137
environmental racism, 7, 52–53, 130, 131, 136–137
Environment and Christian Ethics (Northcott), 16, 38n16
Erasmus of Rotterdam, 59–60, 68, 97n23
ethical ecological responsibility, 48–53, 129

ethics *homo faber, politicus,* and *dialogicus,* 45, 127
Evangelical Lutheran Church of America (ELCA), 140

"Fidelity" (Berry), 118
Foundation of the Christian Religion Gathered in Six Principles (Perkins), 79

Galileo, Galilei, 20, 80–81
Gardiner, Stephen, 50, 52, 54n15
Gebara, Ivone, 28–29, 40n63, 51
Genesis creation narratives, 18, 19, 21, 22–23, 49, 106–107
Gnanadason, Aruna, 12
Gottlieb, Roger, 33, 42n83
Greening Spaces for Worship and Ministry (Torgerson), 49
Gregorious, Paulos, 23–24
Gustafson, James, 45, 54n9

Hale, Matthew, 20–21
Hauerwas, Stanley, 72n45, 131, 132
Hedge, Frederic Henry, 84, 90–92, 133
henotheism, 46, 54n6
"Historical Roots" (White), 13
Hugo, Victor, 157
Hume, David, 83

I-Ens relations, 106, 107
individualism: Humanism, focus on, 80; medieval understanding of, 65; modern emphasis on, vocation affected by, 133, 142; North American region, as reigning in, 59; personalization of vocation, leading to, 80; the problem of, 67–68; quietistic individualism, rise of, 105; religious individualism as abnormal, 92; Romanticism as a response to, 88
instrumental rationality, 143

Jamieson, Dale, 14, 51, 54n16–55n17
Jenkins, Willis, 20, 31, 52, 126n59
Jennings, Willie, 36
John Paul II, Pope, 132
"A Jonquil for Mary Penn" (Berry), 119
Jordan, William, 34

justification, doctrine of: ecological awareness, doing little to raise, 60; Protestants, ongoing focus on, 105, 111, 149, 157; sanctification and, 79; vocation, linking to, 64, 72n40, 76, 78

Kant, Immanuel, 82
Kellert, Stephen, 35–36
kenosis, 68, 110, 111–114, 120, 122, 124n35, 127
kerygmatic approach to salvation, 105
King, Martin Luther, Jr., 136, 138
Kingdom of God theology, 108–109
Klein, Naomi, 55n21
Kolb, Robert, 77

land ethic, 21, 33, 39n35, 41n73, 106
Latour, Bruno, 16, 51, 122n10
Laytham, Brent, 121
Leopold, Aldo, 13, 21, 39n35
Liberation of Life (Cobb/Birch), 31
Livingston, James, 88
Loci Communes Rerum Theologicarum (Melanchthon), 76, 77
Locke, John, 82–83
Lubchenco, Jane, 13
Luria, Isaac, 26
Luther, Martin and Lutheranism: ascriptivism in the works of, 58, 63, 64–65, 73n50; capitalism, Lutheran ethic rejecting, 86; the darkness, acknowledging, 108; as democratizing vocation doctrine, 57, 58, 60, 75, 128; on ethics in terms of vocation, 67; on internal *vs.* external vocation, 132–133; intimate and spiritual understanding of vocation, 81; Melanchthonian expansion of vocation doctrine, 76–78; mindfulness in vocation, exemplifying, 107; natural law tradition, taking for granted, 109; nature, viewing in a theocentric light, 33; neighbors, on vocational service to, 64, 66, 79; obedience to God, vocation as, 82; Philipist Lutheranism, 80; *saeculum,* separating from the eternal, 60; sanctification, contemporary minimization of, 67; Santmire, Lutheran sensibilities of, 8, 103,

104–106, 112; *simul justus et peccator* tradition, 79; vocation, on natural law as expression of, 61; on vocation as a way of life, 62–63, 66; Wittenberg Theses, 500th anniversary of, 157

Macy, Joanna, 152, 153n3
Marion, Jean-Luc, 82, 97n28
Marshall, Paul, 82
the martyr church in sacramental life, 108
Matthew, calling of, 149–150, 151
McFague, Sallie: bodily theology of, 110, 111; on God's relationship with the natural world, 28; on kenosis and radical incarnationalism, 111–112, 124n35; on obligation and desire in vocation, 112–113; on practical vocation, 144; Reformed background, 8, 103, 112; Santmire, building on work of, 104; suffering, on the supernatural purpose of, 145; on vocation as resistance, 109, 113–114, 122
Meister Eckhart, 59–60, 70n14
Melanchthon, Philip, 8, 76, 77, 79, 96n8
missions, accompaniment model of, 140
Moltmann, Jürgen, 25, 26–27, 109, 123n26, 149
Mumford, Lewis, 84, 87
Murdoch, Iris, 112

Nash, James, 28, 40n58
National People of Color Environmental Leadership Summit, 137, 138
"Native Hill" (Berry), 117
natural value theory, 32–33
nature as the new poor, 28, 112
Nature Deficit Disorder, 147
Nature Reborn (Santmire), 106, 122n10
Newton, Isaac, 82, 97n28
Niebuhr, H. Richard: anthropogenic age, ethical approach to, 48; Buber, as inspired by, 106; cathecontic, on the third ethical space as, 62, 159; on ethics *homo dialogicus*, 127; ethics of response and, 57, 58, 71n27, 153n2; on objective relationism, 44–45, 138; radical theocentrism, promoting, 46–47; on self-awareness as an ongoing journey, 150

Nixon, Rob, 51
Northcott, Michael, 16, 38n16
Novum Organum (Bacon), 17, 81

Obama, Barack, 18, 138
objective relationism, 44, 47, 138

panentheism, 25, 28, 71n30, 109, 124n31
pantheism, 24, 29, 40n58
Peacocke, Arthur, 29
Perfect Moral Storm (Gardiner), 50
Perkins, William, 76, 78–80, 88, 97n17, 97n19
personalism, 58, 65, 109, 123n26
Philipists, 78, 80
piety, 62, 77, 78, 82, 86, 105
Plumwood, Val, 43
Pollution and the Death of Man (Schaeffer), 17
Port William narrative, 115, 117–118, 118–119, 120, 121, 125n50
"Pray without Ceasing" (Berry), 120
priesthood, ideology of, 17, 23–25
priesthood of all believers, 59, 65–66, 128
Priestly creation narrative, 18, 21, 22–23, 49, 106, 134, 151
Primitive Origination of Mankind (Hale), 20
Protestant doctrine of vocation: Age of Reflection contributions to doctrine, 81–84; creation, connection to in early doctrine, 130, 131, 132–133; earthly realities, focus on, 64; ethical privatization, release from, 45; industrialism and capitalism, linking to the rise of, 75, 76, 80, 83, 86, 98n46, 133; priesthood of all believers, democratizing effect of, 128; reformation of the doctrine, 128, 138–143; Transcendentalism, impact on, 89–90, 90, 158; Troeltsch, reflections on, 85–87; white sensibilities of, 53. *See also* democratization of vocation; vocation
Protestant Ethic and the Spirit of Capitalism (Weber), 85
Protestant work ethic, 80, 85, 85–86, 133

racism. *See* environmental racism

Radford-Ruether, Rosemary, 28–29
radical incarnationalism, 111
radical monotheism, 46
Rahner, Karl, 26
Rasmussen, Larry, 19, 33–34, 53, 142
Rauschenbusch, Walter: H. Richard Niebuhr, as an influence on, 44; as a prophetic thinker, 136, 138; theology of work, 92–94, 95, 133–134, 134; vocation with luxury, rejecting equivocation of, 90
Remembering (Berry), 118
Rolston, Holmes, III, 23, 32–33
Romanticism, 83, 88, 100n77
Rousseau, Max, 88

sacramentalism, 28–30
sanctification, 67, 78, 79, 82
Sand Country Almanac (Leopold), 13, 39n35, 106
Santmire, H. Paul: on the church's calling to nature, 106–108, 122n5, 122n10; *koinonia*, on all life as sharing, 144–145; Lutheran sensibilities of, 8, 103, 104–106, 112; spirituality of cosmic hope, on the viability of, 152; on vocation as paradox, 104, 108–109, 121–122
Schade, Leah, 9, 142
Schaeffer, Francis, 17–19, 38n20–38n21
Schweitzer, Albert, 11, 46
Schweitzer, William, 141–142
Seventeen Principles of Environmental Justice (document), 137–138
Silent Spring (Carson), 11
Sinden, Amy, 52
Sittler, Joseph, 11–12, 14, 33
Smith, Adam, 83, 98n34–98n35
Social Gospel movement, 92, 100n76, 108, 134, 135
Sölle, Dorothee, 29, 95, 123n27, 136
Spencer, Dan, 25
Steger, Wallace, 117
Stevens, Michael, 117
stewardship, 17, 18, 20–23, 68, 82, 106
Stoll, Mark, 90
Summa Contra Gentiles (Aquinas), 25
Swoboda, A. J., 14

Taylor, Bron, 16, 54n14
Taylor, Charles, 60, 69n8, 72n42
Taylor, Dorceta, 55n31, 131
Teilhard de Chardin, Pierre, 28, 30, 124n33
teleological ethics, 22, 45, 48, 113
terreology: biocentric approaches to, 30–32; Christian ecological ethics and, 15, 103, 104; ecological ethics, reconfiguring, 16; ecological terreology, primary goal of, 47; of Godly dominion, 17–20; of priesthood, 23–25; radical terreology, 45, 46–47; of stewardship, 20–23. *See also* anthropocentrism
theocentric ethical approach: abstraction, tendency towards, 25; cathecontic methodology of, 159; ecological vocation in the context of, 144; of H. Richard Niebuhr, 45, 48; liability of, 47; in the Lutheran tradition, 33; major theocentric approaches, 110–111; as a mediating terreology, 46–47, 71n32; nature, theocentric perspective on, 106; paradigmatic approach, as a framework in, 16; pre-modern theocentric views, 146; radical theocentrism of Santmire, 104; responsibilist commitment to radical theocentrism, 159; sacramentalism and, 28–30; Transcendentalists as influenced by, 89; Trinity, theocentric approach towards, 109
Torgerson, Mark, 10n10, 49
Townes, Emilie, 53
"Toxic Wastes and Race in the United States" (report), 137
Transcendentalism, 89–90, 90–91, 92, 115, 158
Treatise of the Vocations (Perkins), 78, 79
Trinitarianism, 25–27, 28
Trinitarian theology, 19, 25, 29–30, 109, 123n26
Troeltsch, Ernst, 44, 70n13, 73n47, 76, 85–87, 88
Tucker, Mary Evelyn, 36

van Wensveen, Louke, 22
Van Wieren, Gretel, 34, 123n15

virtue: Aristotelian/Thomist virtue tradition, 21, 22; of hope, 144, 151–153; of humility, 144–145, 152; of justice, 144, 149–151, 152; of restraint, 144, 146–147, 149, 152; virtue ethics, 21, 67, 104, 110, 113, 123n13; virtue theory, 146–147; of wisdom, 144, 147–149, 152

vocation: as affection, 114–117; as both a task and a gift, 61–62; Christian ethics, as foundational to, 43, 57, 86; class system, effect on, 93–94; co-creation, as a means of, 95, 131–133; the dignity of work, 134–136, 141; as embodied, 59, 60, 62, 64, 76, 77–78, 106, 130–131, 133, 137; as knowledge, 80–84; in mundane life, 62–63, 65, 91, 94, 95, 142; as obligation and desire, 112–113; as paradox, 104, 108–109; personalization of, 65, 80, 109; in Port William stories, 117–121; as privilege, 88–90, 92, 95; as production, 84–87; recasting of, 87, 95, 105, 109, 127–128, 138–139, 159; as resistance, 109–110, 113–114; as retreat, 83–84, 88, 89, 90, 91, 128, 130, 158; social and ecological justice, link between, 136–138; theology of, 69n9, 85–87; virtues linked to, 52, 67, 78, 116, 123n13, 143–153, 159; as a way of life, 58, 58–59, 66–67, 67–68; as worship, 76, 78–80, 97n19, 147. *See also* democratization of vocation; Protestant doctrine of vocation

Volf, Miroslav, 83, 131, 132, 133, 143

Waldo, Peter, 59, 60
Warren County, PCB dumping in, 136–137, 138
Wealth of the Nations (Smith), 83
Weber, Max, 76, 78, 80, 85, 88
Wendell Berry and the Restoration of Life (Bonzo/Stevens), 117
White, Christopher, 34
White, Lynn, 13–14, 15, 17, 31–32, 60
"The Wild Birds" (Berry), 121
Williams, Jordan, 25
Wingren, Gustaf, 60, 64, 72n40
Wirzba, Norman, 15, 35

Yahwist creation narrative, 18, 21, 22, 49

Zizioulas, John, 23–24, 25, 40n46

About the Author

Kiara A. Jorgenson is assistant professor of religion and environmental studies and the director of the environmental conversations program at St. Olaf College in Northfield, Minnesota.

www.ingramcontent.com/pod-product-compliance
Lightning Source LLC
Chambersburg PA
CBHW032149010526
44111CB00035B/1422